ONE

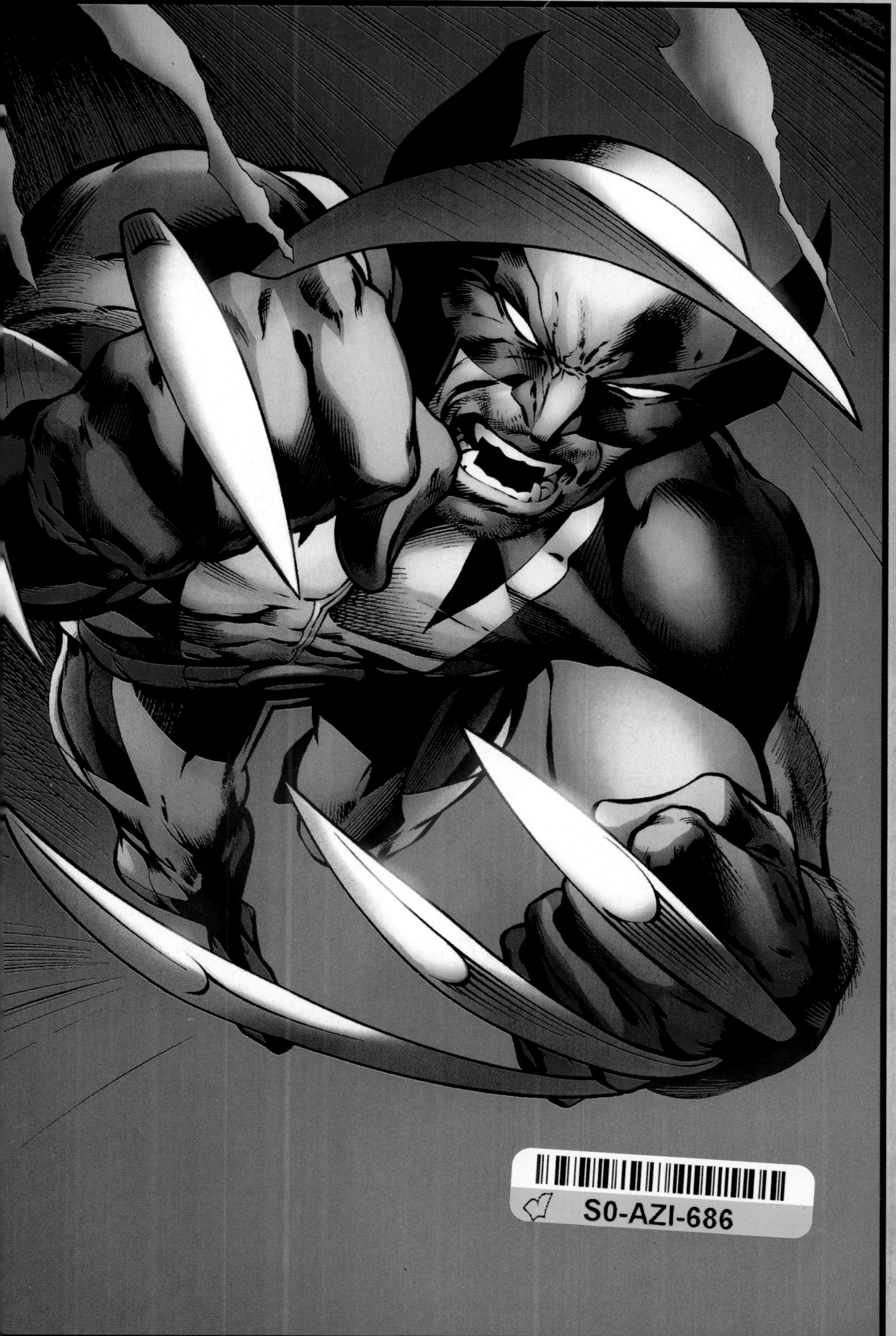

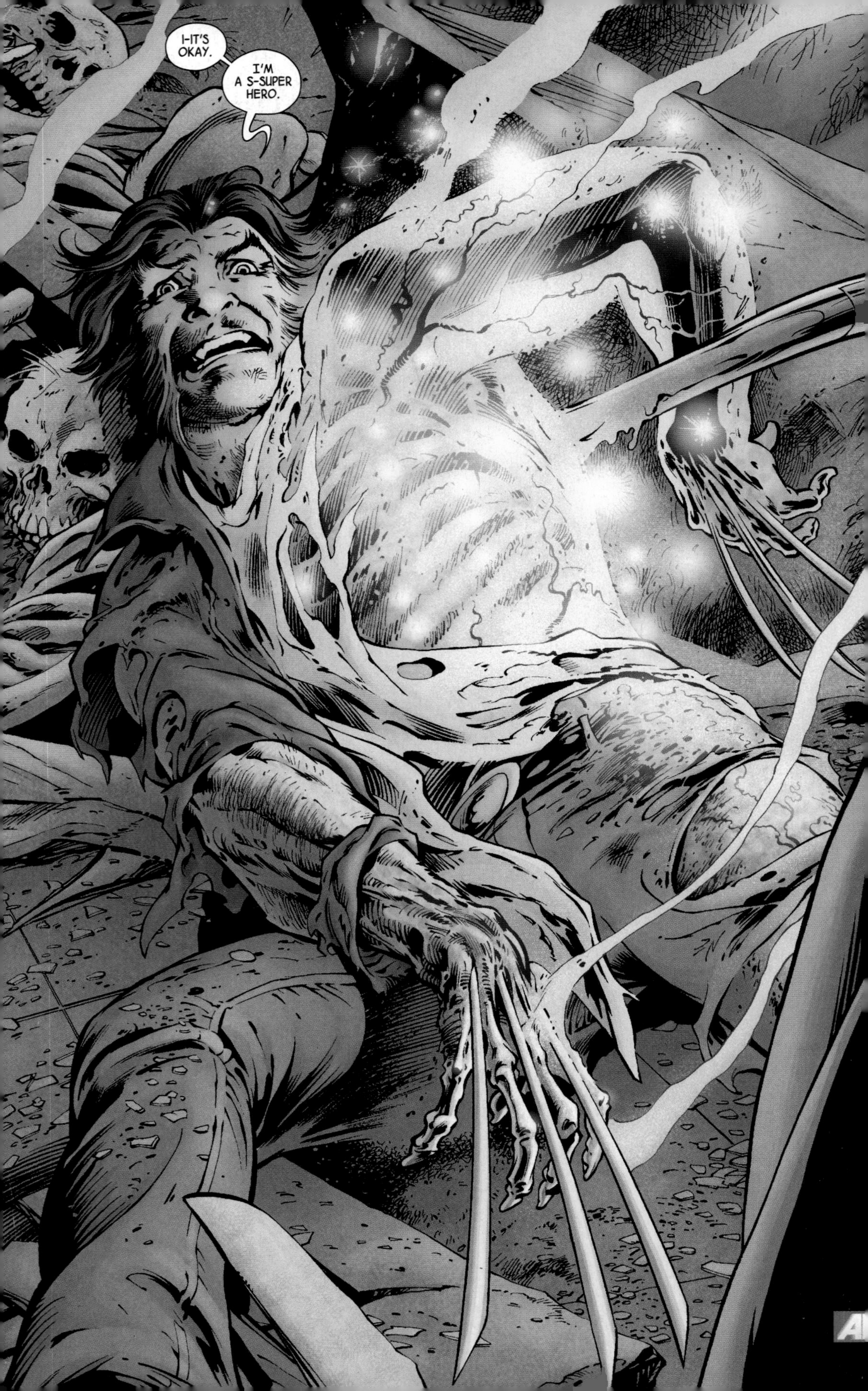
I-IT'S OKAY.
I'M A S-SUPER HERO.

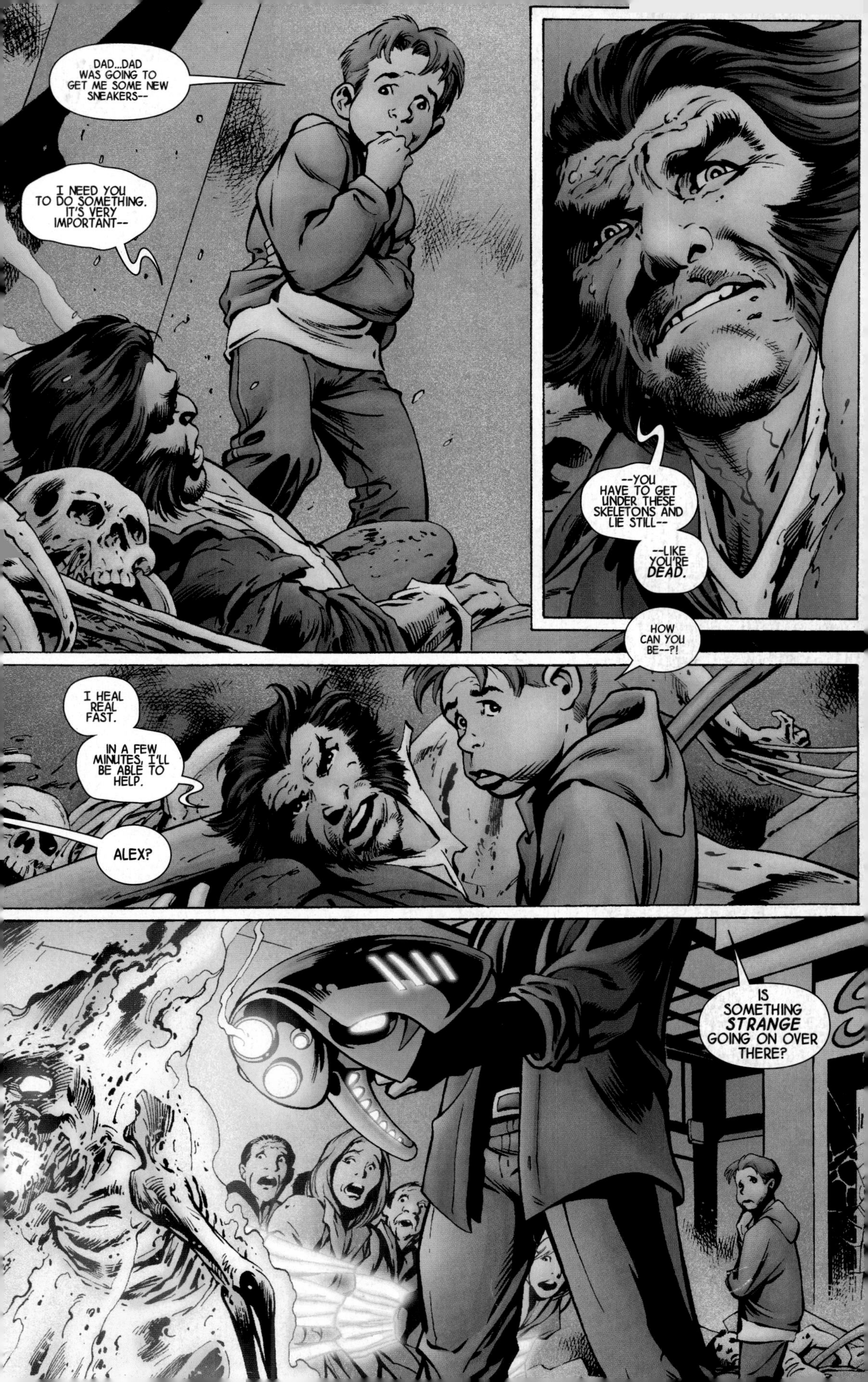
DAD...DAD WAS GOING TO GET ME SOME NEW SNEAKERS--
I NEED YOU TO DO SOMETHING. IT'S VERY IMPORTANT--
--YOU HAVE TO GET UNDER THESE SKELETONS AND LIE STILL--
--LIKE YOU'RE DEAD.
HOW CAN YOU BE--?!
I HEAL REAL FAST.
IN A FEW MINUTES, I'LL BE ABLE TO HELP.
ALEX?
IS SOMETHING STRANGE GOING ON OVER THERE?

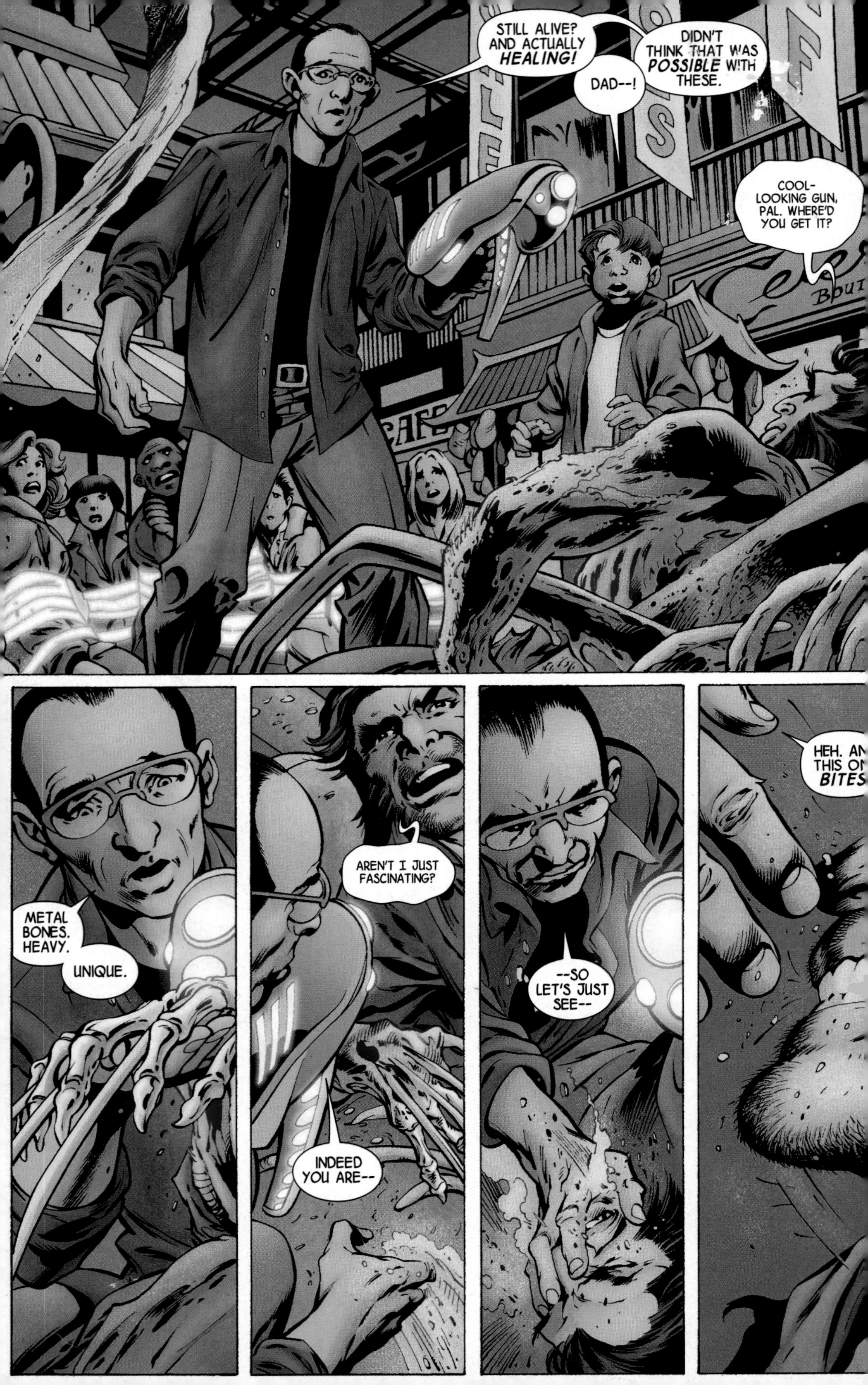
STILL ALIVE? AND ACTUALLY HEALING!
DIDN'T THINK THAT WAS POSSIBLE WITH THESE.
DAD--!
COOL-LOOKING GUN, PAL. WHERE'D YOU GET IT?
METAL BONES. HEAVY.
UNIQUE.
AREN'T I JUST FASCINATING?
INDEED YOU ARE--
--SO LET'S JUST SEE--
HEH. AN
THIS ON
BITES

WOLVERINE

VOLUME ONE

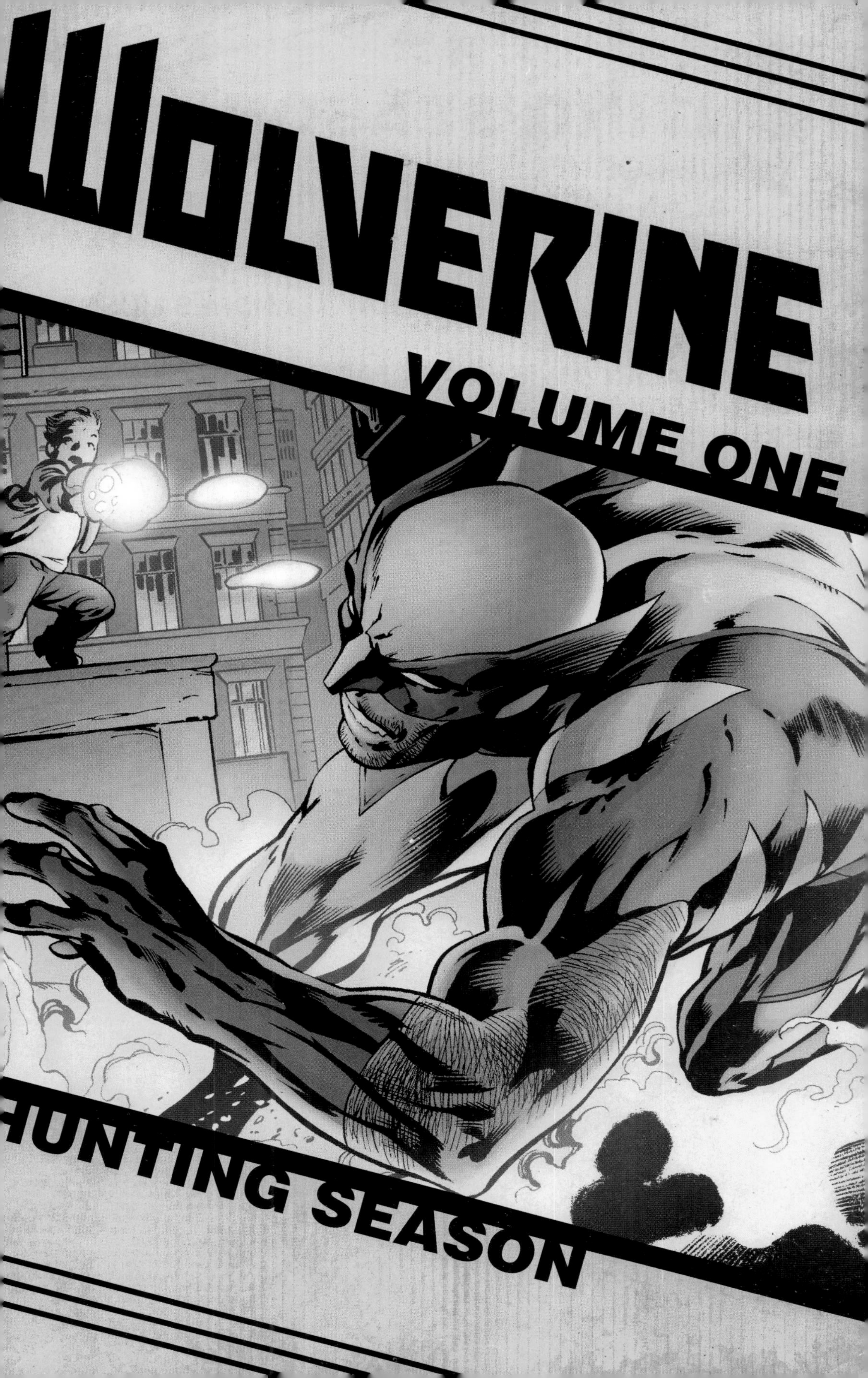

HUNTING SEASON

HUNTING SEASON

WRITER **PAUL CORNELL**

PENCILERS **ALAN DAVIS** (#1-4) & **MIRCO PIERFEDERICI** (#5-6)

INKERS **MARK FARMER** (#1-4), **KARL KESEL** WITH **ZACH FISCHER** (#5) & **TOM PALMER** (#6)

COLORISTS **MATT HOLLINGSWORTH** (#1-4) & **ANDRES MOSSA** (#5-6)

LETTERER **VC'S CORY PETIT**

COVER ARTISTS **ALAN DAVIS** & **MARK FARMER** WITH **JASON KEITH** (#1 & #6) & **MATT HOLLINGSWORTH** (#2-5)

ASSISTANT EDITOR **JENNIFER M. SMITH**

EDITOR **JEANINE SCHAEFER**

GROUP EDITOR **NICK LOWE**

COLLECTION EDITC
CORY LEVIN
ASSISTANT EDITOR
ALEX STARBUCK & **NELSON RIBEIR**
EDITORS, SPECIAL PROJECT
JENNIFER GRÜNWALD & **MARK D. BEAZLE**
SENIOR EDITOR, SPECIAL PROJECT
JEFF YOUNGQUIS
SVP OF PRINT & DIGITAL PUBLISHING SALE
DAVID GABRIE
BOOK DESIG
JEFF POWELL & **CORY LEVIN**

EDITOR IN CHIE
AXEL ALONS
CHIEF CREATIVE OFFICE
JOE QUESAD
PUBLISHE
DAN BUCKLE
EXECUTIVE PRODUCE
ALAN FIN

WOLVERINE VOL. 1: HUNTING SEASON. Contains material origin
published in magazine form as WOLVERINE #1-6. First printing 20
ISBN# 978-0-7851-8396-9. Published by MARVEL WORLDW
INC., a subsidiary of MARVEL ENTERTAINMENT, LLC. OFFICE
PUBLICATION: 135 West 50th Street, New York, NY 10020. Copyr
© 2013 Marvel Characters, Inc. All rights reserved. All charac
featured in this issue and the distinctive names and likenes
thereof, and all related indicia are trademarks of Marvel Charact
Inc. No similarity between any of the names, characters, perso
and/or institutions in this magazine with those of any living or de
person or institution is intended, and any such similarity wh
may exist is purely coincidental. **Printed in the U.S.A.** ALAN FI
EVP - Office of the President, Marvel Worldwide, Inc. and EVP
CMO Marvel Characters B.V.; DAN BUCKLEY, Publisher & Presid
- Print, Animation & Digital Divisions; JOE QUESADA, Chief Crea
Officer; TOM BREVOORT, SVP of Publishing; DAVID BOGART, S
of Operations & Procurement, Publishing; C.B. CEBULSKI, SVP
Creator & Content Development; DAVID GABRIEL, SVP of Prin
Digital Publishing Sales; JIM O'KEEFE, VP of Operations & Logist
DAN CARR, Executive Director of Publishing Technology; SUS
CRESPI, Editorial Operations Manager; ALEX MORALES, Publish
Operations Manager; STAN LEE, Chairman Emeritus. For informat
regarding advertising in Marvel Comics or on Marvel.com, plea
contact Niza Disla, Director of Marvel Partnerships, at ndisla@mar
com. For Marvel subscription inquiries, please call 800-217-91
Manufactured between 6/21/2013 and 7/29/2013 by QUA
GRAPHICS ST. CLOUD, ST. CLOUD, MN, USA.

10 9 8 7 6 5 4 3 2 1

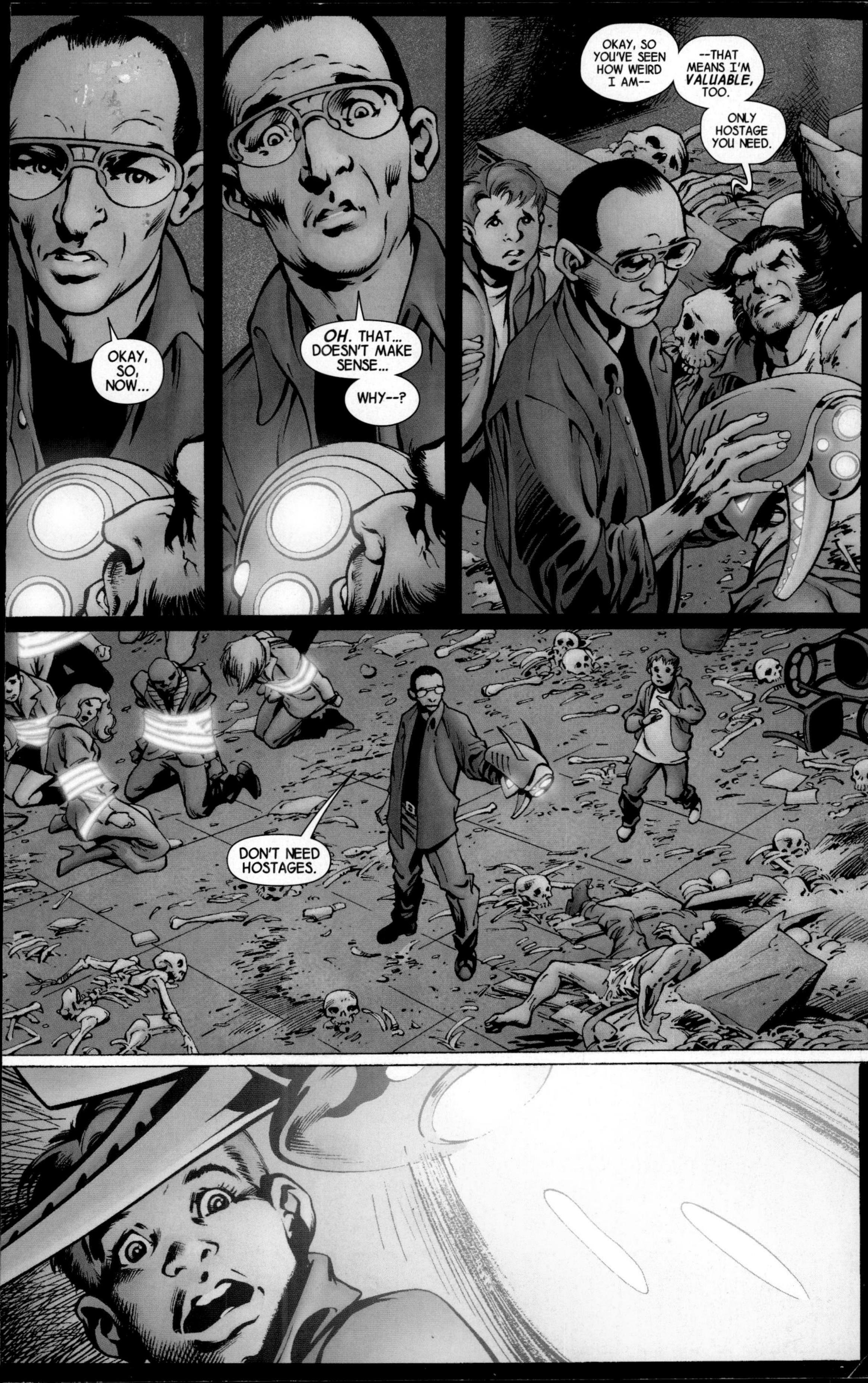
OKAY, SO, NOW...
OH. THAT... DOESN'T MAKE SENSE...
WHY--?
OKAY, SO YOU'VE SEEN HOW WEIRD I AM--
--THAT MEANS I'M VALUABLE, TOO.
ONLY HOSTAGE YOU NEED.
DON'T NEED HOSTAGES.

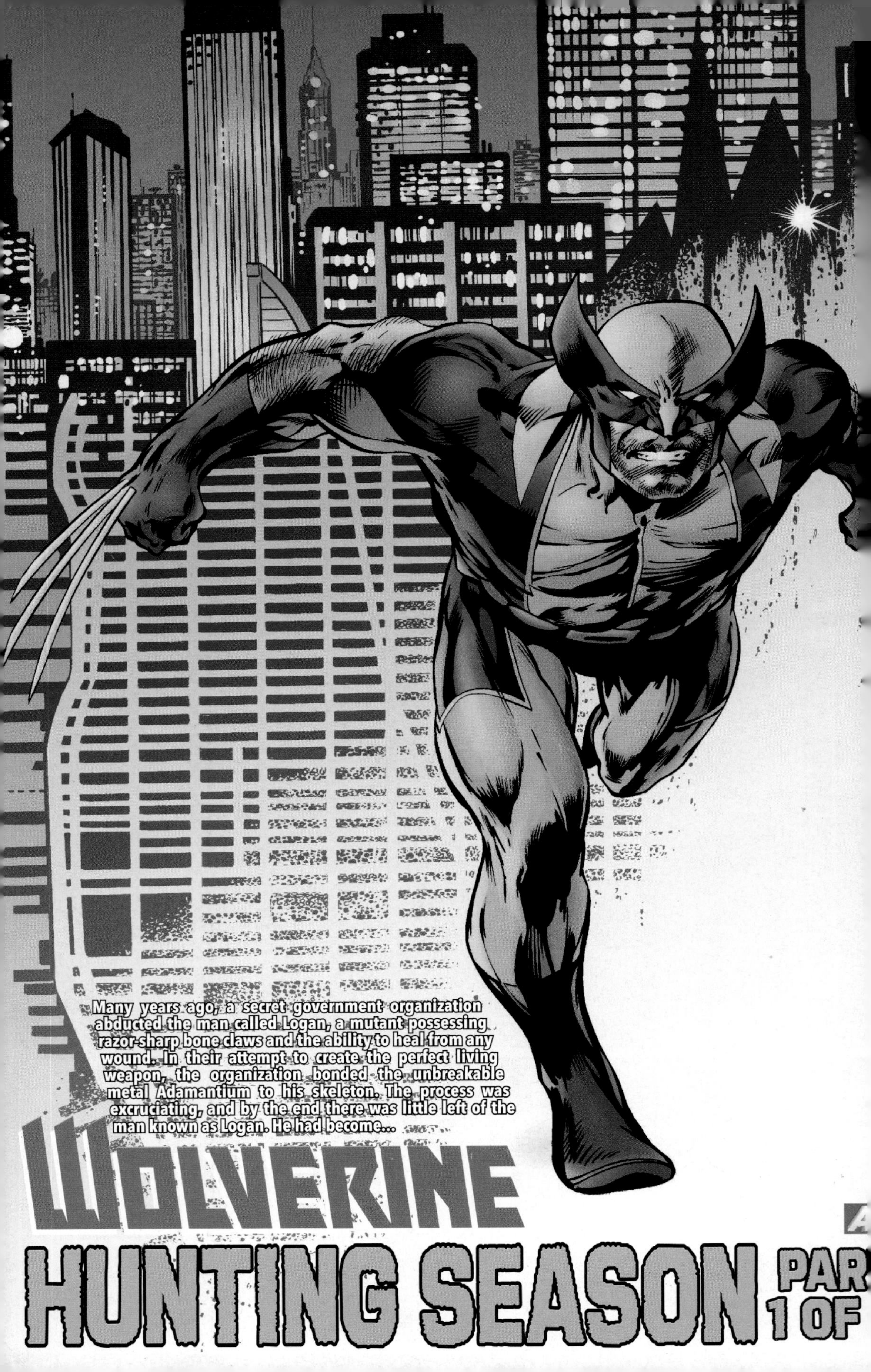
Many years ago, a secret government organization abducted the man called Logan, a mutant possessing razor-sharp bone claws and the ability to heal from any wound. In their attempt to create the perfect living weapon, the organization bonded the unbreakable metal Adamantium to his skeleton. The process was excruciating, and by the end there was little left of the man known as Logan. He had become...
WOLVERINE
HUNTING SEASON
PAR
1 OF

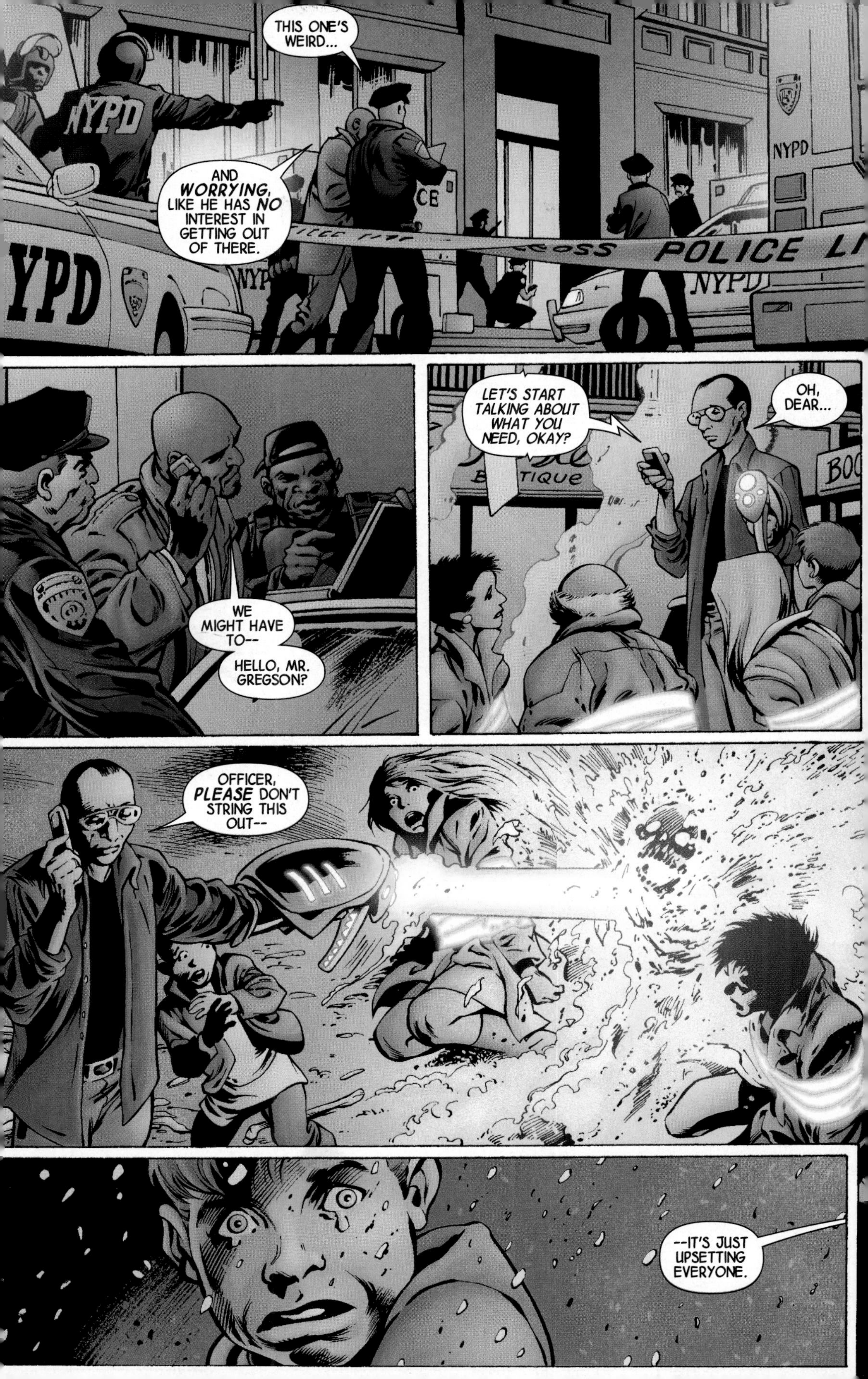
THIS ONE'S WEIRD...
AND WORRYING, LIKE HE HAS NO INTEREST IN GETTING OUT OF THERE.
NYPD
POLICE
NYPD
NYPD
NYPD
WE MIGHT HAVE TO--
HELLO, MR. GREGSON?
LET'S START TALKING ABOUT WHAT YOU NEED, OKAY?
OH, DEAR...
OFFICER, PLEASE DON'T STRING THIS OUT--
--IT'S JUST UPSETTING EVERYONE.

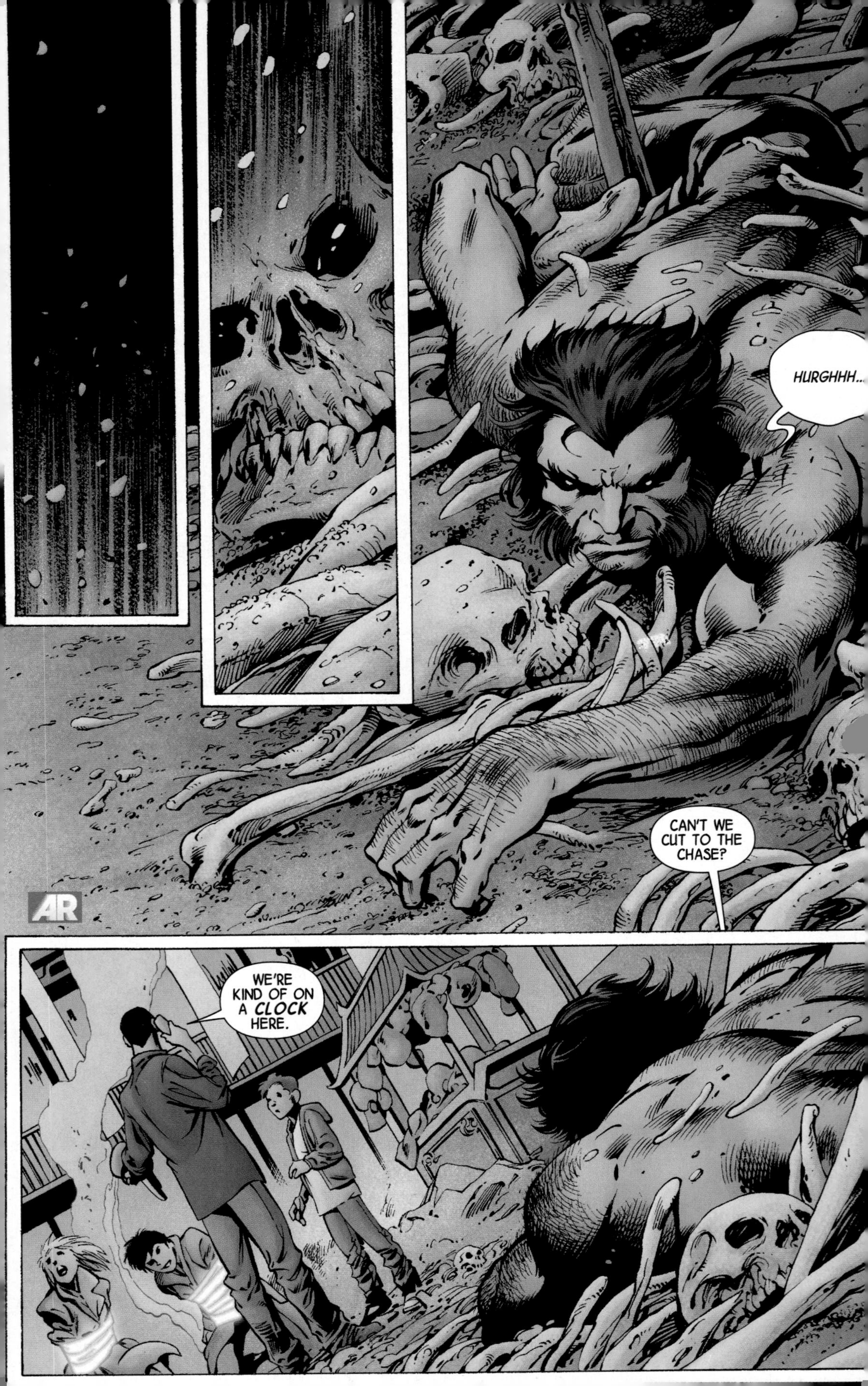
HURGHHH...
CAN'T WE CUT TO THE CHASE?
WE'RE KIND OF ON A CLOCK HERE.

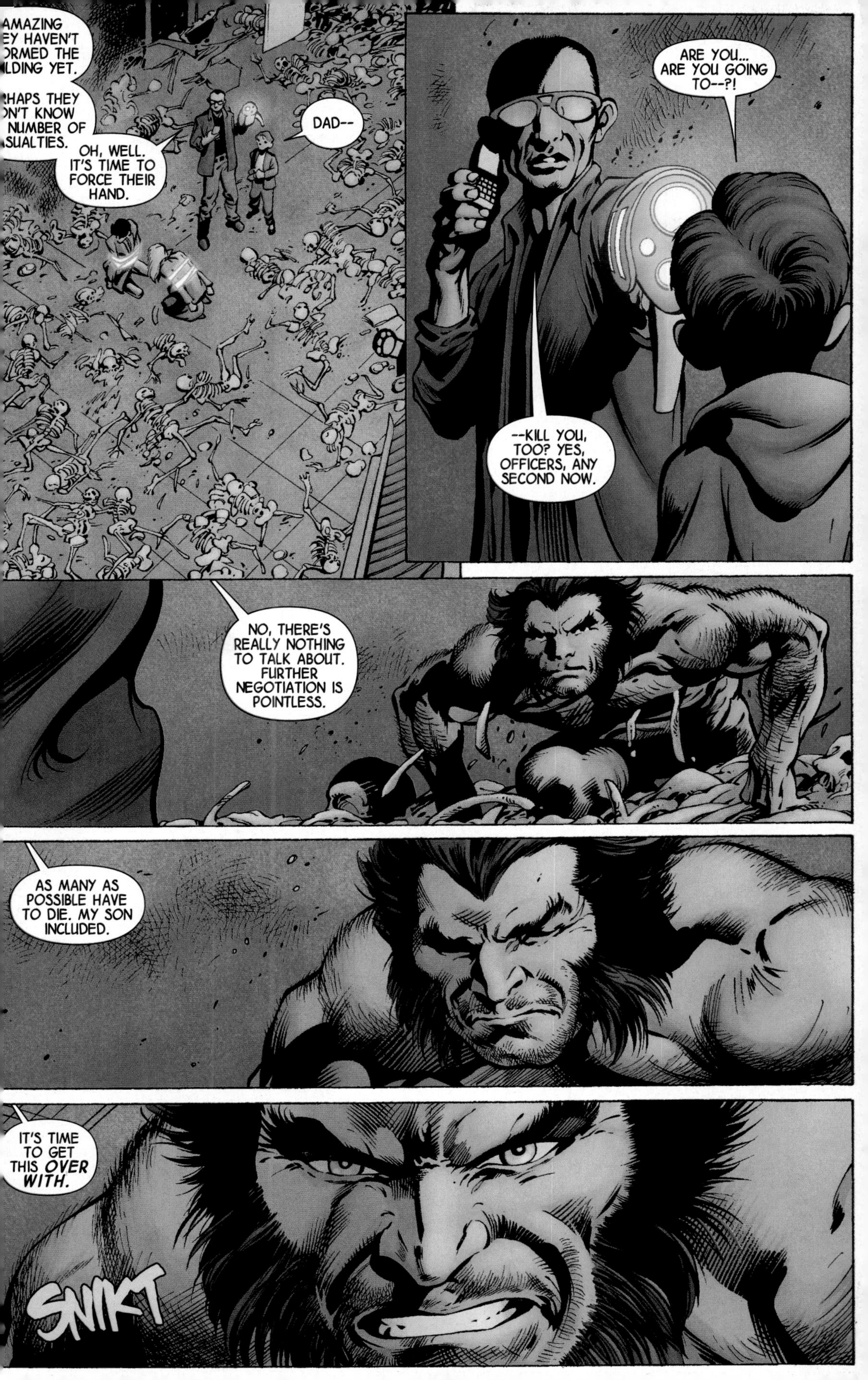
AMAZING
EY HAVEN'T
ORMED THE
ILDING YET.
RHAPS THEY
N'T KNOW
NUMBER OF
SUALTIES.
OH, WELL. IT'S TIME TO FORCE THEIR HAND.
DAD--
ARE YOU... ARE YOU GOING TO--?!
--KILL YOU, TOO? YES, OFFICERS, ANY SECOND NOW.
NO, THERE'S REALLY NOTHING TO TALK ABOUT. FURTHER NEGOTIATION IS POINTLESS.
AS MANY AS POSSIBLE HAVE TO DIE. MY SON INCLUDED.
IT'S TIME TO GET THIS OVER WITH.
SNIKT

RAGGHHH!

WHAT?!

YOU'RE *STILL* NOT--?!

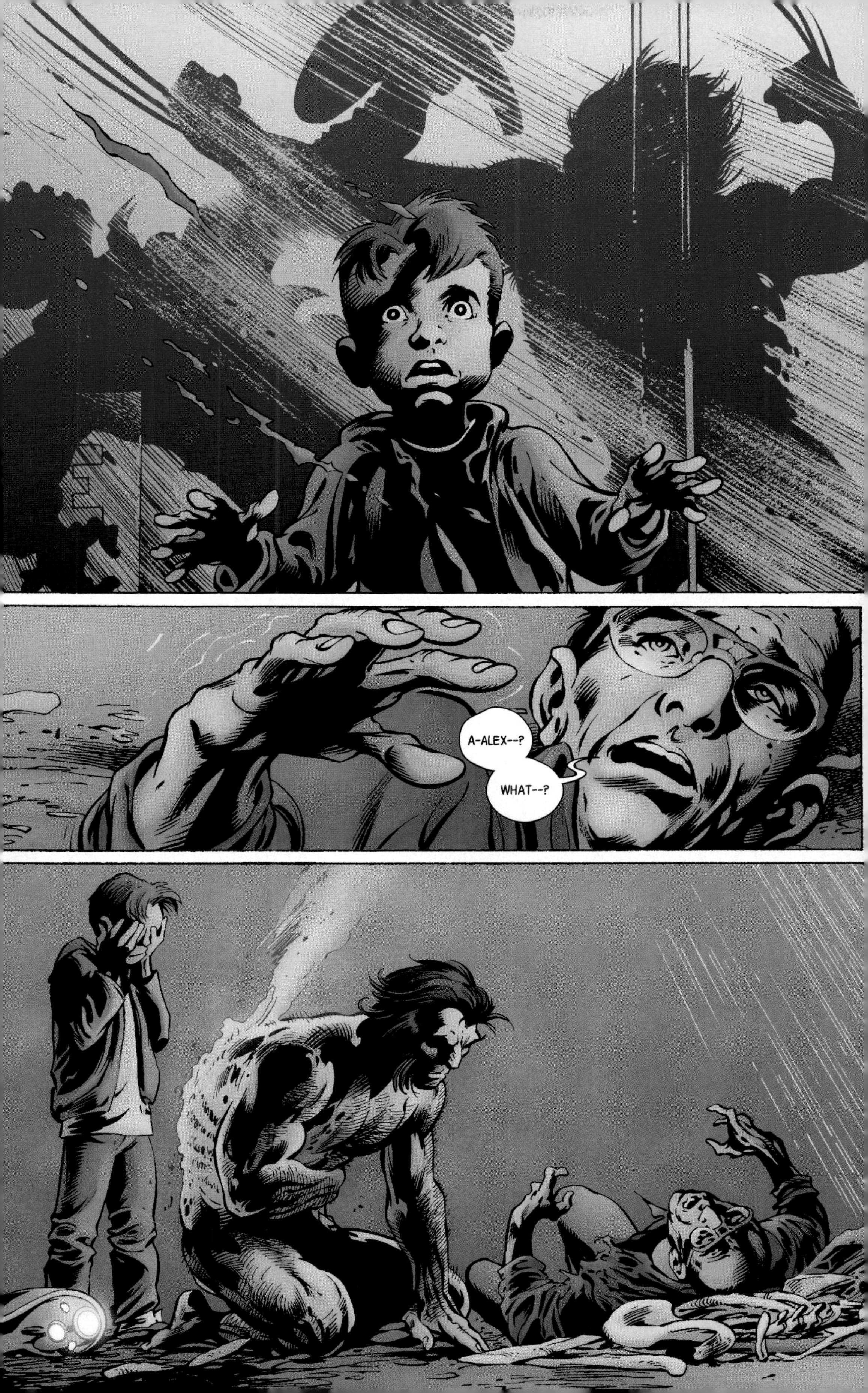
A-ALEX--?
WHAT--?

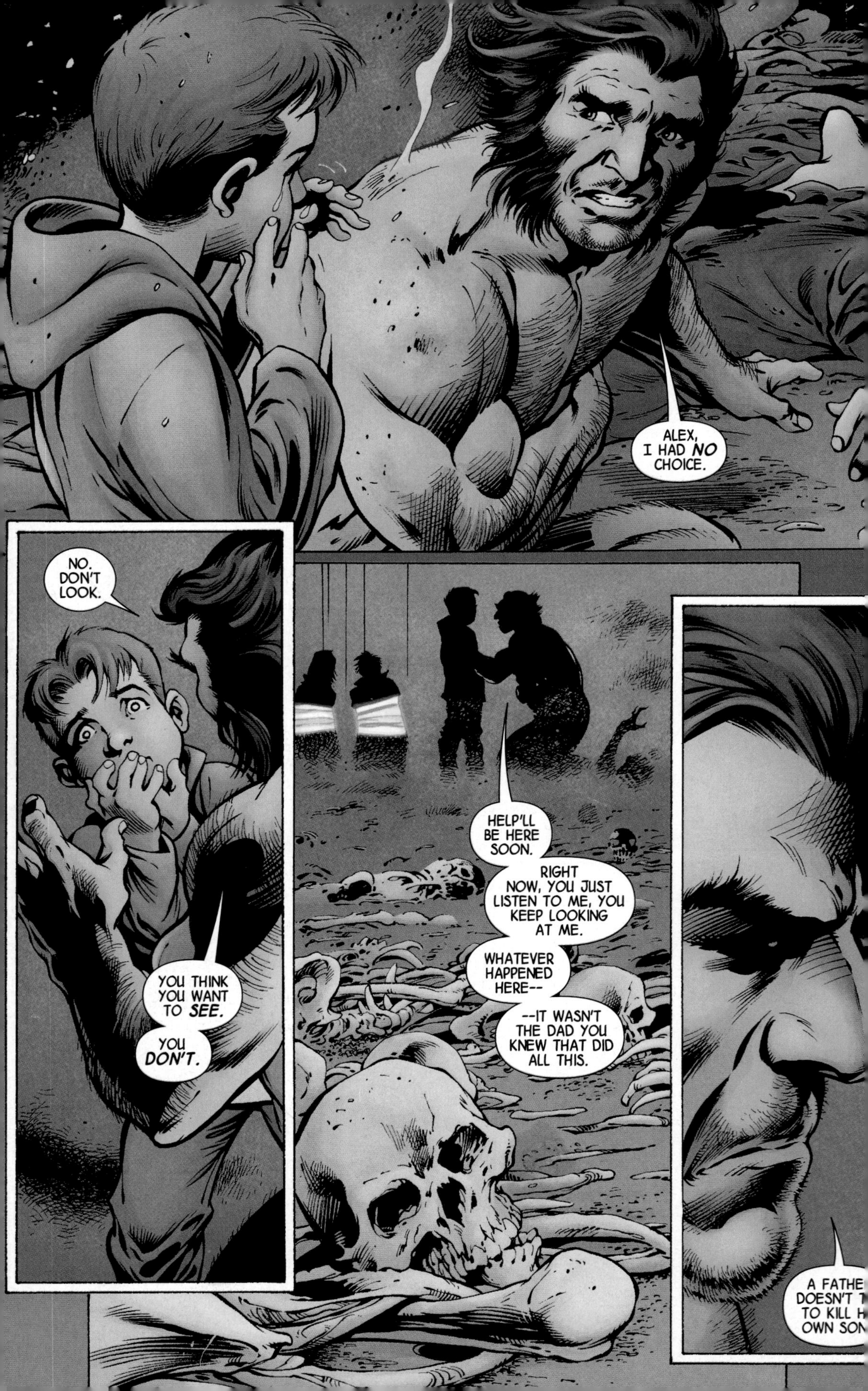
ALEX, I HAD NO CHOICE.
NO. DON'T LOOK.
YOU THINK YOU WANT TO SEE.
YOU DON'T.
HELP'LL BE HERE SOON.
RIGHT NOW, YOU JUST LISTEN TO ME, YOU KEEP LOOKING AT ME.
WHATEVER HAPPENED HERE--
--IT WASN'T THE DAD YOU KNEW THAT DID ALL THIS.

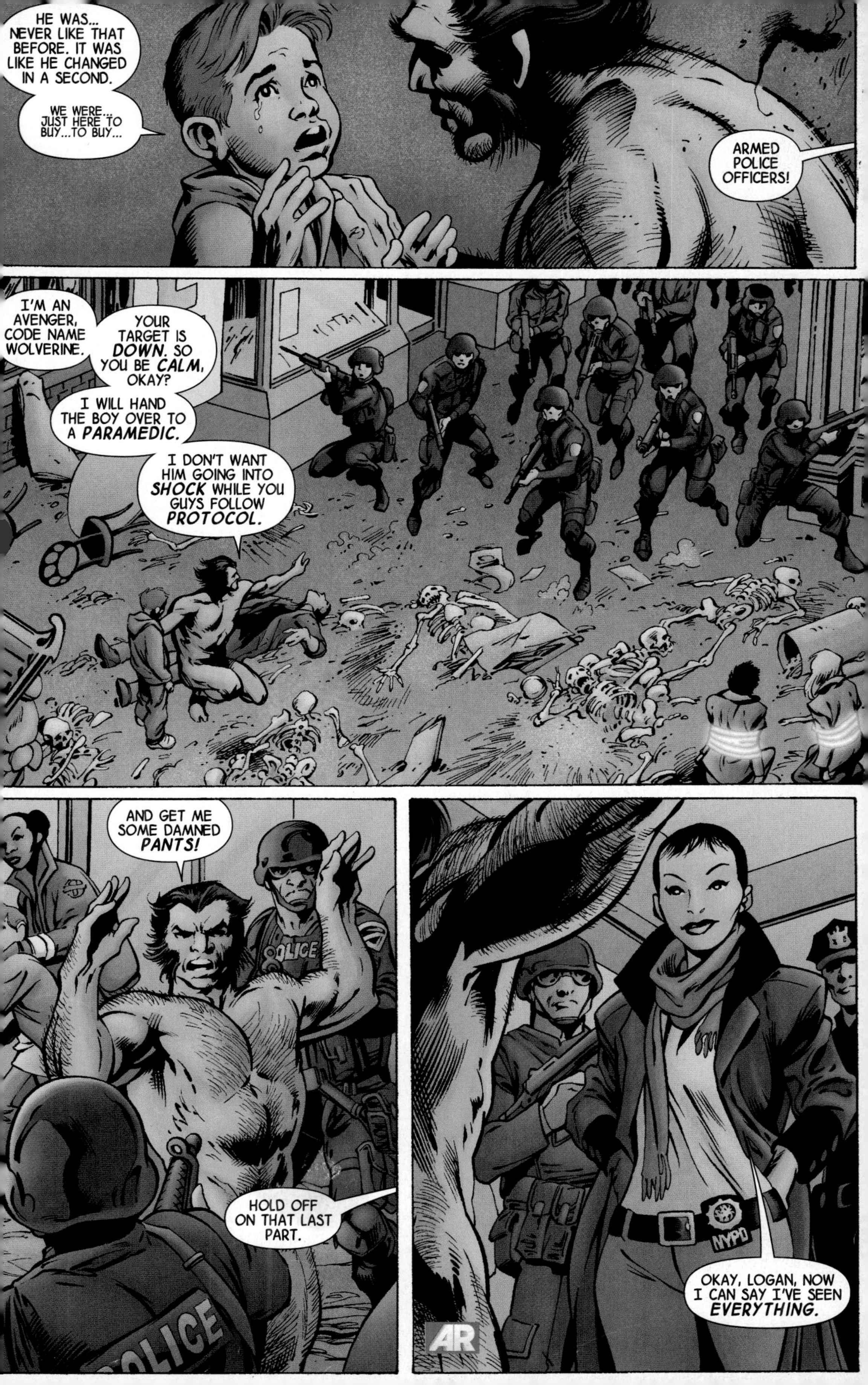
HE WAS... NEVER LIKE THAT BEFORE. IT WAS LIKE HE CHANGED IN A SECOND.
WE WERE... JUST HERE TO BUY...TO BUY...
ARMED POLICE OFFICERS!
I'M AN AVENGER, CODE NAME WOLVERINE.
YOUR TARGET IS DOWN. SO YOU BE CALM, OKAY?
I WILL HAND THE BOY OVER TO A PARAMEDIC.
I DON'T WANT HIM GOING INTO SHOCK WHILE YOU GUYS FOLLOW PROTOCOL.
AND GET ME SOME DAMNED PANTS!
HOLD OFF ON THAT LAST PART.
OKAY, LOGAN, NOW I CAN SAY I'VE SEEN EVERYTHING.

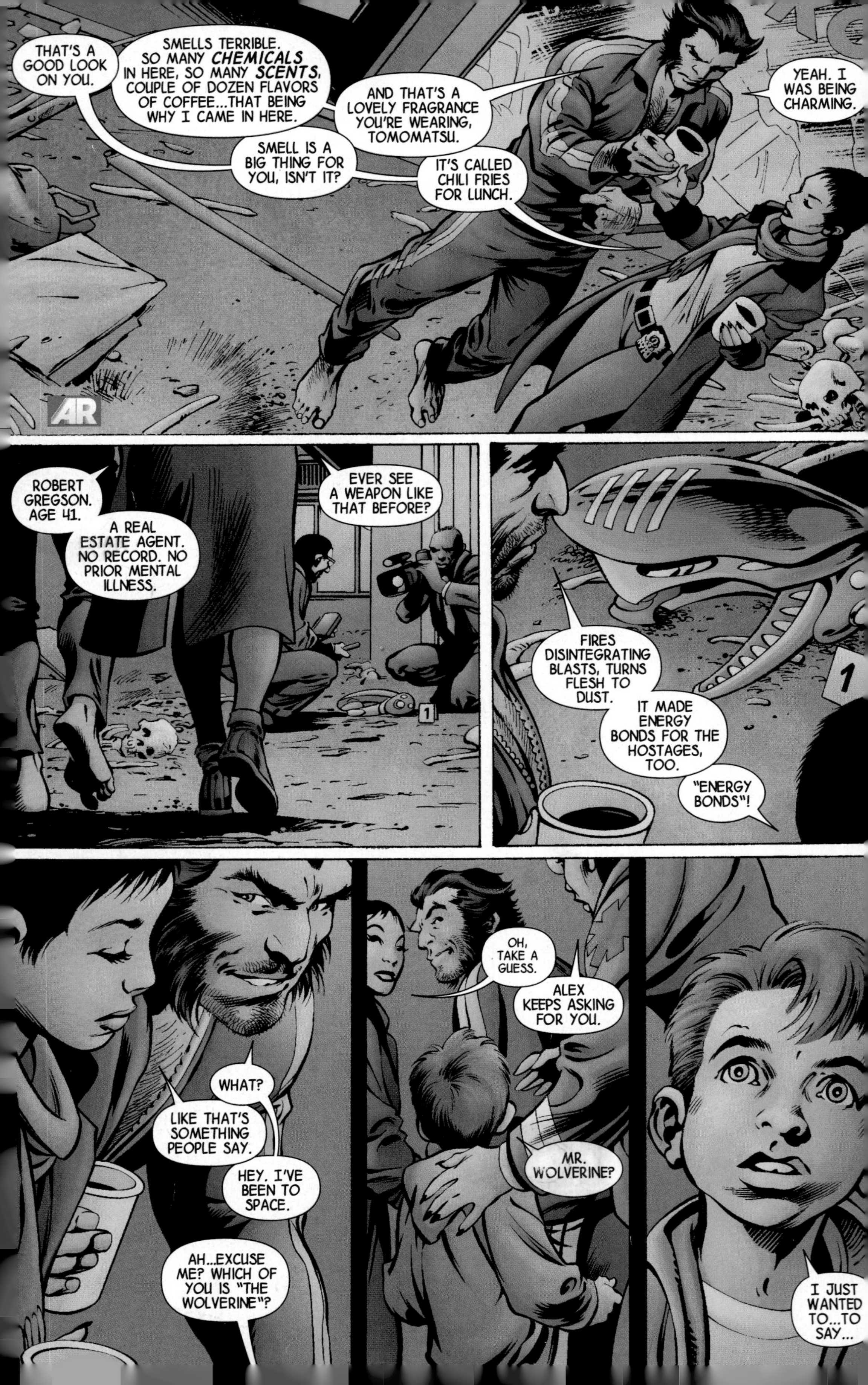
SMELLS TERRIBLE. SO MANY CHEMICALS IN HERE, SO MANY SCENTS, COUPLE OF DOZEN FLAVORS OF COFFEE...THAT BEING WHY I CAME IN HERE.
THAT'S A GOOD LOOK ON YOU.
AND THAT'S A LOVELY FRAGRANCE YOU'RE WEARING, TOMOMATSU.
YEAH. I WAS BEING CHARMING.
SMELL IS A BIG THING FOR YOU, ISN'T IT?
IT'S CALLED CHILI FRIES FOR LUNCH.
AR
ROBERT GREGSON. AGE 41.
A REAL ESTATE AGENT. NO RECORD. NO PRIOR MENTAL ILLNESS.
EVER SEE A WEAPON LIKE THAT BEFORE?
1
FIRES DISINTEGRATING BLASTS, TURNS FLESH TO DUST.
IT MADE ENERGY BONDS FOR THE HOSTAGES, TOO.
"ENERGY BONDS"!
1
WHAT?
LIKE THAT'S SOMETHING PEOPLE SAY.
HEY. I'VE BEEN TO SPACE.
AH...EXCUSE ME? WHICH OF YOU IS "THE WOLVERINE"?
OH, TAKE A GUESS.
ALEX KEEPS ASKING FOR YOU.
MR. WOLVERINE?
I JUST WANTED TO...TO SAY...

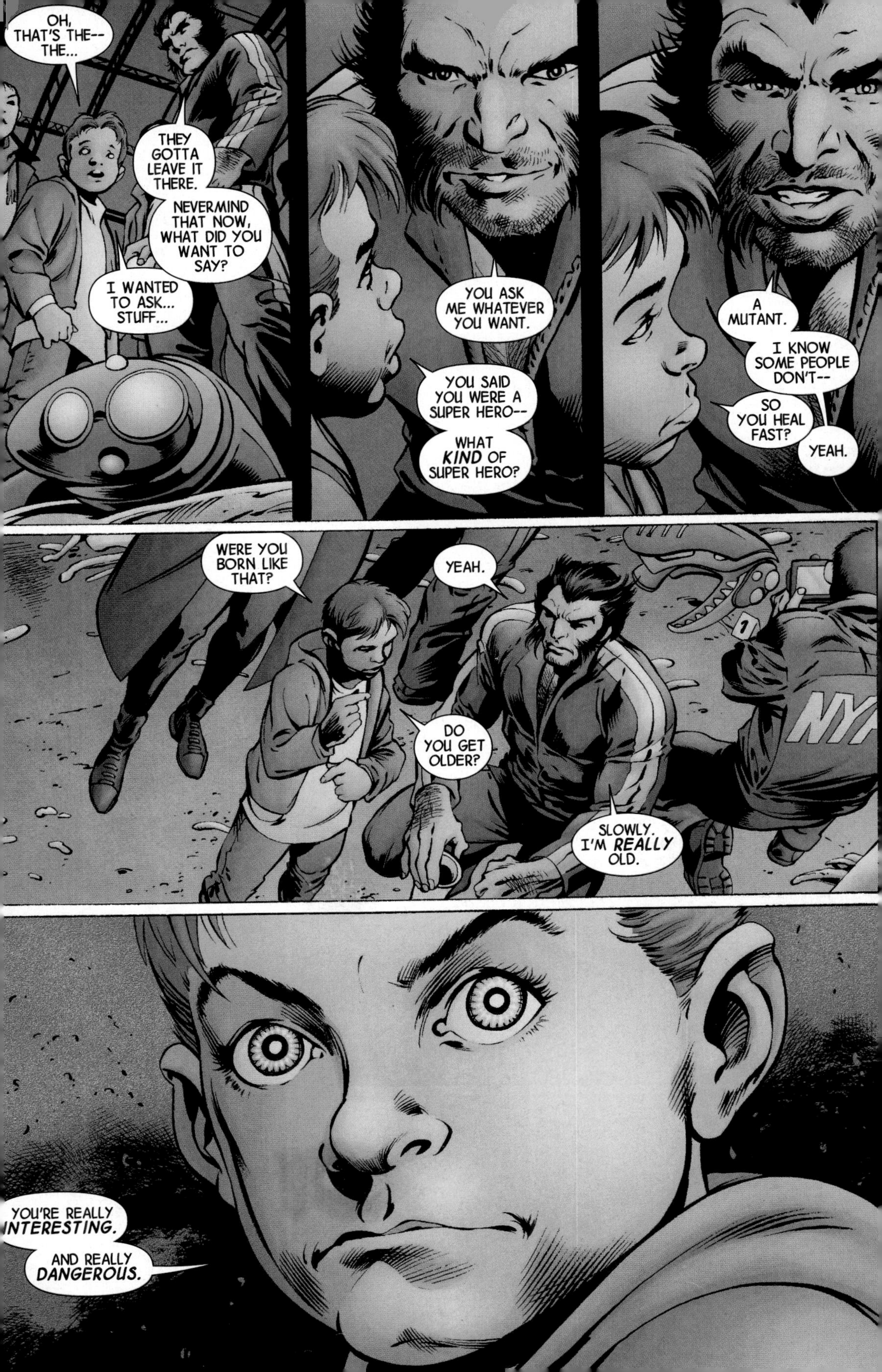
OH, THAT'S THE-- THE...
THEY GOTTA LEAVE IT THERE.
NEVERMIND THAT NOW, WHAT DID YOU WANT TO SAY?
I WANTED TO ASK... STUFF...
YOU ASK ME WHATEVER YOU WANT.
YOU SAID YOU WERE A SUPER HERO--
WHAT KIND OF SUPER HERO?
A MUTANT.
I KNOW SOME PEOPLE DON'T--
SO YOU HEAL FAST?
YEAH.
WERE YOU BORN LIKE THAT?
YEAH.
DO YOU GET OLDER?
SLOWLY. I'M REALLY OLD.
NY
YOU'RE REALLY INTERESTING.
AND REALLY DANGEROUS.

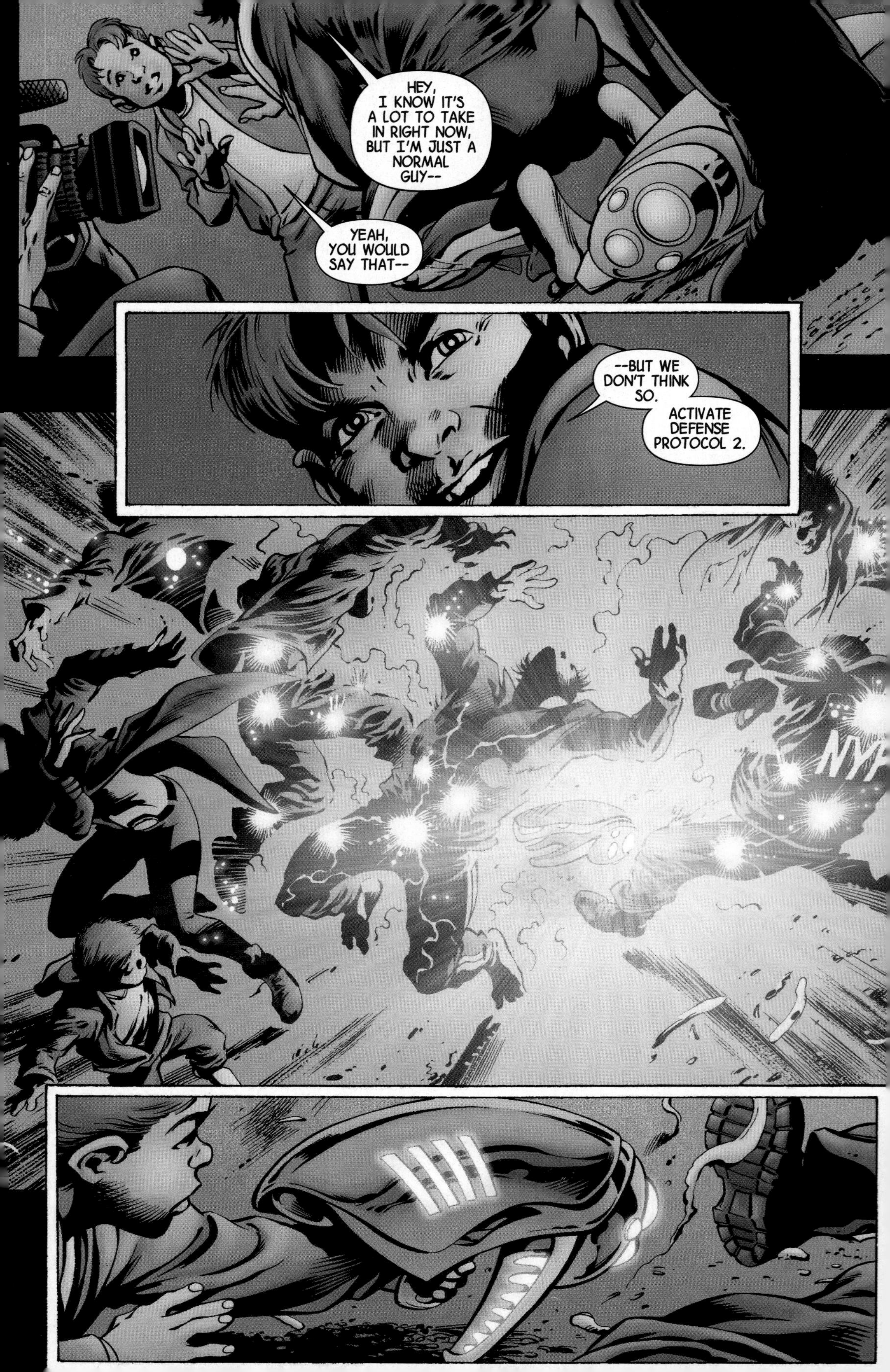
HEY, I KNOW IT'S A LOT TO TAKE IN RIGHT NOW, BUT I'M JUST A NORMAL GUY--
YEAH, YOU WOULD SAY THAT--
--BUT WE DON'T THINK SO.
ACTIVATE DEFENSE PROTOCOL 2.

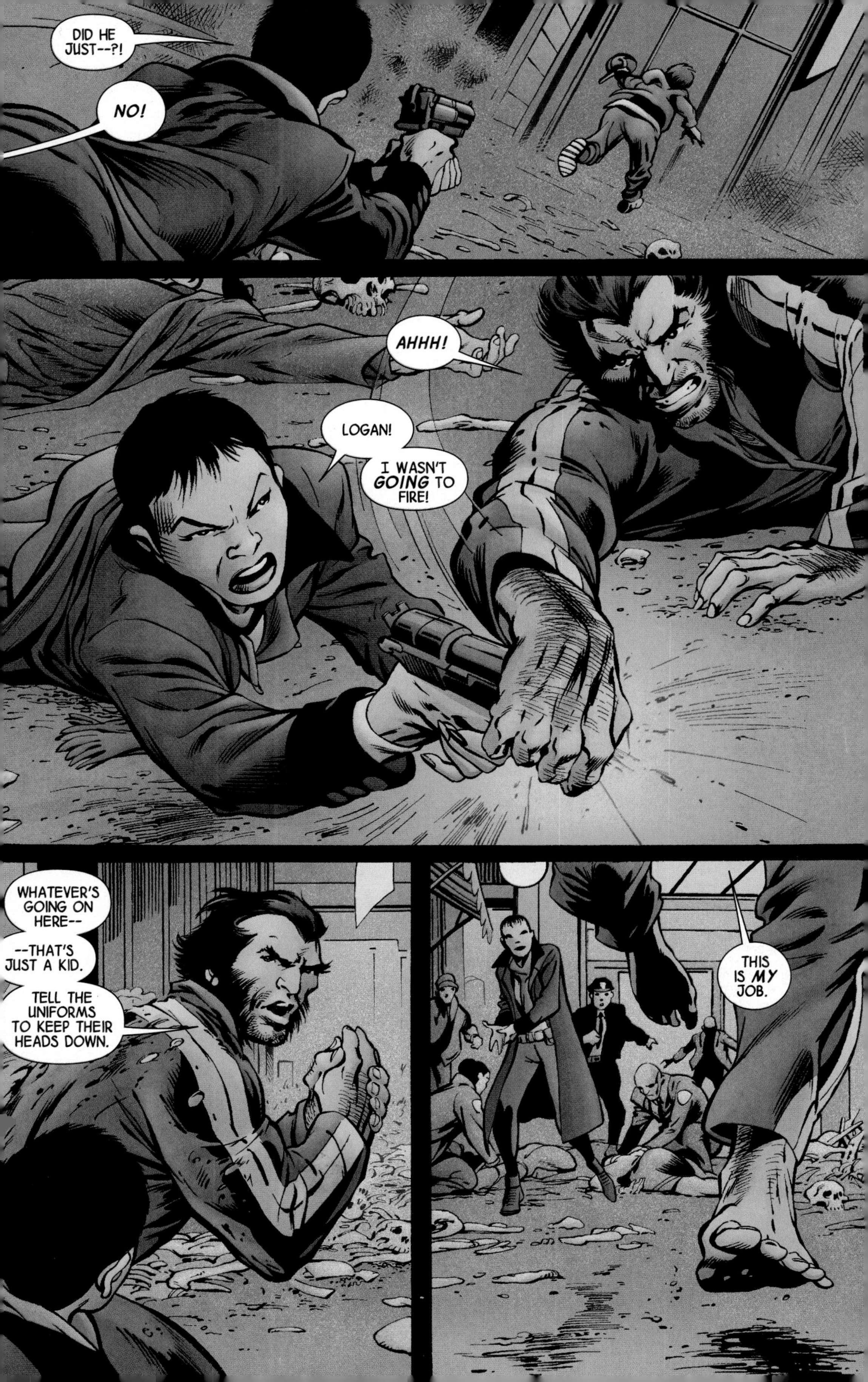
DID HE JUST--?!
NO!
AHHH!
LOGAN!
I WASN'T GOING TO FIRE!
WHATEVER'S GOING ON HERE--
--THAT'S JUST A KID.
TELL THE UNIFORMS TO KEEP THEIR HEADS DOWN.
THIS IS MY JOB.

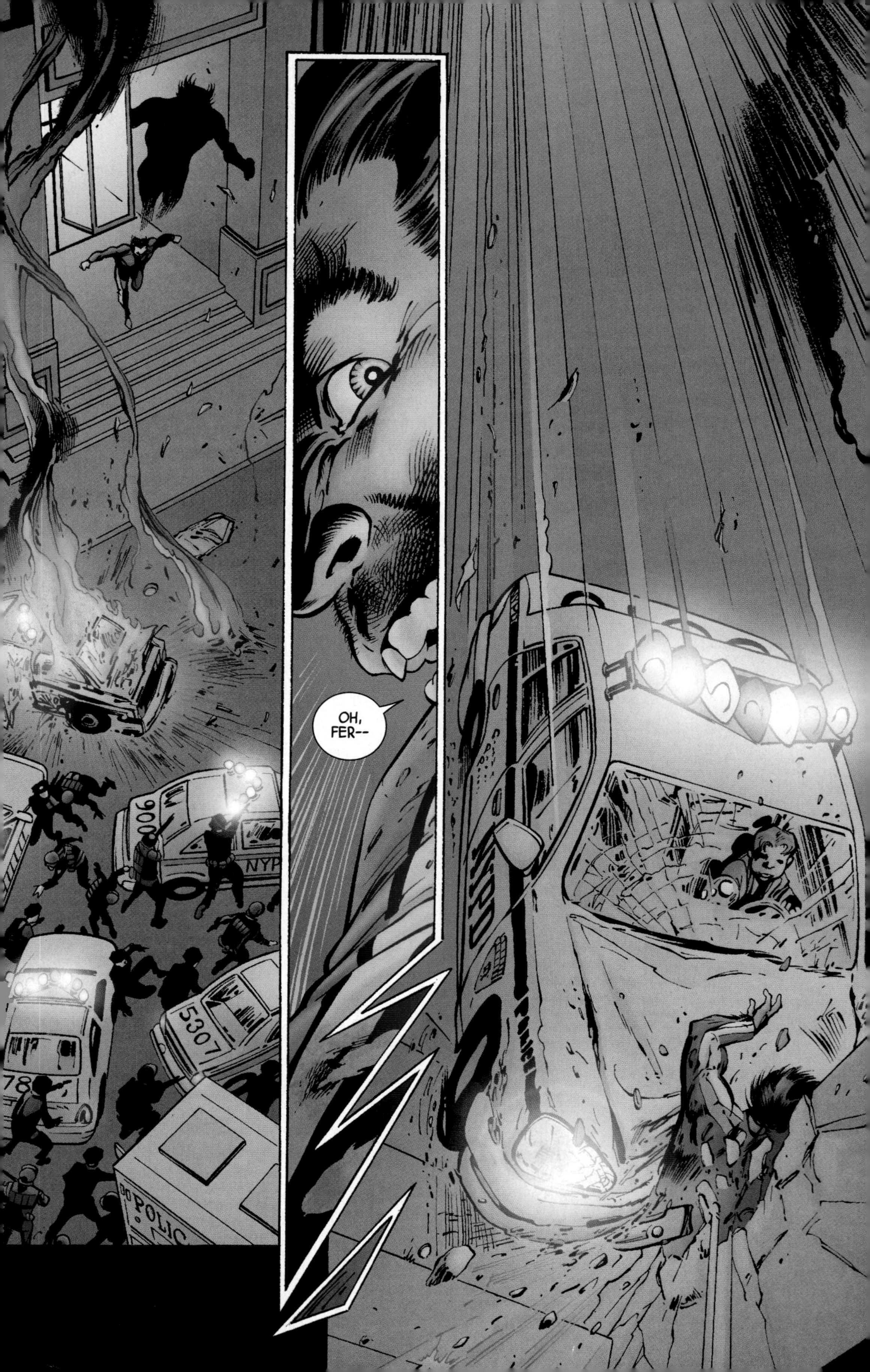
OH, FER--

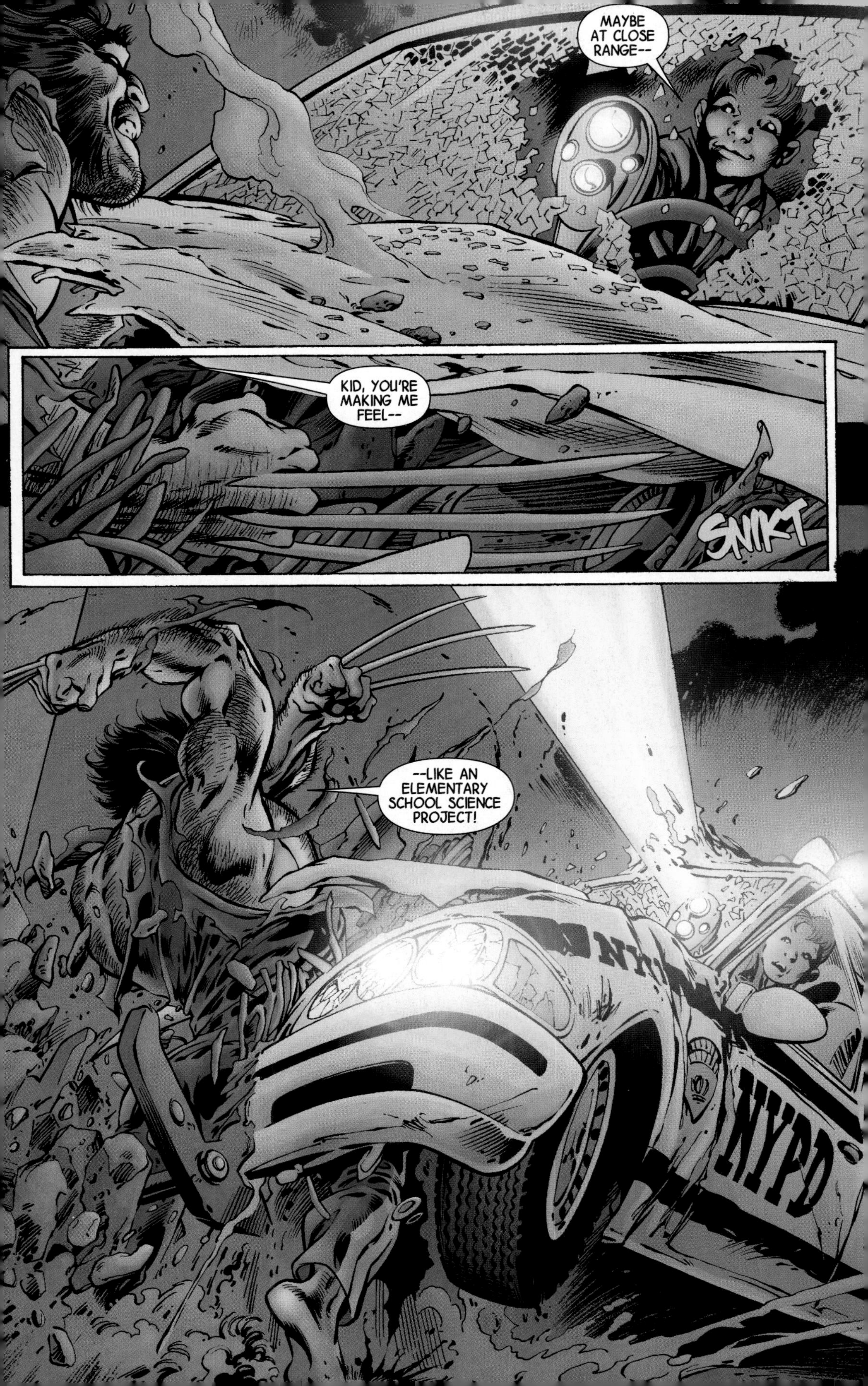
MAYBE AT CLOSE RANGE--
KID, YOU'RE MAKING ME FEEL--
SNIKT
--LIKE AN ELEMENTARY SCHOOL SCIENCE PROJECT!
NYPD
NYPD

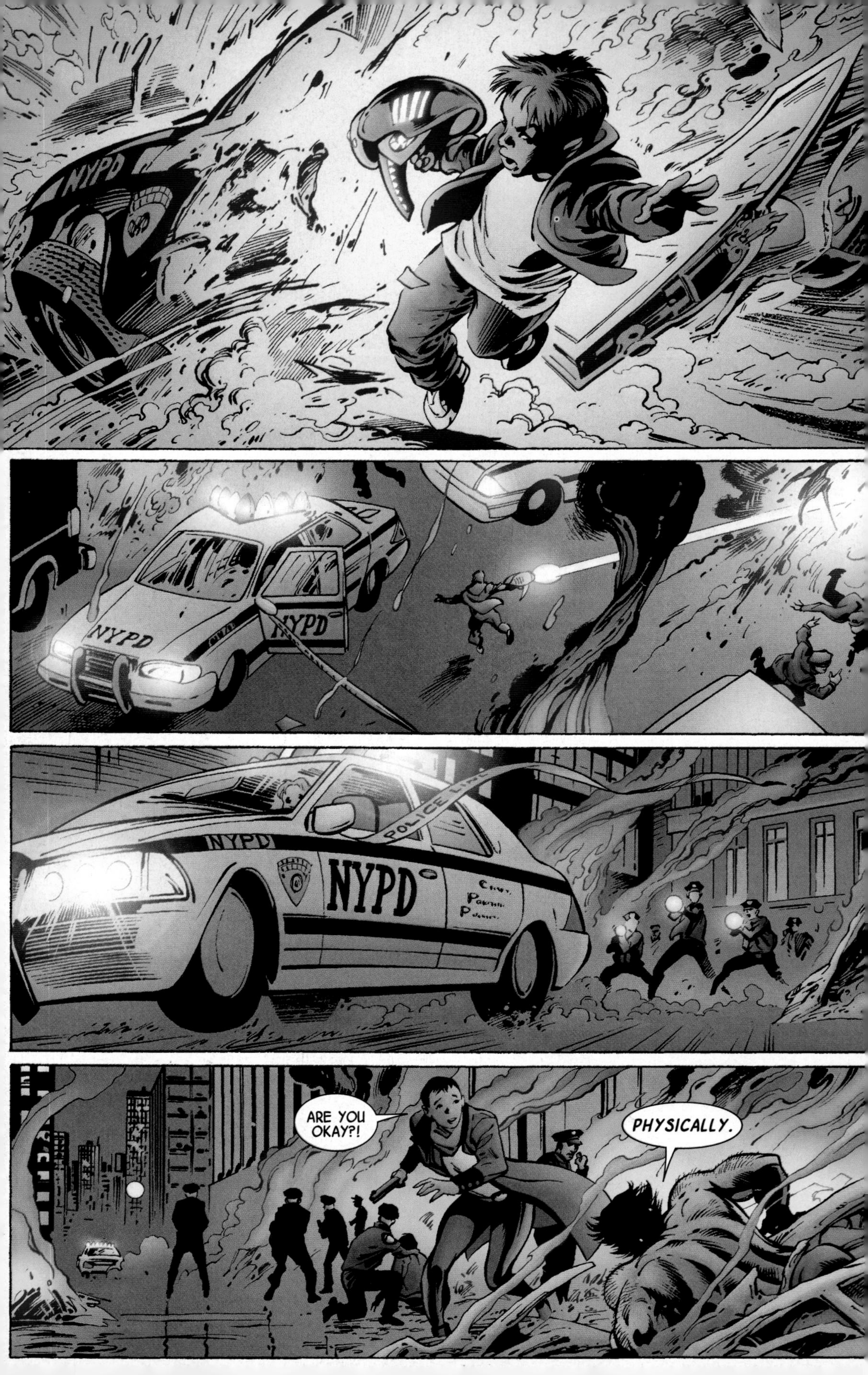
NYPD
NYPD
NYPD
NYPD
POLICE LINE
ARE YOU OKAY?!
PHYSICALLY.

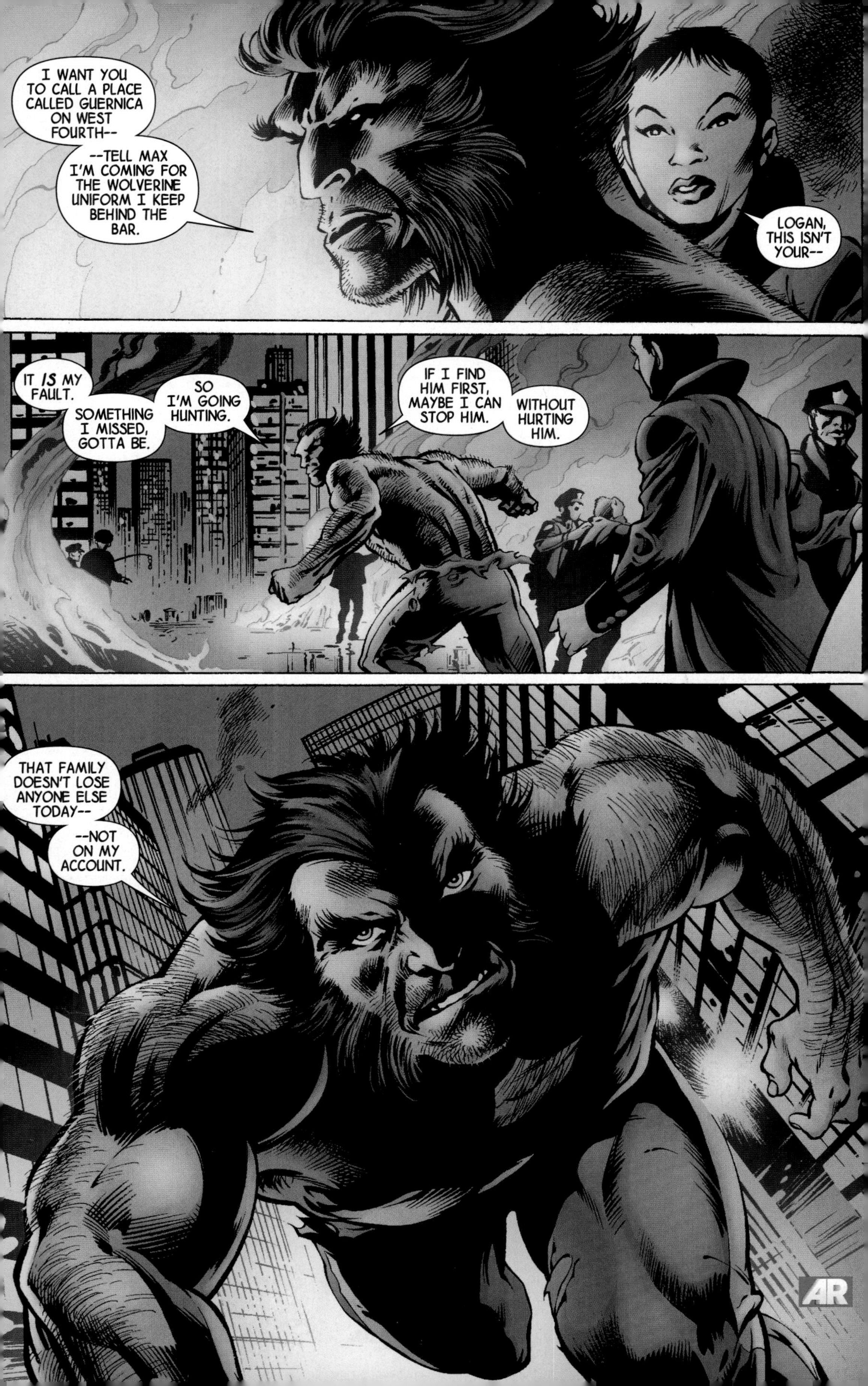
I WANT YOU TO CALL A PLACE CALLED GUERNICA ON WEST FOURTH--
--TELL MAX I'M COMING FOR THE WOLVERINE UNIFORM I KEEP BEHIND THE BAR.
LOGAN, THIS ISN'T YOUR--
IT IS MY FAULT.
SOMETHING I MISSED, GOTTA BE.
SO I'M GOING HUNTING.
IF I FIND HIM FIRST, MAYBE I CAN STOP HIM.
WITHOUT HURTING HIM.
THAT FAMILY DOESN'T LOSE ANYONE ELSE TODAY--
--NOT ON MY ACCOUNT.
AR

TWO

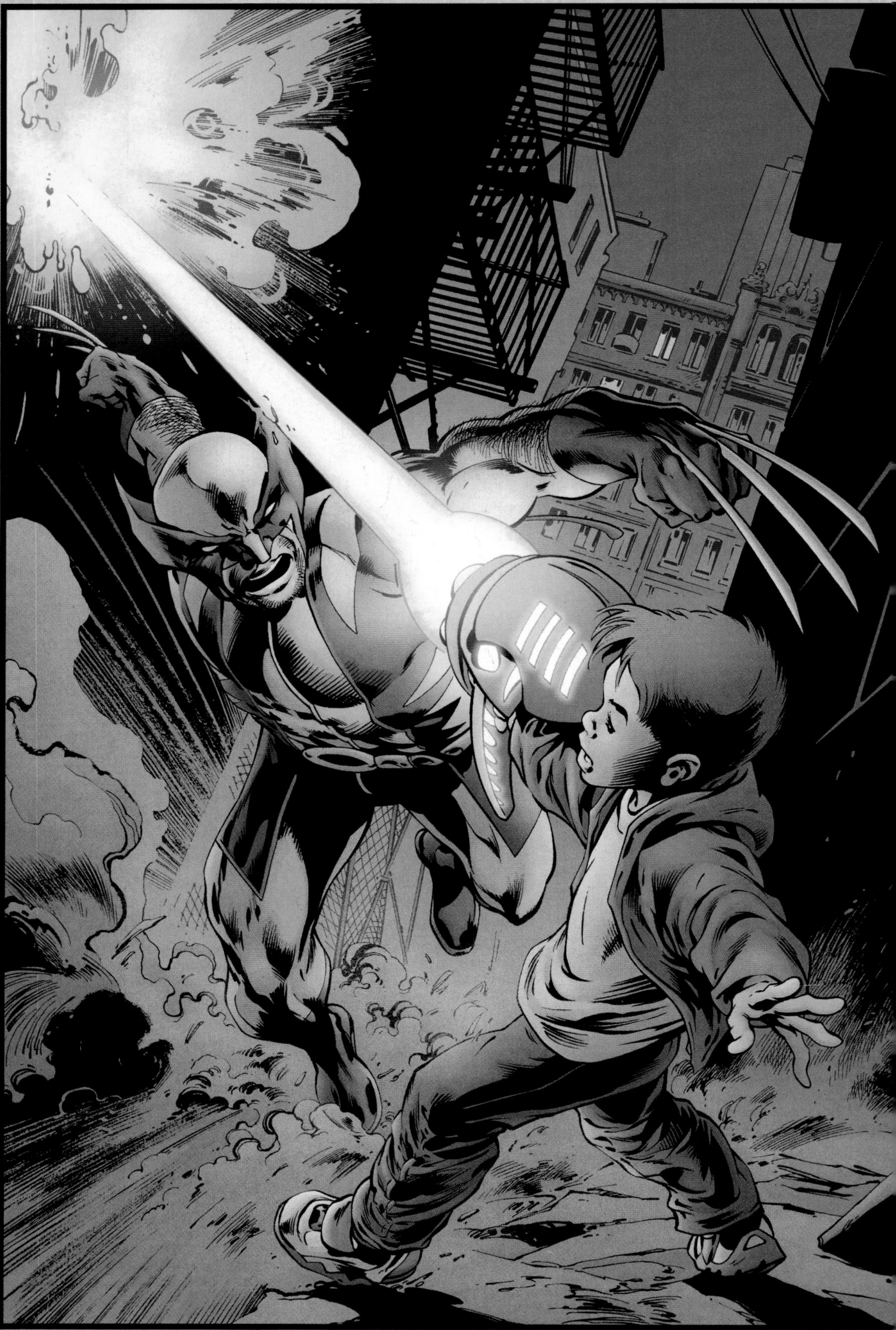

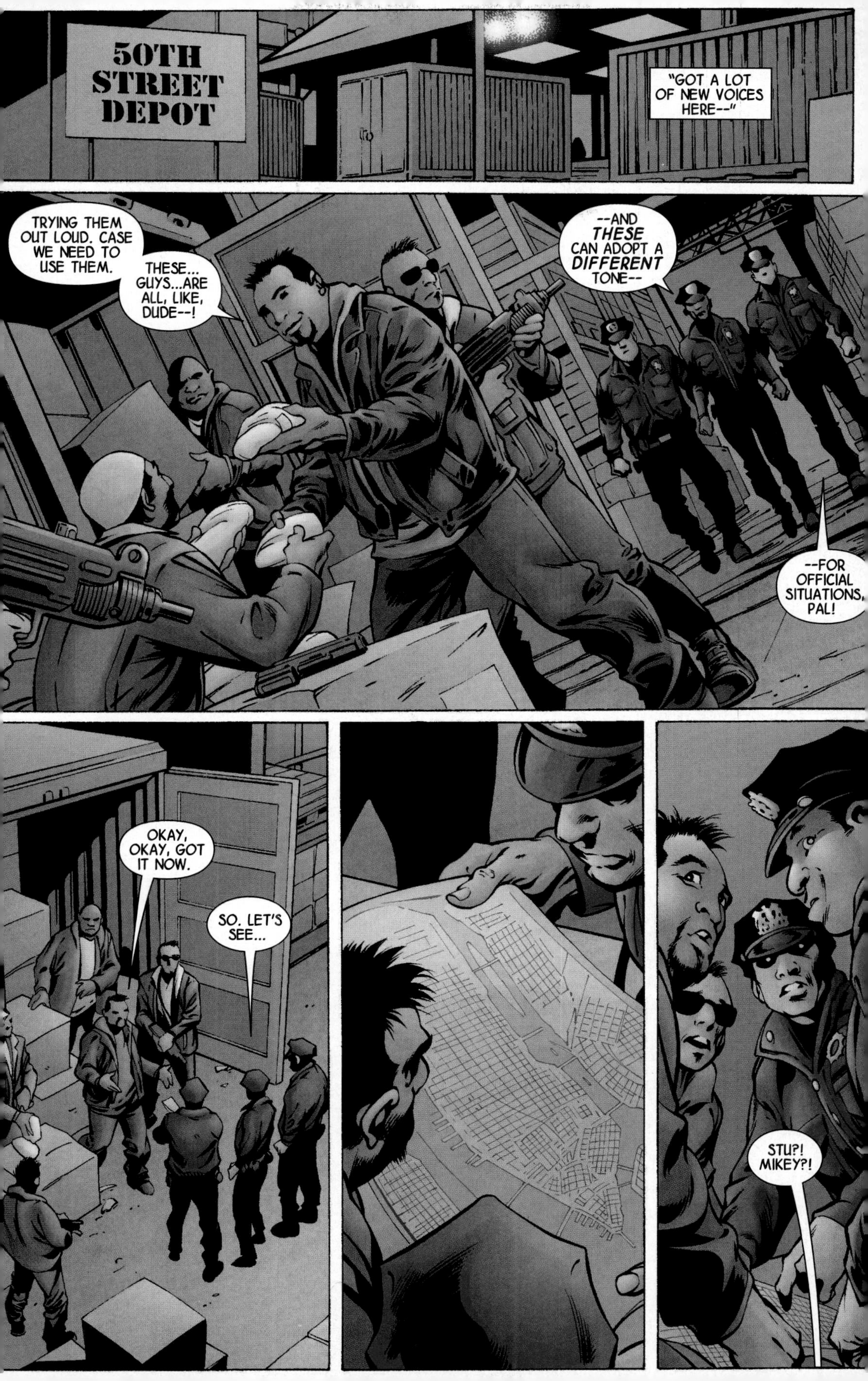
50TH STREET DEPOT
"GOT A LOT OF NEW VOICES HERE--"
TRYING THEM OUT LOUD. CASE WE NEED TO USE THEM.
THESE... GUYS...ARE ALL, LIKE, DUDE--!
--AND THESE CAN ADOPT A DIFFERENT TONE--
--FOR OFFICIAL SITUATIONS, PAL!
OKAY, OKAY, GOT IT NOW.
SO. LET'S SEE...
STU?! MIKEY?!

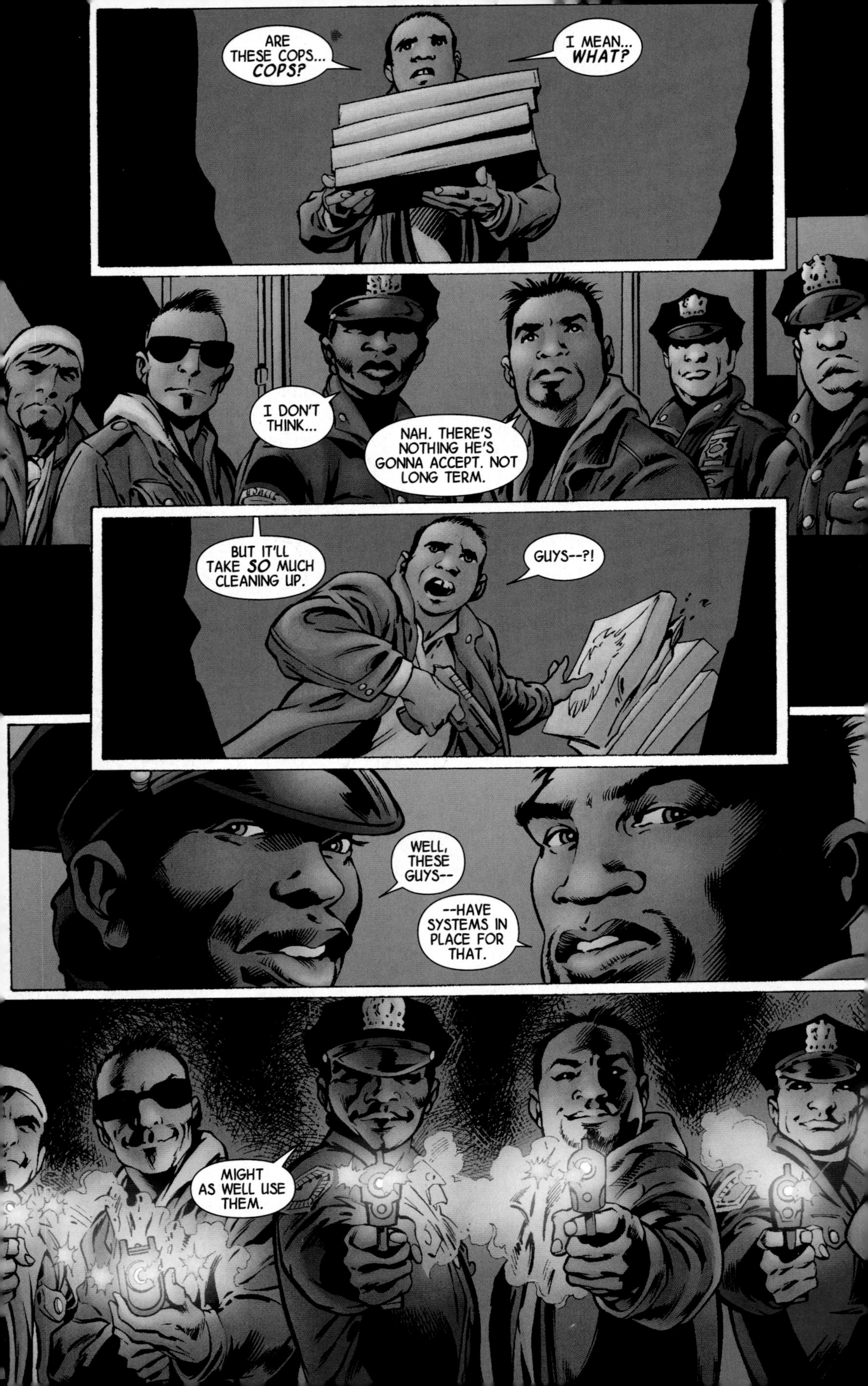
ARE THESE COPS... COPS?
I MEAN... WHAT?
I DON'T THINK...
NAH. THERE'S NOTHING HE'S GONNA ACCEPT. NOT LONG TERM.
BUT IT'LL TAKE SO MUCH CLEANING UP.
GUYS--?!
WELL, THESE GUYS--
--HAVE SYSTEMS IN PLACE FOR THAT.
MIGHT AS WELL USE THEM.

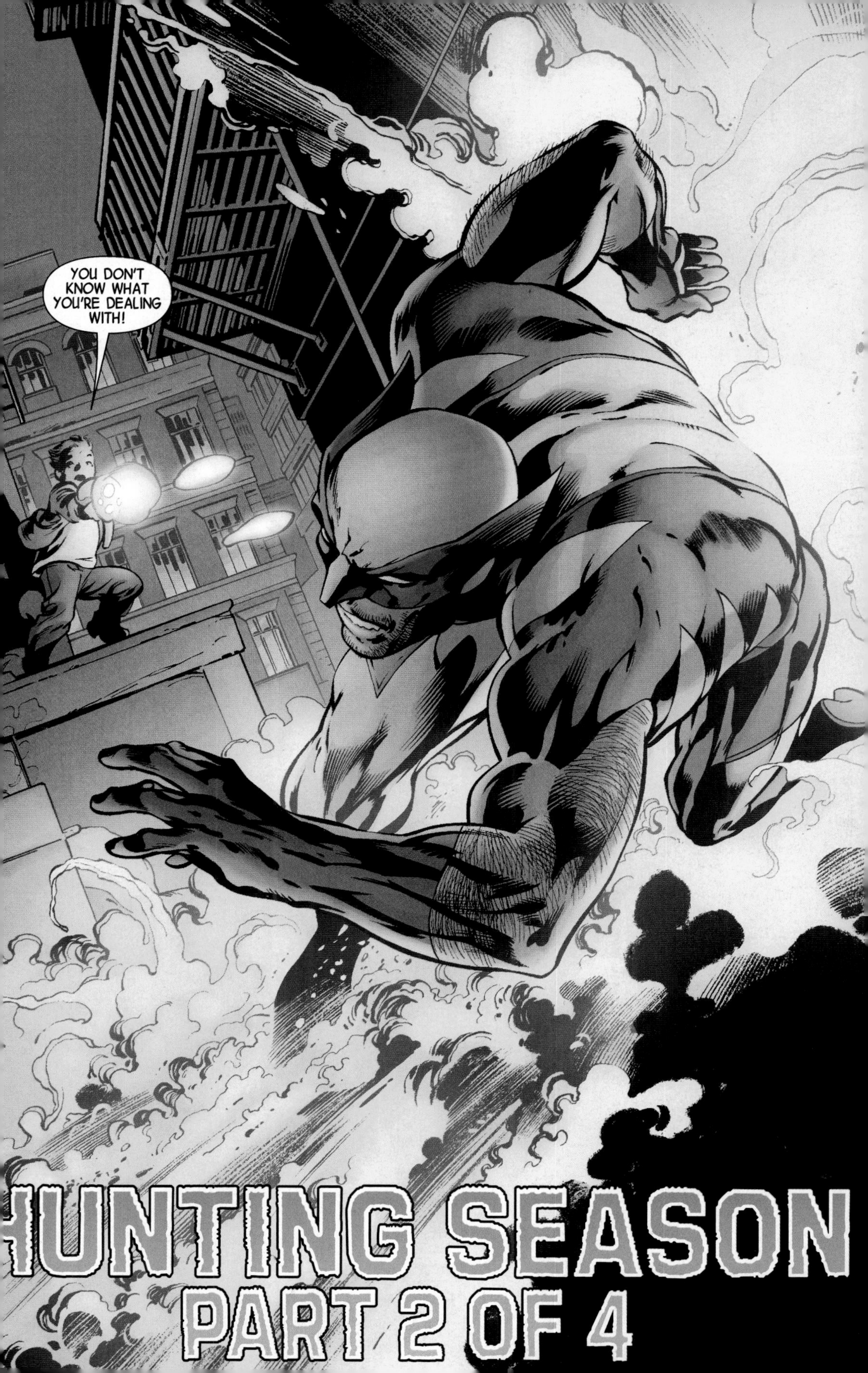
YOU DON'T KNOW WHAT YOU'RE DEALING WITH!
HUNTING SEASON
PART 2 OF 4

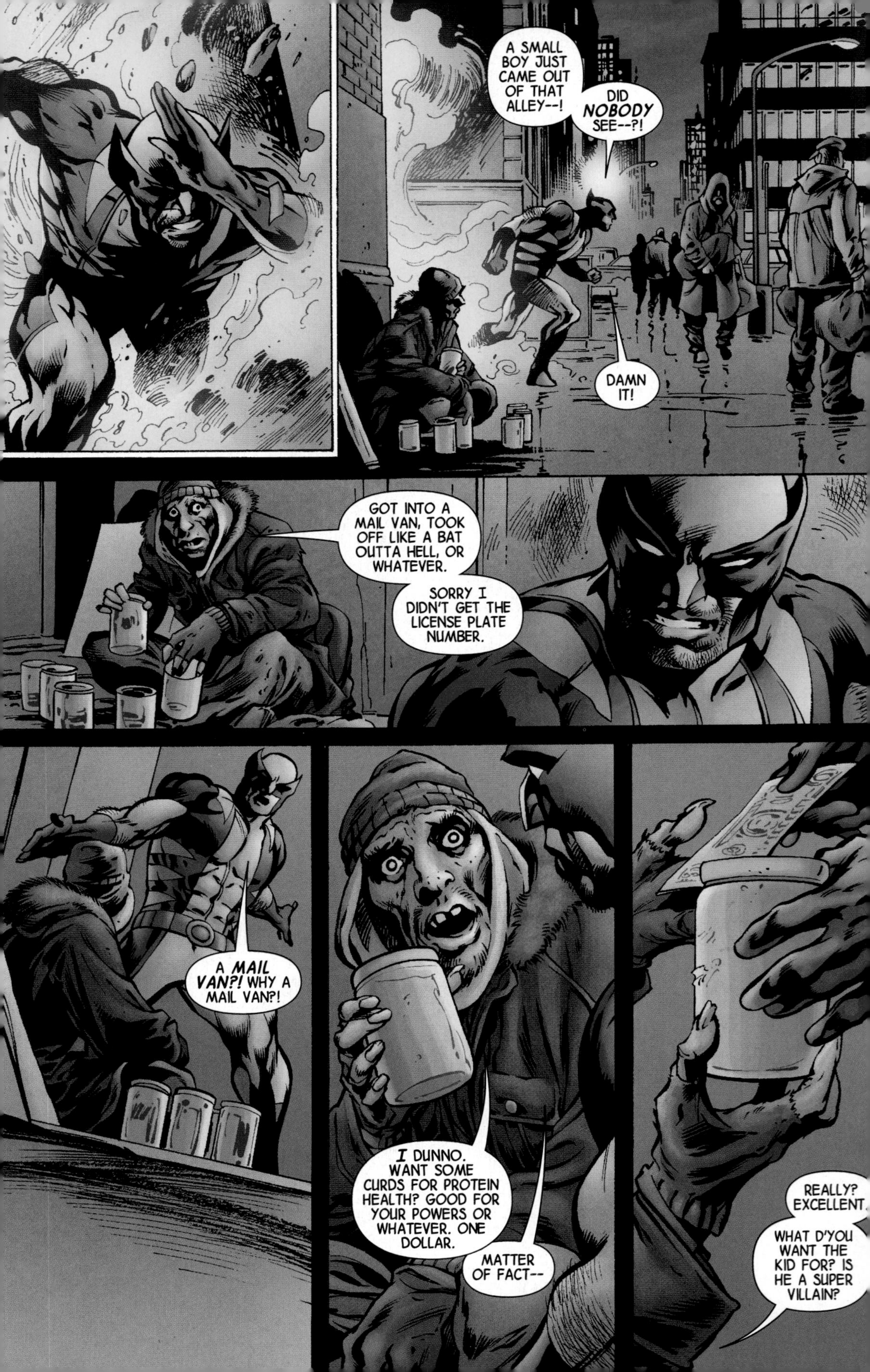
A SMALL BOY JUST CAME OUT OF THAT ALLEY--!
DID *NOBODY* SEE--?!
DAMN IT!
GOT INTO A MAIL VAN, TOOK OFF LIKE A BAT OUTTA HELL, OR WHATEVER.
SORRY I DIDN'T GET THE LICENSE PLATE NUMBER.
A *MAIL VAN?!* WHY A MAIL VAN?!
I DUNNO. WANT SOME CURDS FOR PROTEIN HEALTH? GOOD FOR YOUR POWERS OR WHATEVER. ONE DOLLAR.
MATTER OF FACT--
REALLY? EXCELLENT.
WHAT D'YOU WANT THE KID FOR? IS HE A SUPER VILLAIN?

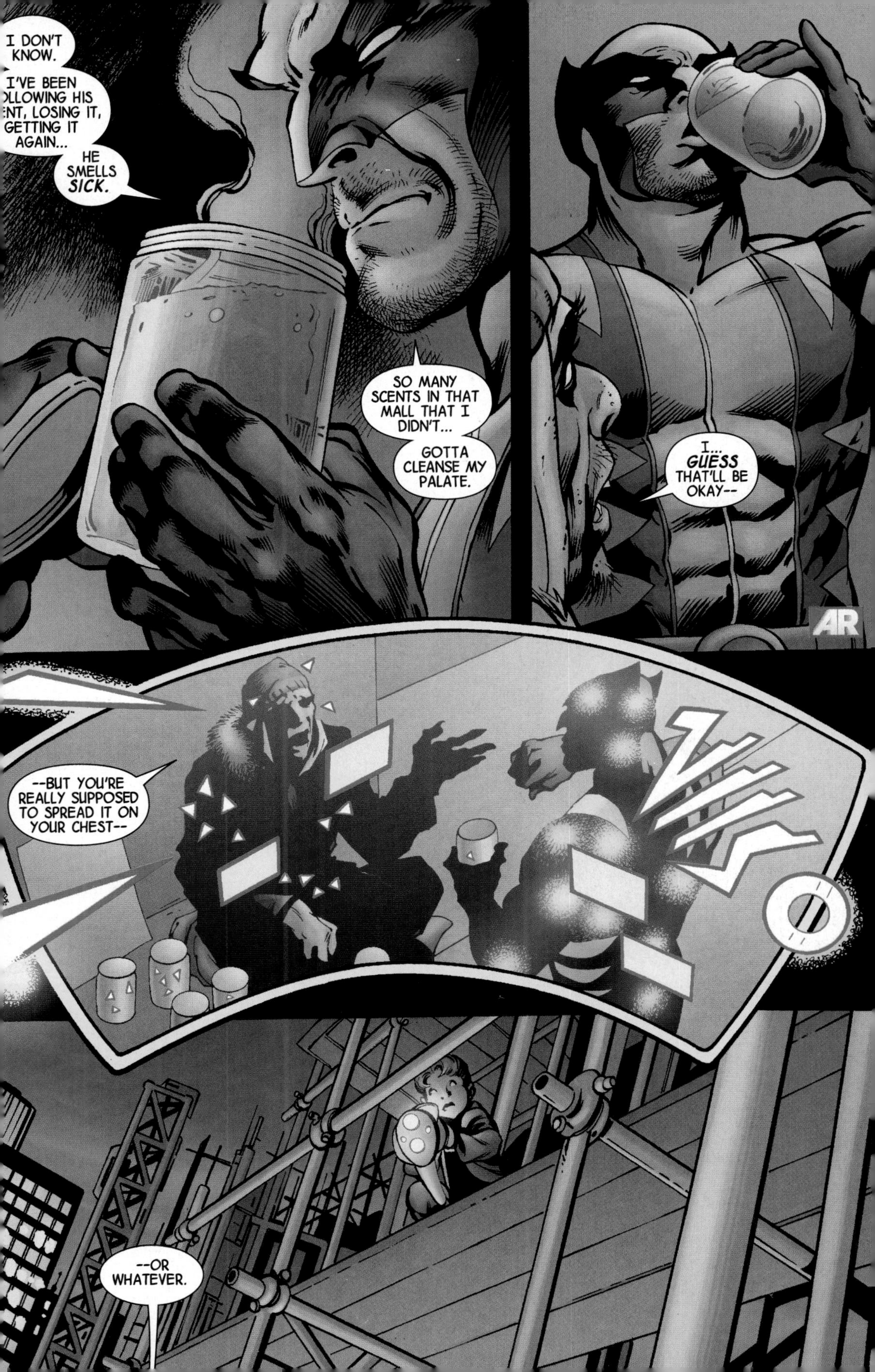
I DON'T KNOW.
I'VE BEEN
LLOWING HIS
ENT, LOSING IT,
GETTING IT
AGAIN...
HE SMELLS *SICK.*
SO MANY SCENTS IN THAT MALL THAT I DIDN'T...
GOTTA CLEANSE MY PALATE.
I... *GUESS* THAT'LL BE OKAY--
--BUT YOU'RE REALLY SUPPOSED TO SPREAD IT ON YOUR CHEST--
--OR WHATEVER.

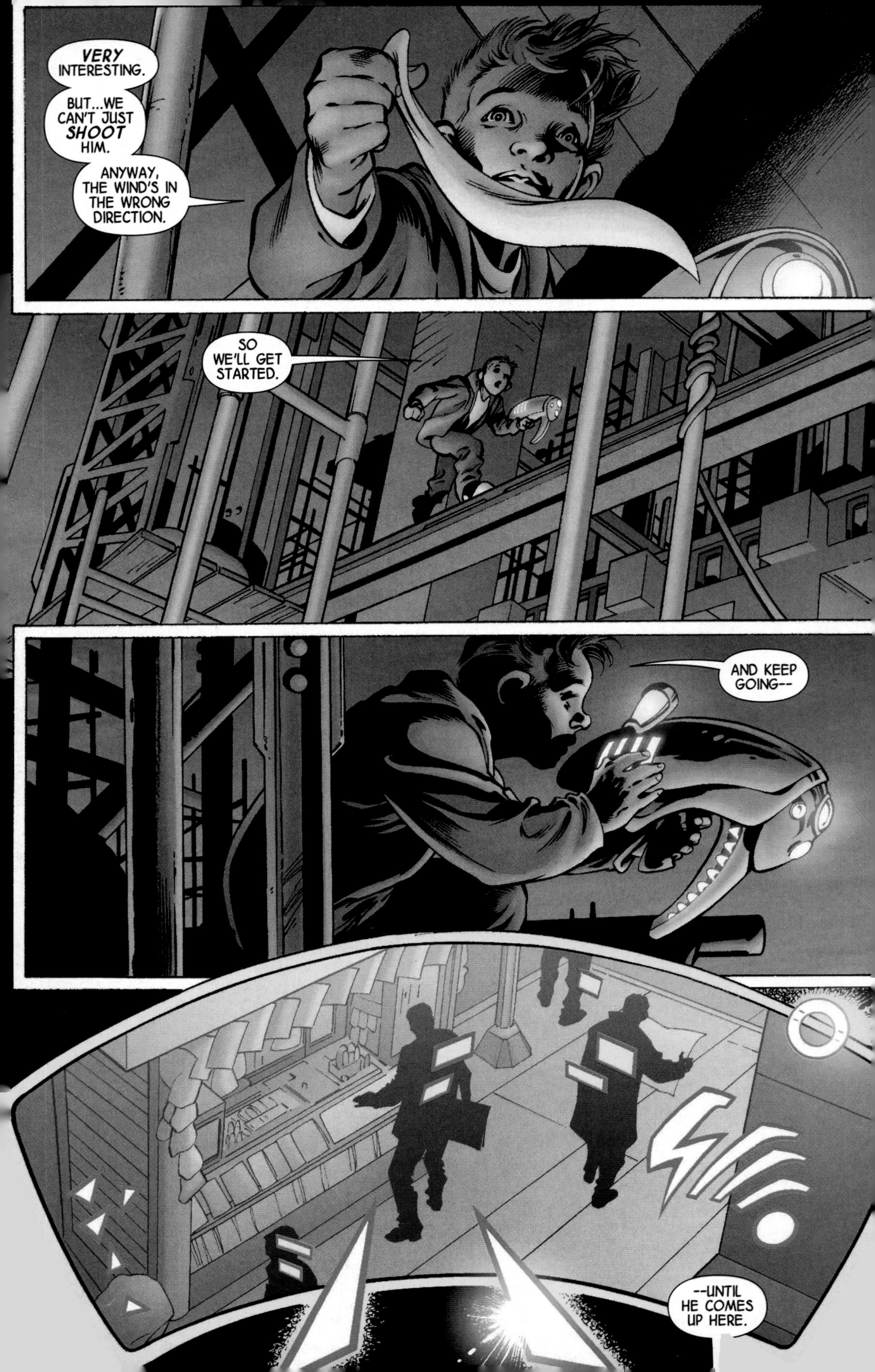
VERY INTERESTING.
BUT...WE CAN'T JUST SHOOT HIM.
ANYWAY, THE WIND'S IN THE WRONG DIRECTION.
SO WE'LL GET STARTED.
AND KEEP GOING--
--UNTIL HE COMES UP HERE.

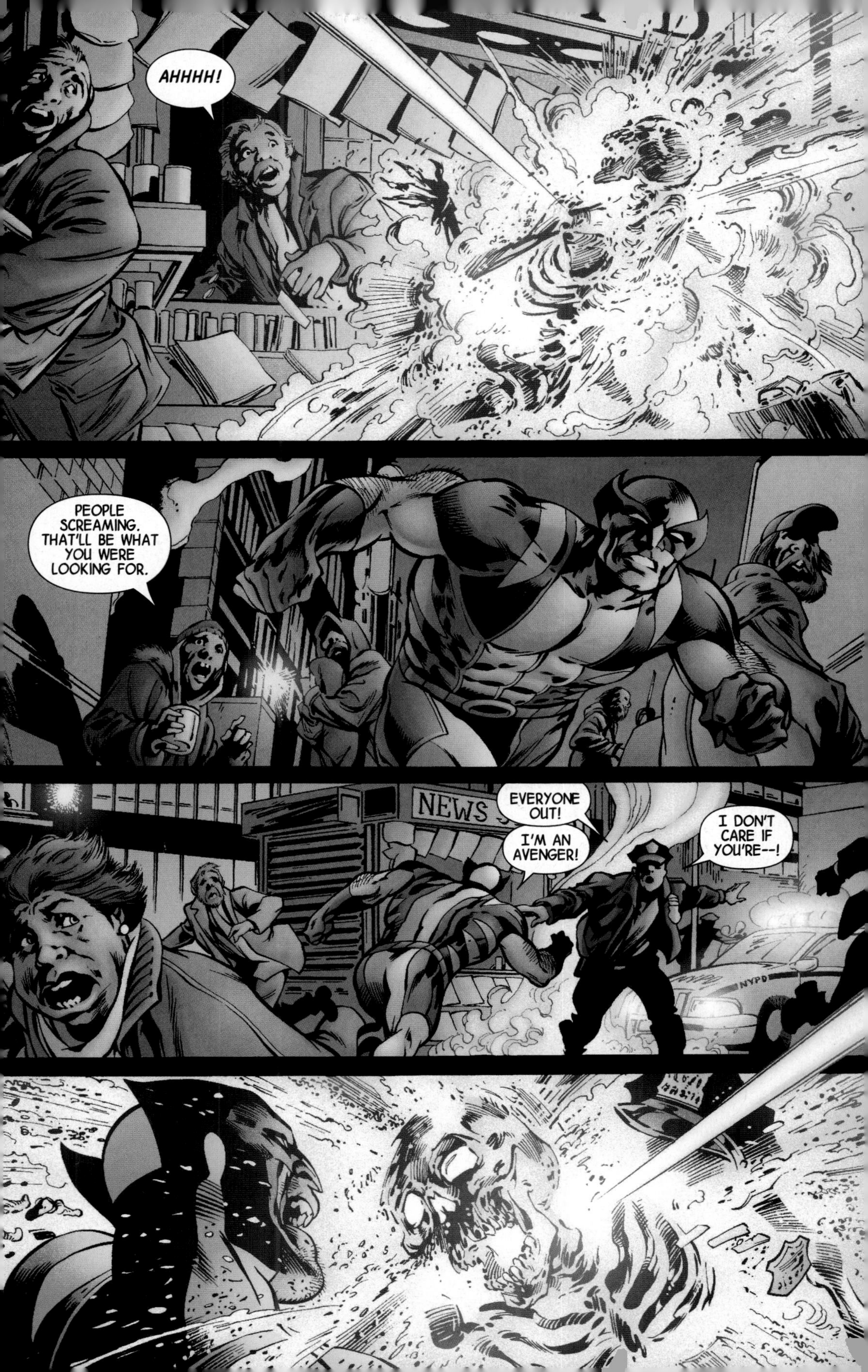
AHHHH!
PEOPLE SCREAMING. THAT'LL BE WHAT YOU WERE LOOKING FOR.
NEWS
EVERYONE OUT!
I'M AN AVENGER!
I DON'T CARE IF YOU'RE--!
NYPD

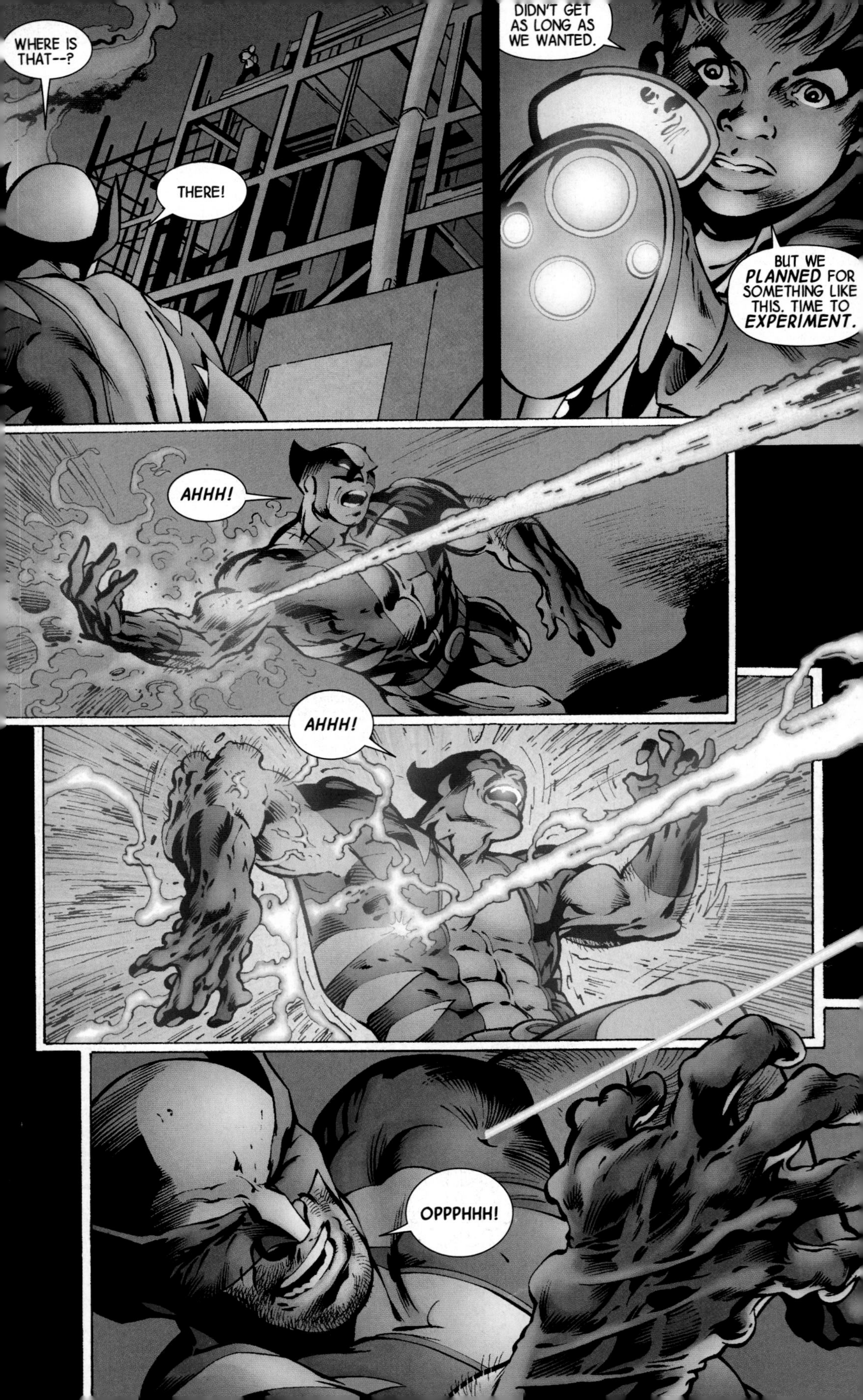
WHERE IS THAT--?
THERE!
DIDN'T GET AS LONG AS WE WANTED.
BUT WE *PLANNED* FOR SOMETHING LIKE THIS. TIME TO *EXPERIMENT.*
AHHH!
AHHH!
OPPPHHH!

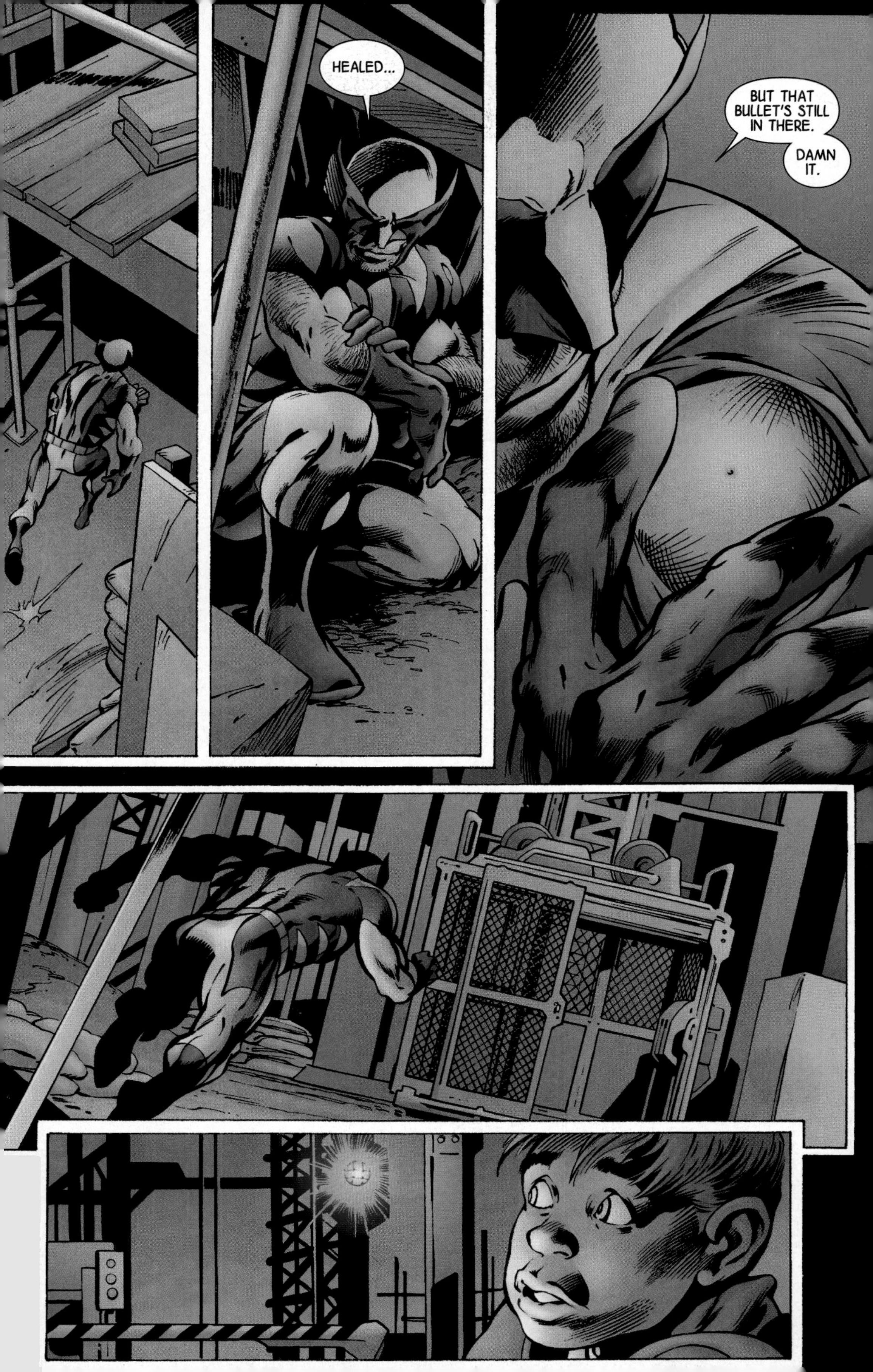
HEALED...
BUT THAT BULLET'S STILL IN THERE.
DAMN IT.

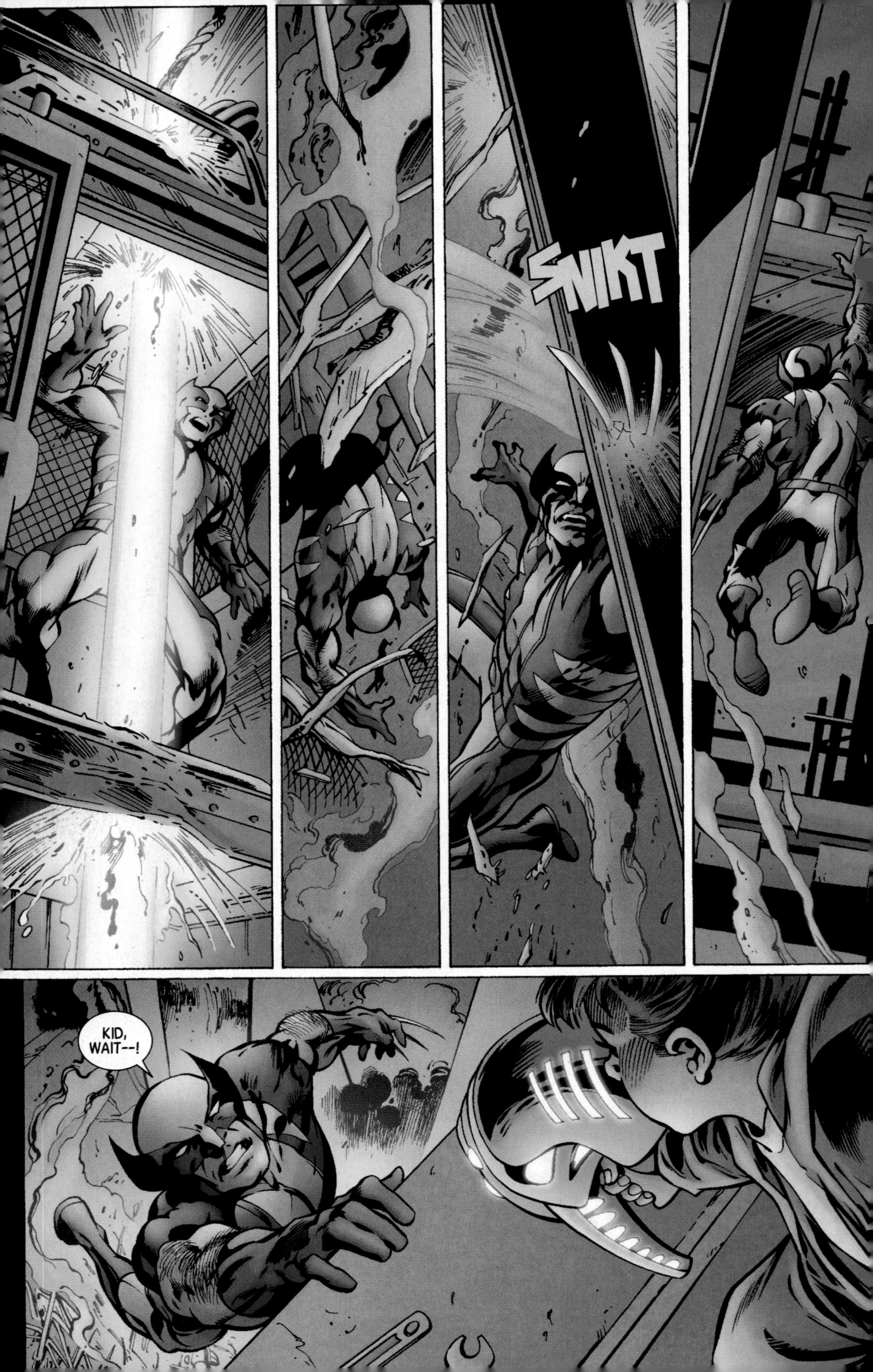
SNIKT
KID, WAIT--!

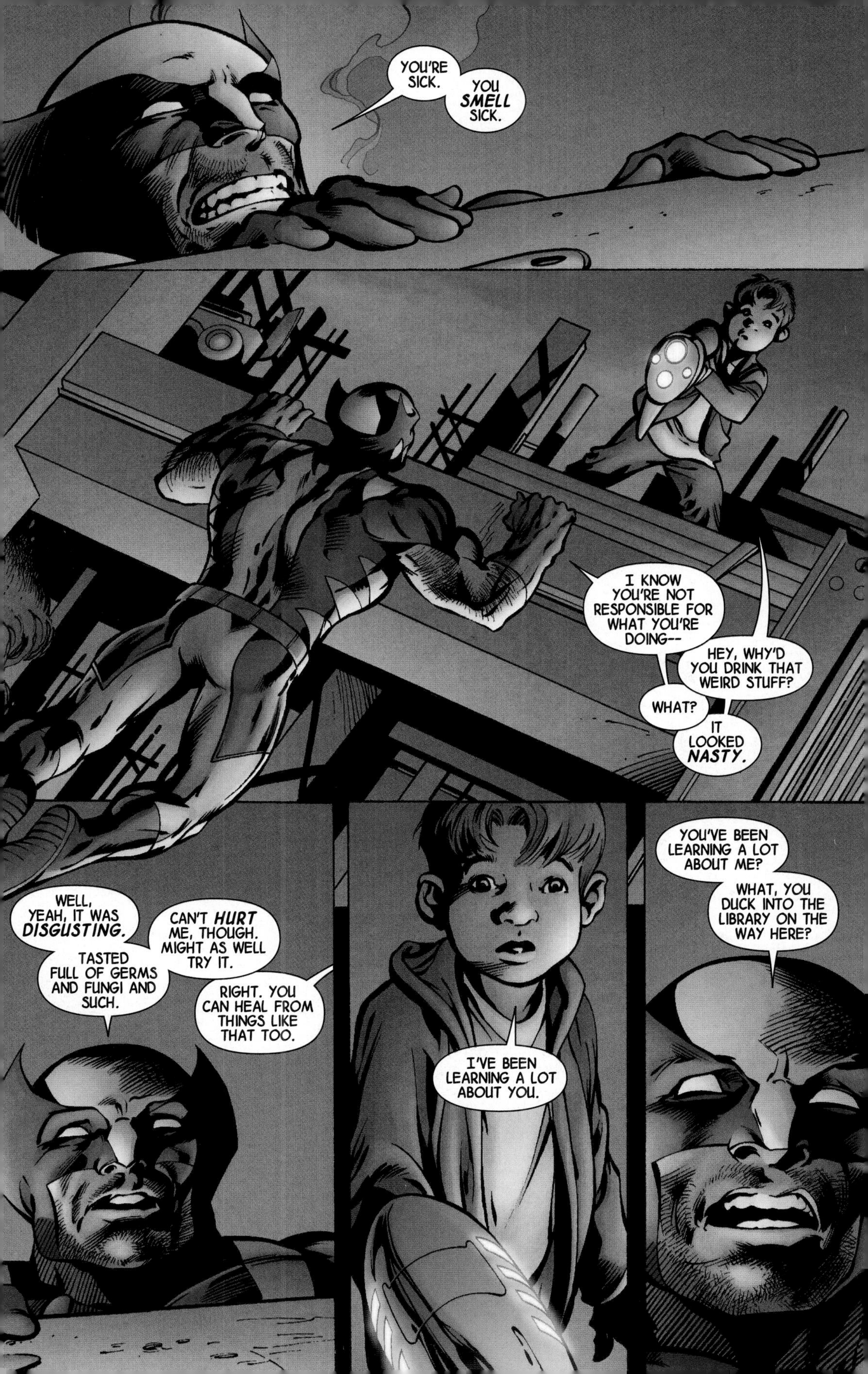
YOU'RE SICK.
YOU SMELL SICK.
I KNOW YOU'RE NOT RESPONSIBLE FOR WHAT YOU'RE DOING--
HEY, WHY'D YOU DRINK THAT WEIRD STUFF?
WHAT?
IT LOOKED NASTY.
WELL, YEAH, IT WAS DISGUSTING.
TASTED FULL OF GERMS AND FUNGI AND SUCH.
CAN'T HURT ME, THOUGH. MIGHT AS WELL TRY IT.
RIGHT. YOU CAN HEAL FROM THINGS LIKE THAT TOO.
I'VE BEEN LEARNING A LOT ABOUT YOU.
YOU'VE BEEN LEARNING A LOT ABOUT ME?
WHAT, YOU DUCK INTO THE LIBRARY ON THE WAY HERE?

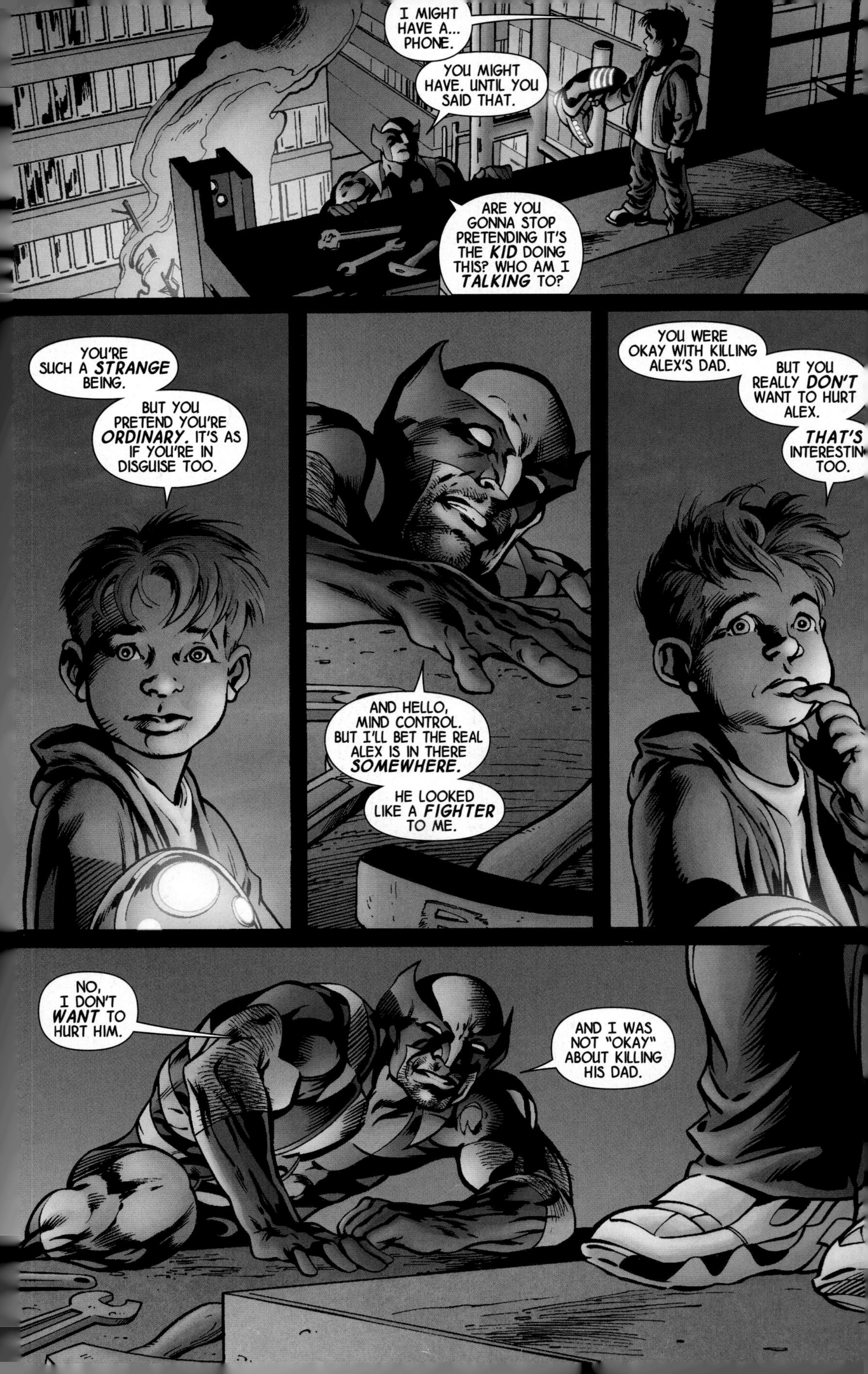
I MIGHT HAVE A... PHONE.
YOU MIGHT HAVE. UNTIL YOU SAID THAT.
ARE YOU GONNA STOP PRETENDING IT'S THE KID DOING THIS? WHO AM I TALKING TO?
YOU'RE SUCH A STRANGE BEING.
BUT YOU PRETEND YOU'RE ORDINARY. IT'S AS IF YOU'RE IN DISGUISE TOO.
AND HELLO, MIND CONTROL. BUT I'LL BET THE REAL ALEX IS IN THERE SOMEWHERE.
HE LOOKED LIKE A FIGHTER TO ME.
YOU WERE OKAY WITH KILLING ALEX'S DAD.
BUT YOU REALLY DON'T WANT TO HURT ALEX.
THAT'S INTERESTIN TOO.
NO, I DON'T WANT TO HURT HIM.
AND I WAS NOT "OKAY" ABOUT KILLING HIS DAD.

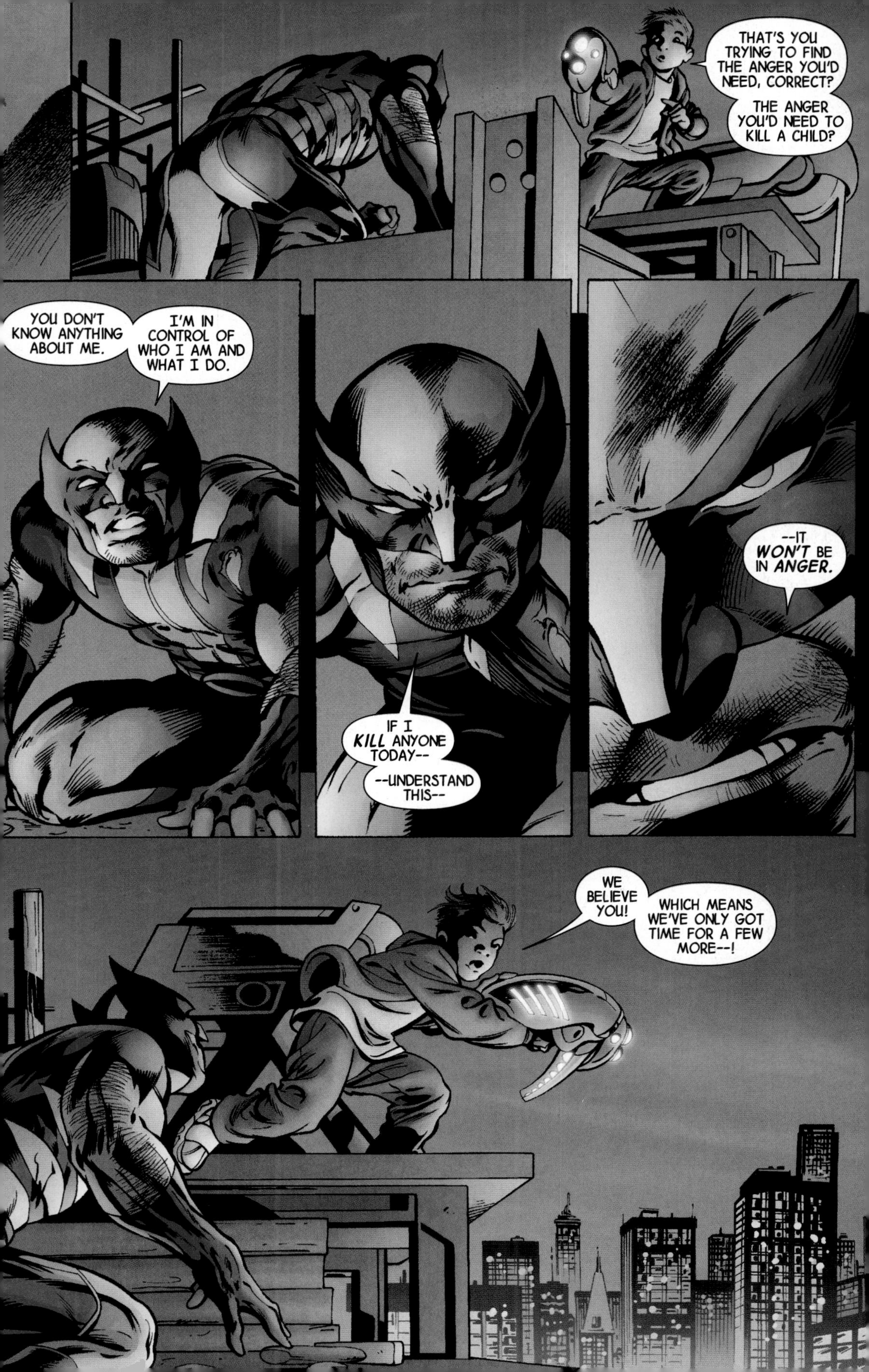
THAT'S YOU TRYING TO FIND THE ANGER YOU'D NEED, CORRECT?
THE ANGER YOU'D NEED TO KILL A CHILD?
YOU DON'T KNOW ANYTHING ABOUT ME.
I'M IN CONTROL OF WHO I AM AND WHAT I DO.
IF I KILL ANYONE TODAY--
--UNDERSTAND THIS--
--IT WON'T BE IN ANGER.
WE BELIEVE YOU!
WHICH MEANS WE'VE ONLY GOT TIME FOR A FEW MORE--!

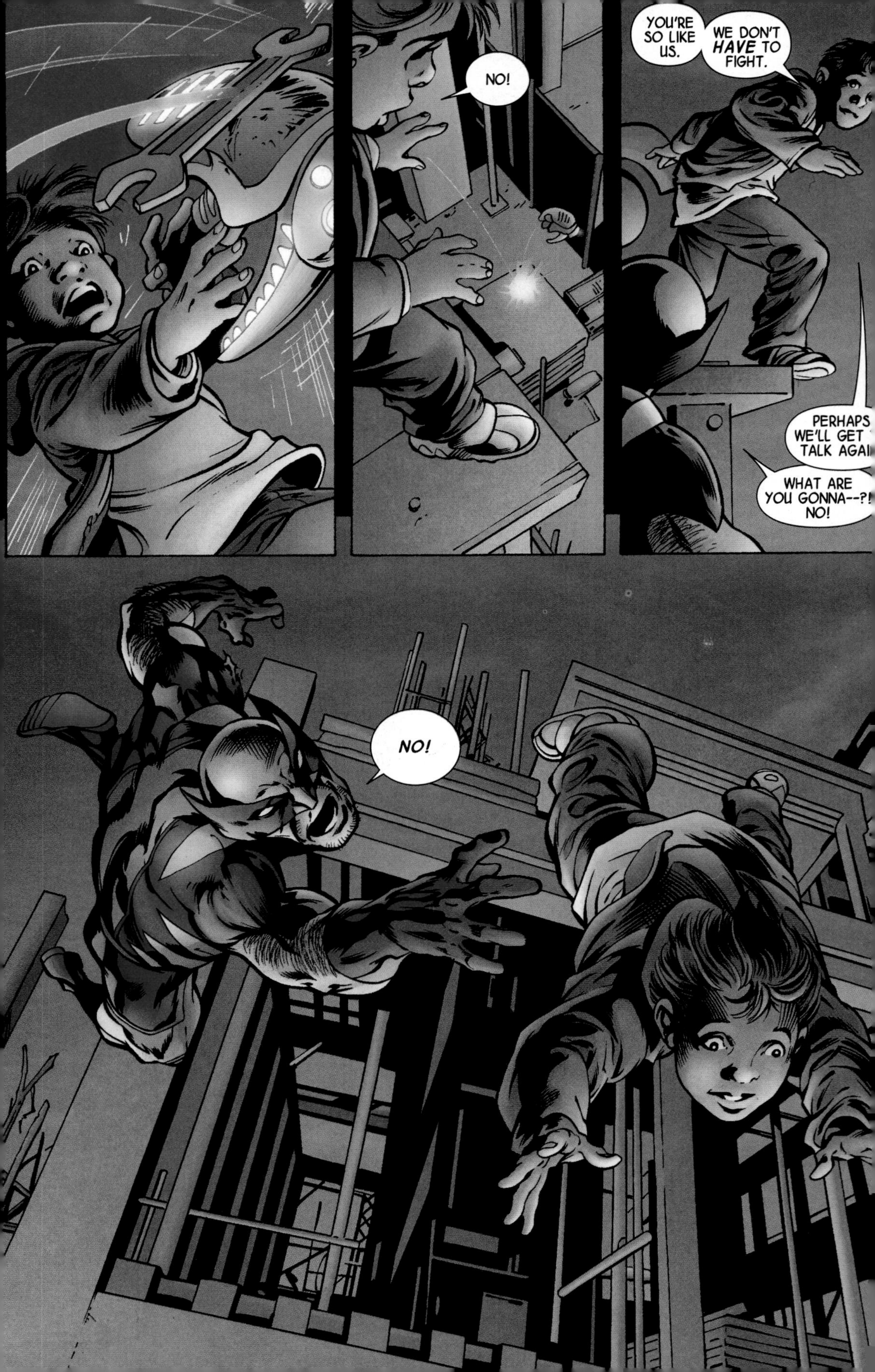
NO!
YOU'RE SO LIKE US.
WE DON'T *HAVE* TO FIGHT.
WHAT ARE YOU GONNA--?! NO!
NO!

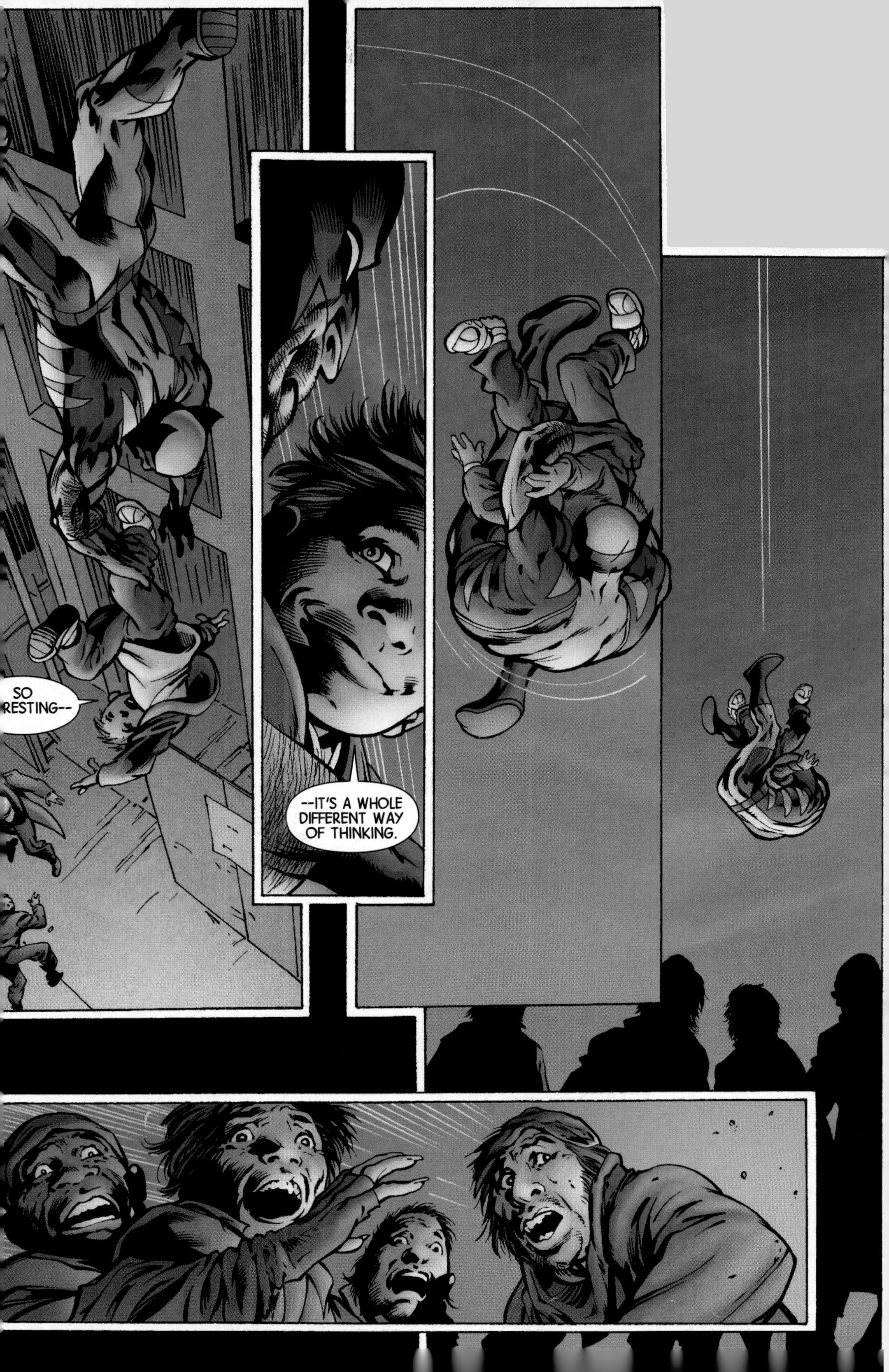
SO
RESTING--
--IT'S A WHOLE DIFFERENT WAY OF THINKING.

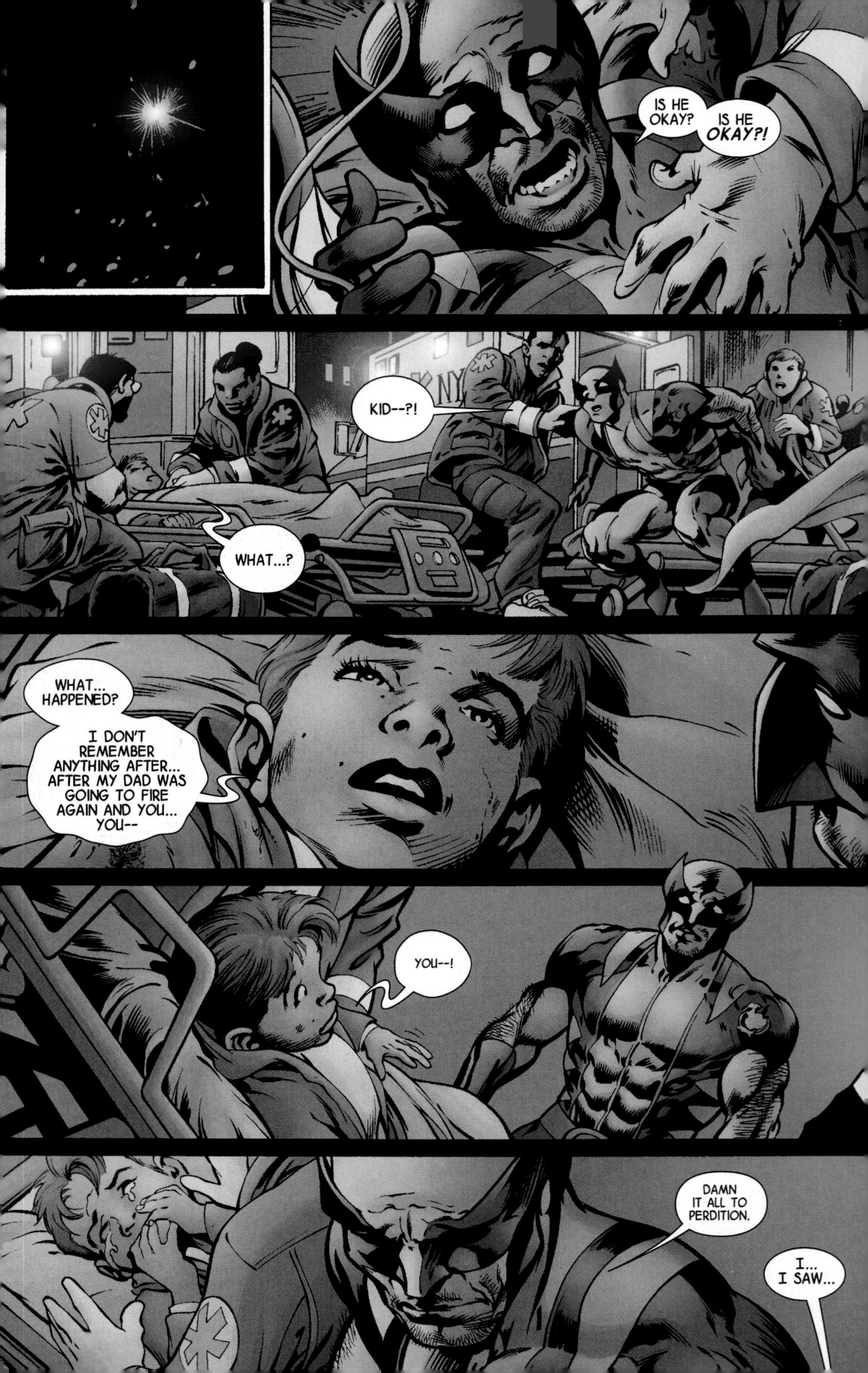
IS HE OKAY?
IS HE OKAY?!
KID--?!
WHAT...?
WHAT... HAPPENED?
I DON'T REMEMBER ANYTHING AFTER... AFTER MY DAD WAS GOING TO FIRE AGAIN AND YOU... YOU--
YOU--!
DAMN IT ALL TO PERDITION.
I... I SAW...

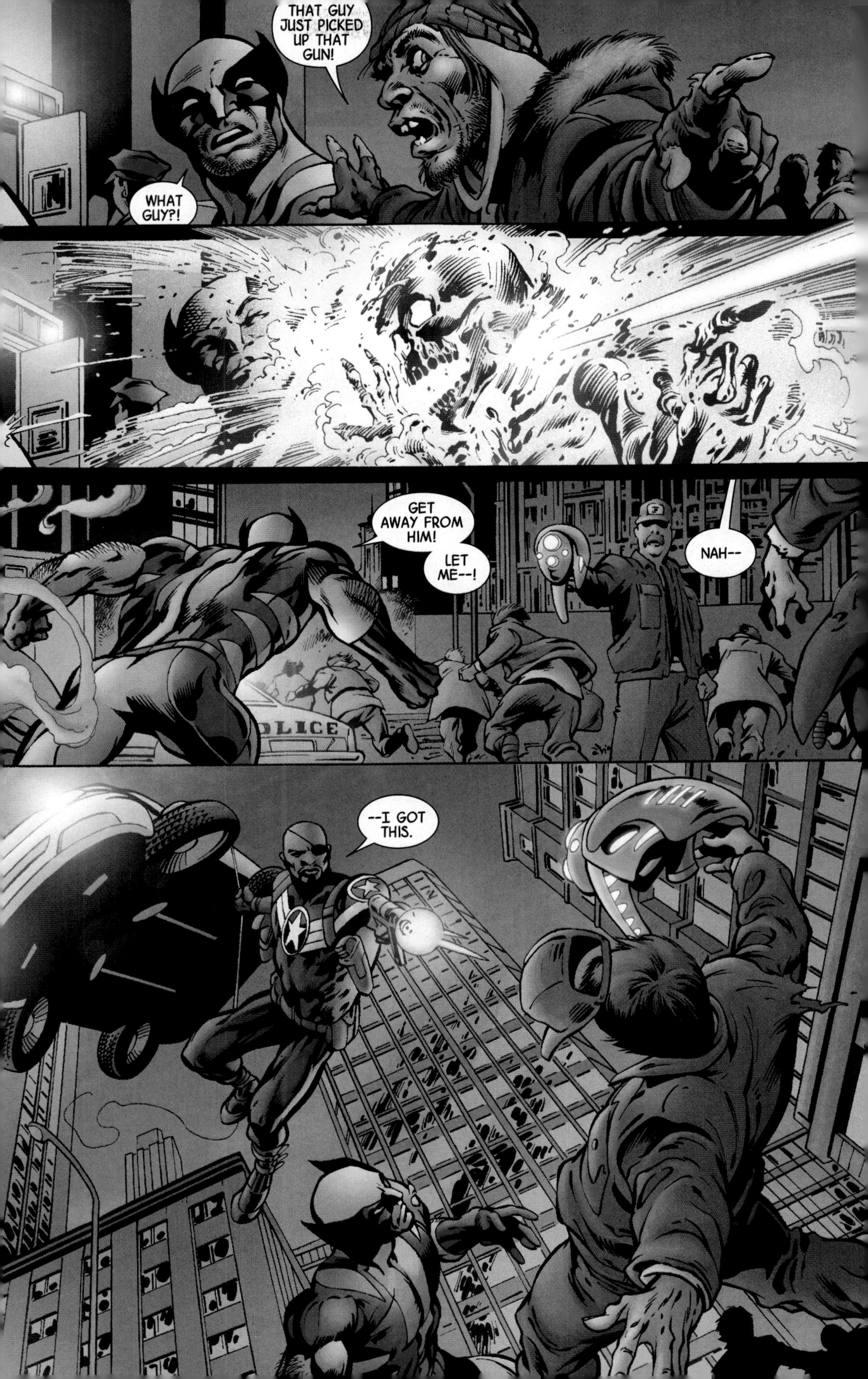
THAT GUY JUST PICKED UP THAT GUN!
WHAT GUY?!
GET AWAY FROM HIM!
LET ME--!
NAH--
--I GOT THIS.

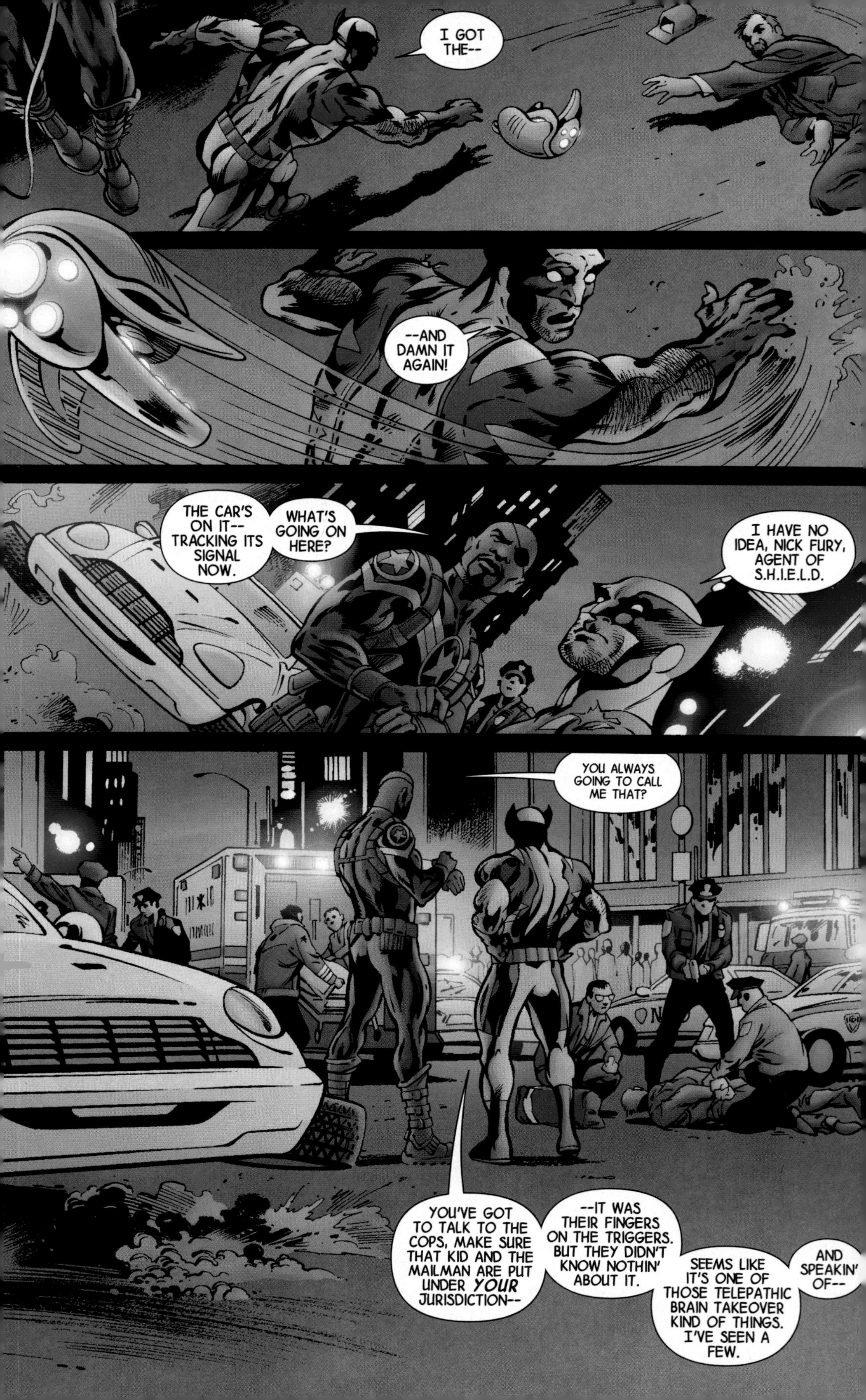
I GOT THE--
--AND DAMN IT AGAIN!
THE CAR'S ON IT-- TRACKING ITS SIGNAL NOW.
WHAT'S GOING ON HERE?
I HAVE NO IDEA, NICK FURY, AGENT OF S.H.I.E.L.D.
YOU ALWAYS GOING TO CALL ME THAT?
YOU'VE GOT TO TALK TO THE COPS, MAKE SURE THAT KID AND THE MAILMAN ARE PUT UNDER YOUR JURISDICTION--
--IT WAS THEIR FINGERS ON THE TRIGGERS. BUT THEY DIDN'T KNOW NOTHIN' ABOUT IT.
SEEMS LIKE IT'S ONE OF THOSE TELEPATHIC BRAIN TAKEOVER KIND OF THINGS. I'VE SEEN A FEW.
AND SPEAKIN' OF--

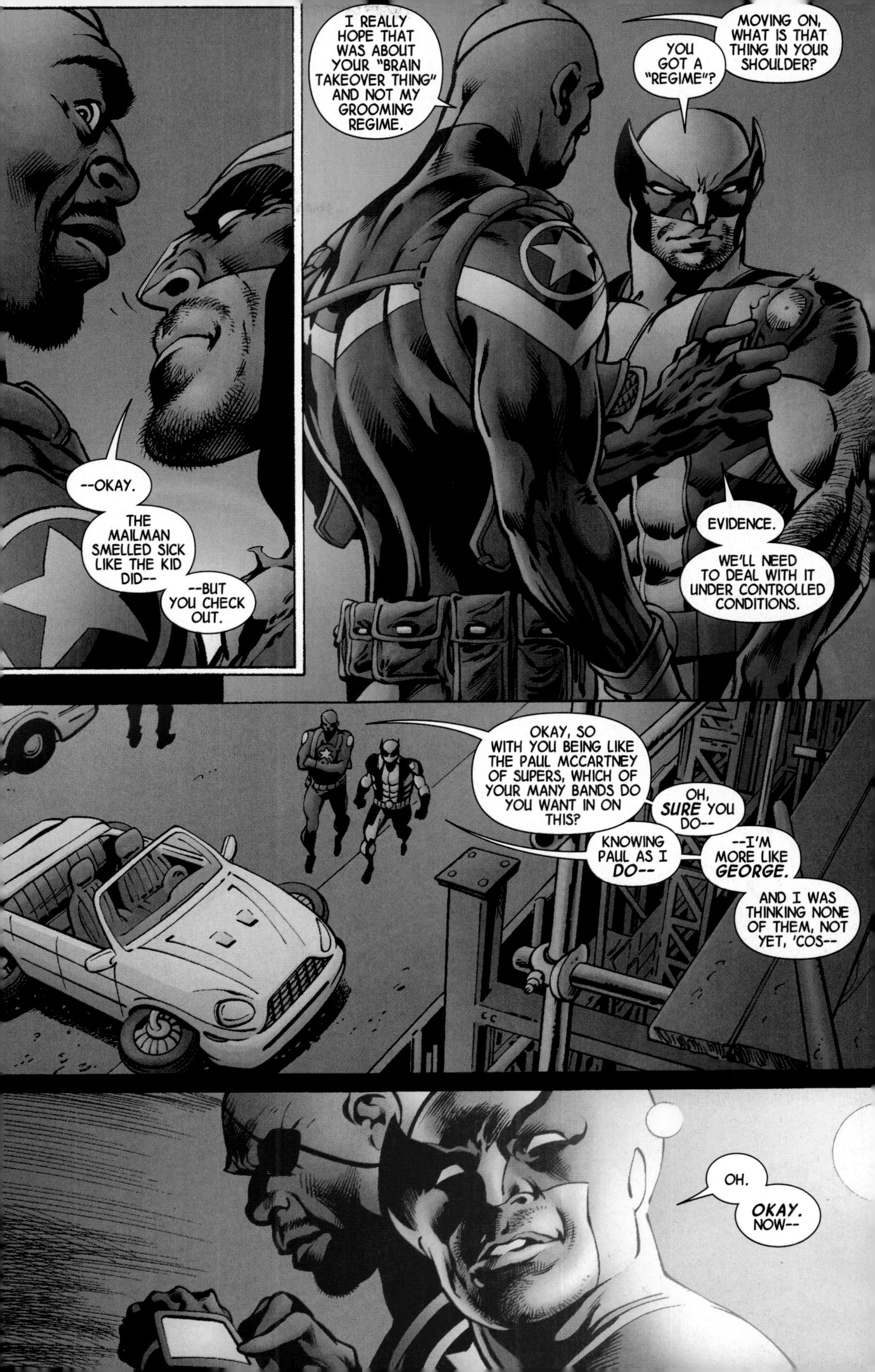
--OKAY.
THE MAILMAN SMELLED SICK LIKE THE KID DID--
--BUT YOU CHECK OUT.
I REALLY HOPE THAT WAS ABOUT YOUR "BRAIN TAKEOVER THING" AND NOT MY GROOMING REGIME.
YOU GOT A "REGIME"?
MOVING ON, WHAT IS THAT THING IN YOUR SHOULDER?
EVIDENCE.
WE'LL NEED TO DEAL WITH IT UNDER CONTROLLED CONDITIONS.
OKAY, SO WITH YOU BEING LIKE THE PAUL McCARTNEY OF SUPERS, WHICH OF YOUR MANY BANDS DO YOU WANT IN ON THIS?
OH, *SURE* YOU DO--
KNOWING PAUL AS I *DO*--
--I'M MORE LIKE *GEORGE.*
AND I WAS THINKING NONE OF THEM, NOT YET, 'COS--
OH.
OKAY. NOW--

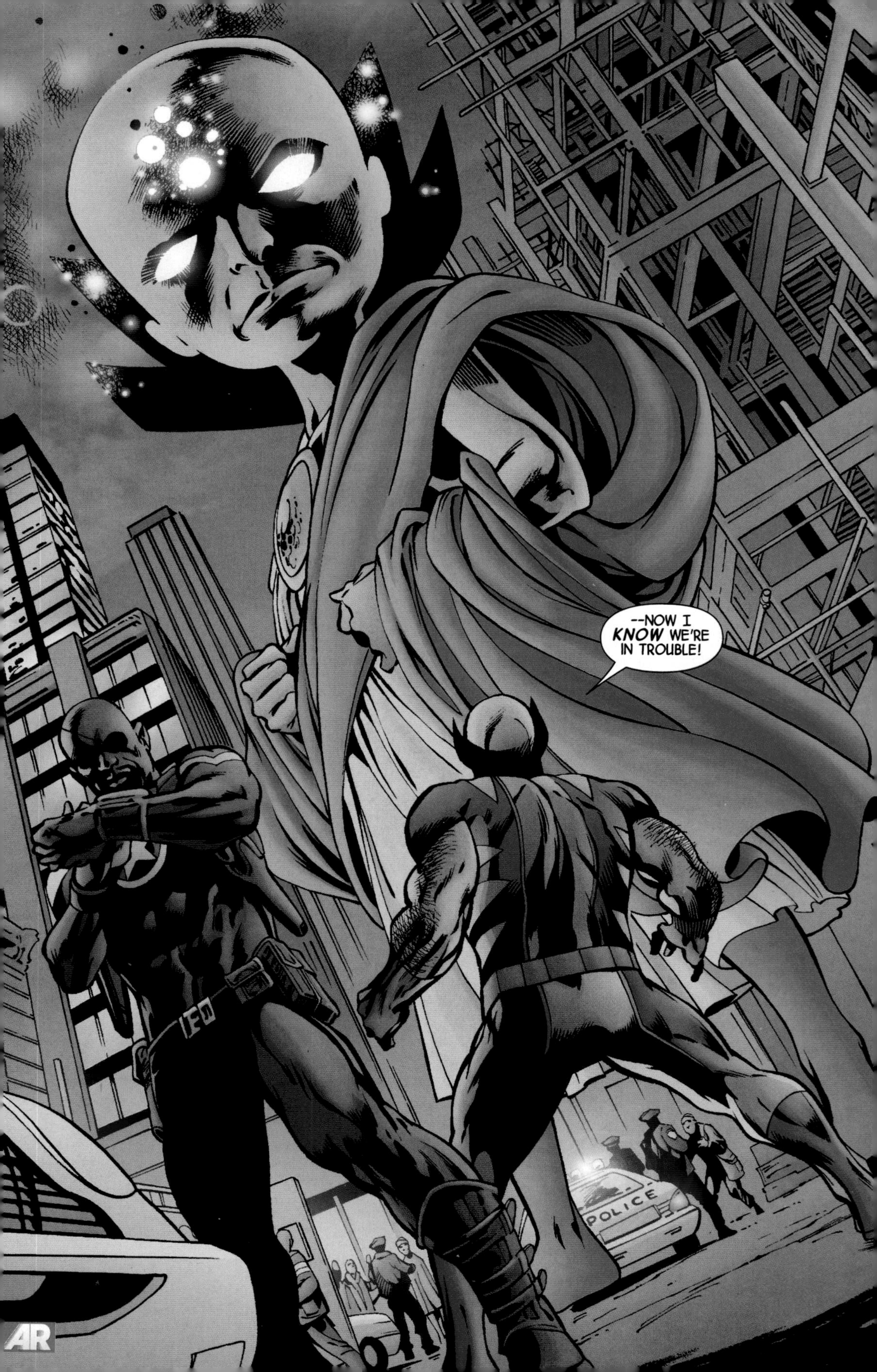
--NOW I KNOW WE'RE IN TROUBLE!
POLICE

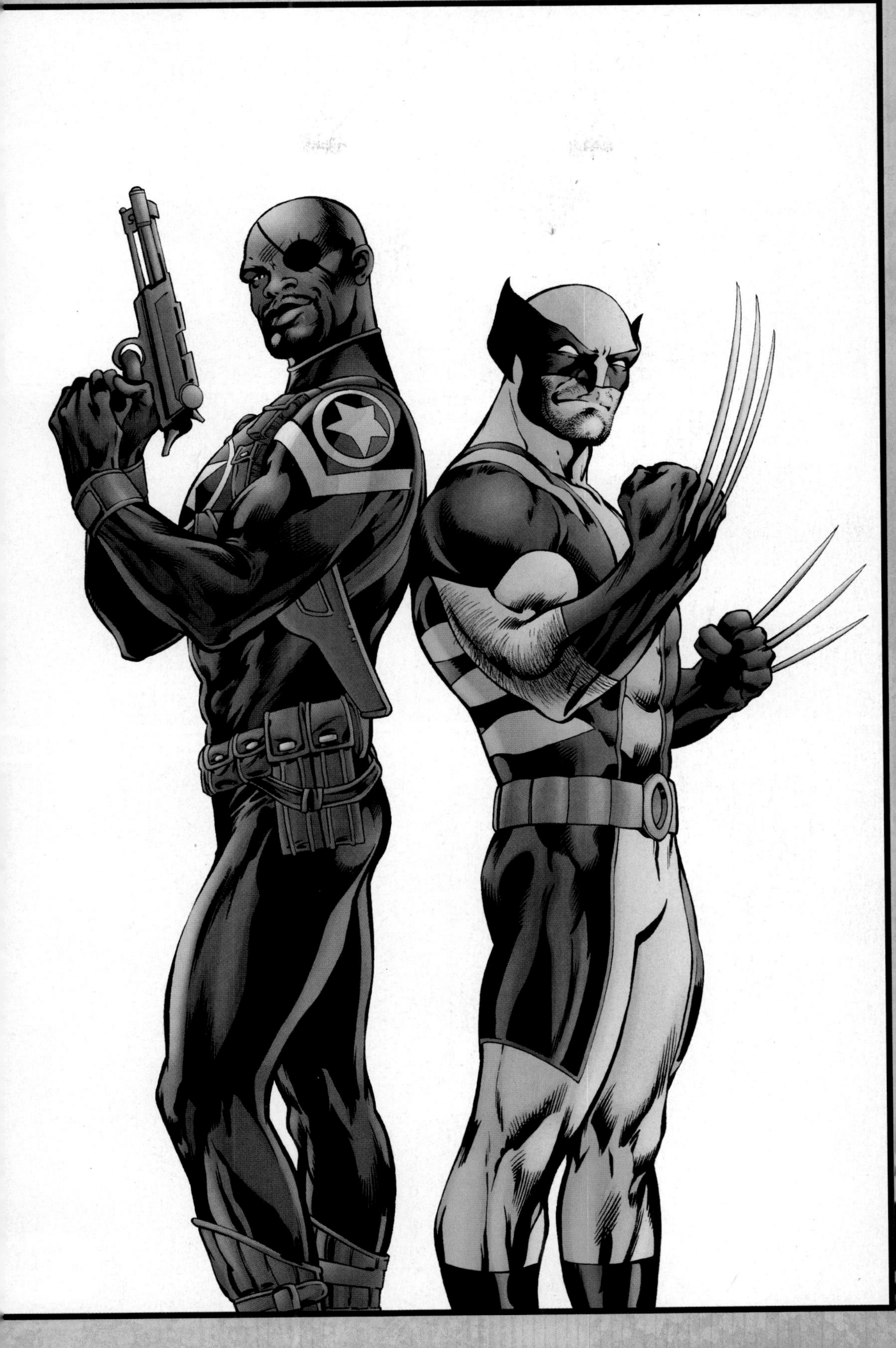

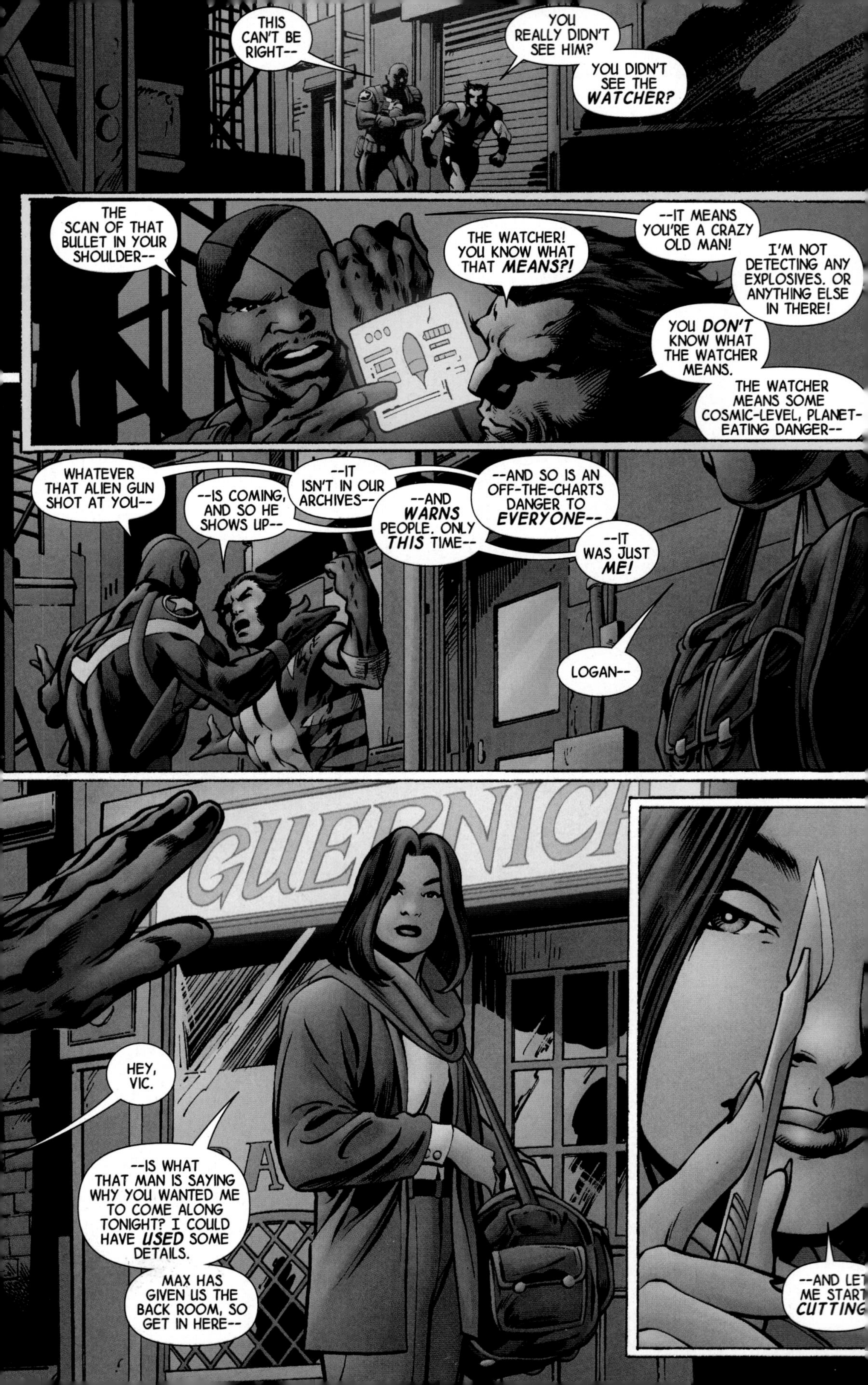
THIS CAN'T BE RIGHT--
YOU REALLY DIDN'T SEE HIM?
YOU DIDN'T SEE THE WATCHER?
THE SCAN OF THAT BULLET IN YOUR SHOULDER--
THE WATCHER! YOU KNOW WHAT THAT MEANS?!
--IT MEANS YOU'RE A CRAZY OLD MAN!
I'M NOT DETECTING ANY EXPLOSIVES. OR ANYTHING ELSE IN THERE!
YOU DON'T KNOW WHAT THE WATCHER MEANS.
THE WATCHER MEANS SOME COSMIC-LEVEL, PLANET-EATING DANGER--
WHATEVER THAT ALIEN GUN SHOT AT YOU--
--IS COMING, AND SO HE SHOWS UP--
--IT ISN'T IN OUR ARCHIVES--
--AND WARNS PEOPLE. ONLY THIS TIME--
--AND SO IS AN OFF-THE-CHARTS DANGER TO EVERYONE--
--IT WAS JUST ME!
LOGAN--
GUERNICA
HEY, VIC.
--IS WHAT THAT MAN IS SAYING WHY YOU WANTED ME TO COME ALONG TONIGHT? I COULD HAVE USED SOME DETAILS.
MAX HAS GIVEN US THE BACK ROOM, SO GET IN HERE--
--AND LET ME START CUTTING

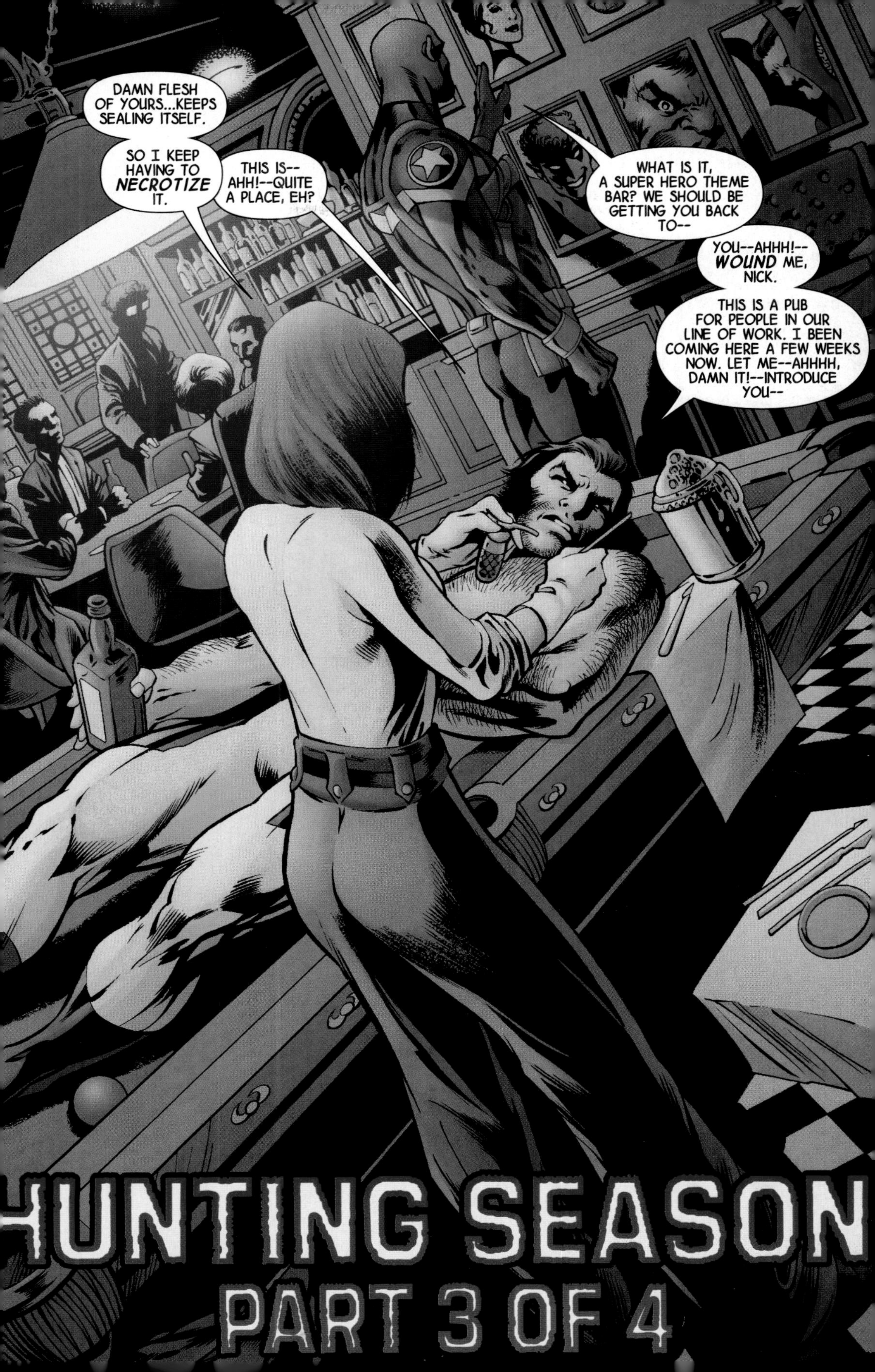
DAMN FLESH OF YOURS...KEEPS SEALING ITSELF.
SO I KEEP HAVING TO NECROTIZE IT.
THIS IS--AHH!--QUITE A PLACE, EH?
WHAT IS IT, A SUPER HERO THEME BAR? WE SHOULD BE GETTING YOU BACK TO--
YOU--AHHH!--WOUND ME, NICK.
THIS IS A PUB FOR PEOPLE IN OUR LINE OF WORK. I BEEN COMING HERE A FEW WEEKS NOW. LET ME--AHHHH, DAMN IT!--INTRODUCE YOU--
HUNTING SEASON
PART 3 OF 4

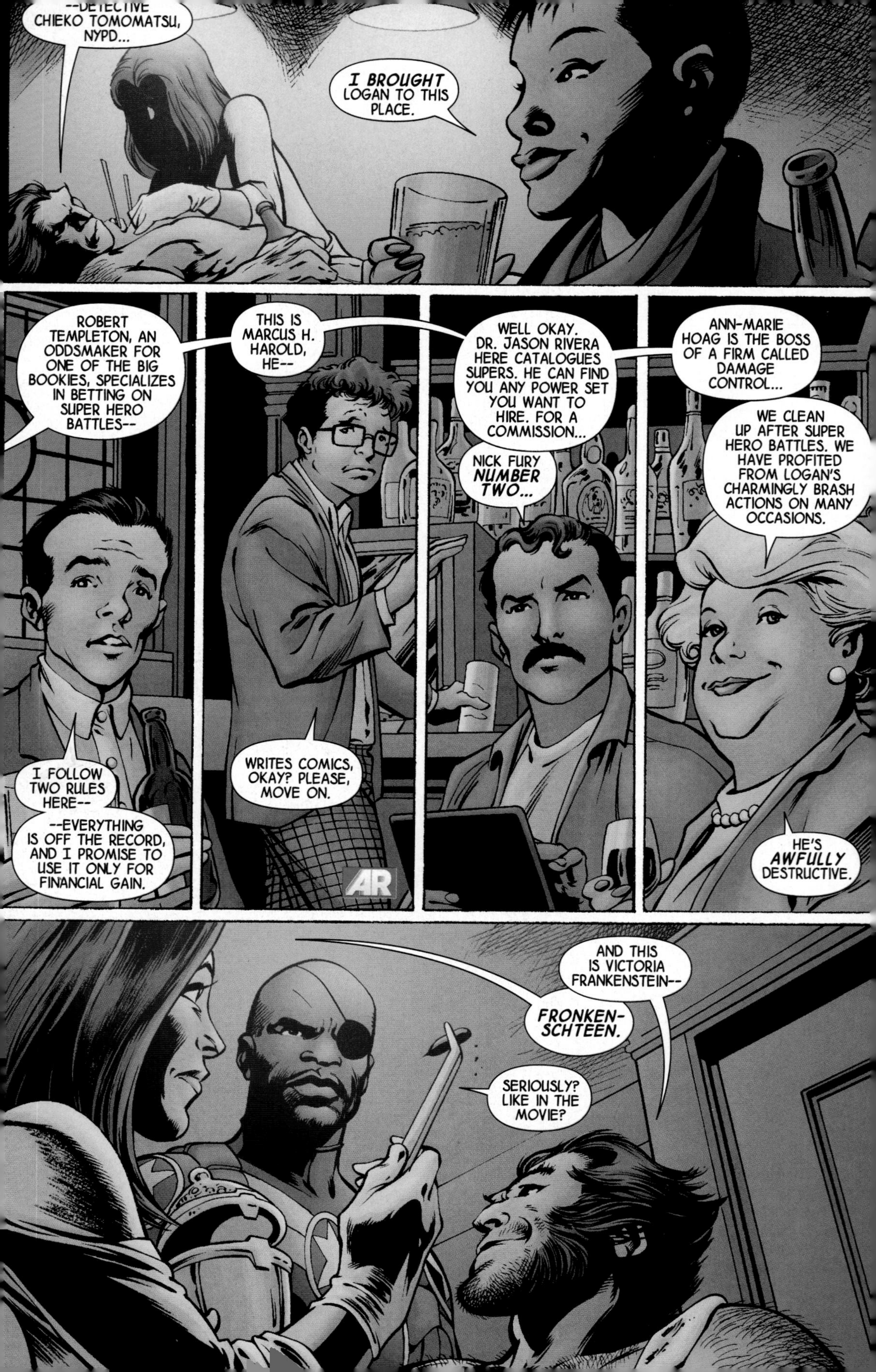
--DETECTIVE CHIEKO TOMOMATSU, NYPD...
I BROUGHT LOGAN TO THIS PLACE.
ROBERT TEMPLETON, AN ODDSMAKER FOR ONE OF THE BIG BOOKIES, SPECIALIZES IN BETTING ON SUPER HERO BATTLES--
I FOLLOW TWO RULES HERE--
--EVERYTHING IS OFF THE RECORD, AND I PROMISE TO USE IT ONLY FOR FINANCIAL GAIN.
THIS IS MARCUS H. HAROLD, HE--
WRITES COMICS, OKAY? PLEASE, MOVE ON.
WELL OKAY. DR. JASON RIVERA HERE CATALOGUES SUPERS. HE CAN FIND YOU ANY POWER SET YOU WANT TO HIRE. FOR A COMMISSION...
NICK FURY NUMBER TWO...
ANN-MARIE HOAG IS THE BOSS OF A FIRM CALLED DAMAGE CONTROL...
WE CLEAN UP AFTER SUPER HERO BATTLES. WE HAVE PROFITED FROM LOGAN'S CHARMINGLY BRASH ACTIONS ON MANY OCCASIONS.
HE'S AWFULLY DESTRUCTIVE.
AR
AND THIS IS VICTORIA FRANKENSTEIN--
FRONKEN-SCHTEEN.
SERIOUSLY? LIKE IN THE MOVIE?

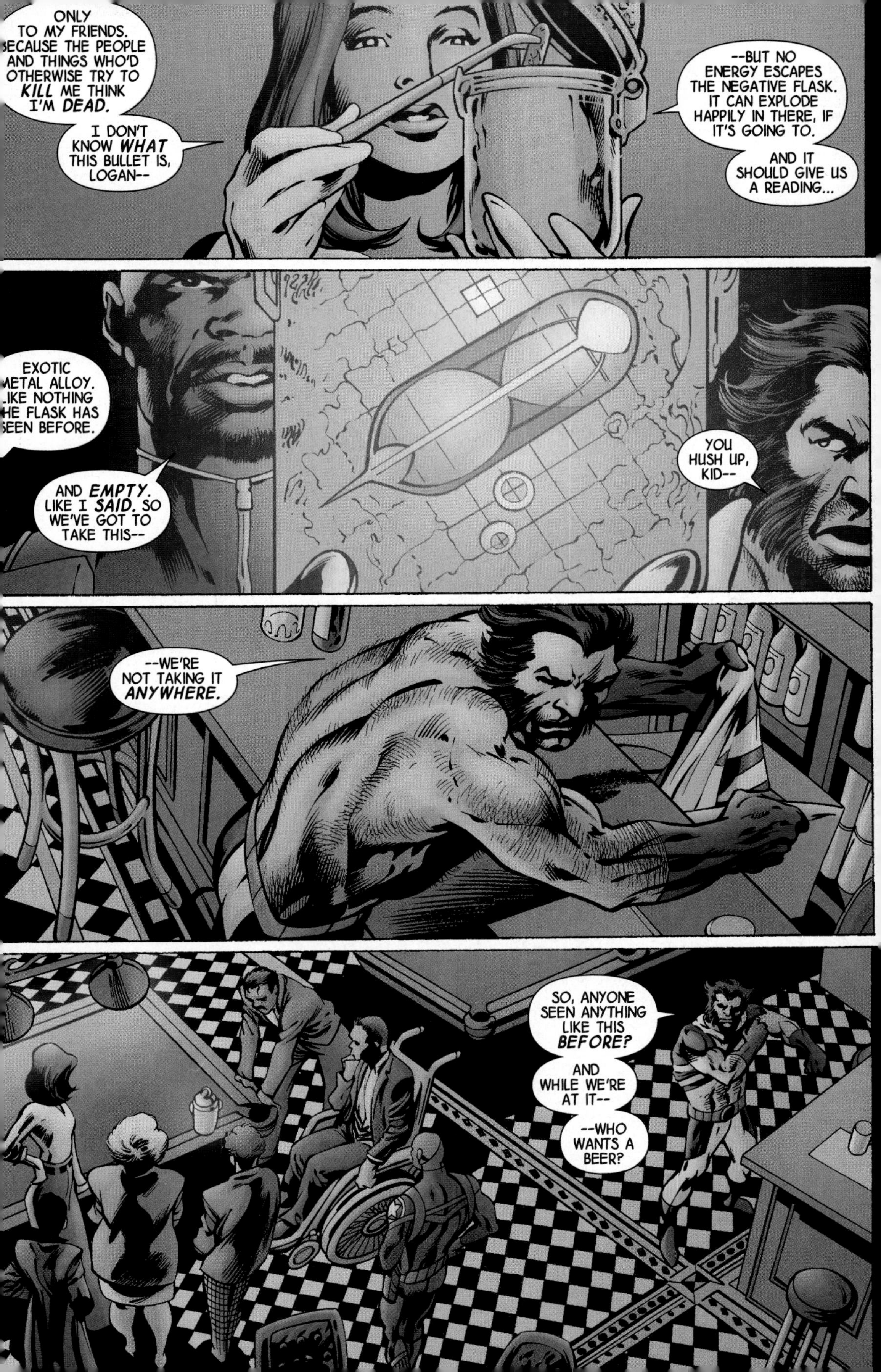
ONLY TO MY FRIENDS. BECAUSE THE PEOPLE AND THINGS WHO'D OTHERWISE TRY TO KILL ME THINK I'M DEAD.
I DON'T KNOW WHAT THIS BULLET IS, LOGAN--
--BUT NO ENERGY ESCAPES THE NEGATIVE FLASK. IT CAN EXPLODE HAPPILY IN THERE, IF IT'S GOING TO.
AND IT SHOULD GIVE US A READING...
EXOTIC METAL ALLOY. LIKE NOTHING THE FLASK HAS SEEN BEFORE.
AND EMPTY. LIKE I SAID. SO WE'VE GOT TO TAKE THIS--
YOU HUSH UP, KID--
--WE'RE NOT TAKING IT ANYWHERE.
SO, ANYONE SEEN ANYTHING LIKE THIS BEFORE?
AND WHILE WE'RE AT IT--
--WHO WANTS A BEER?

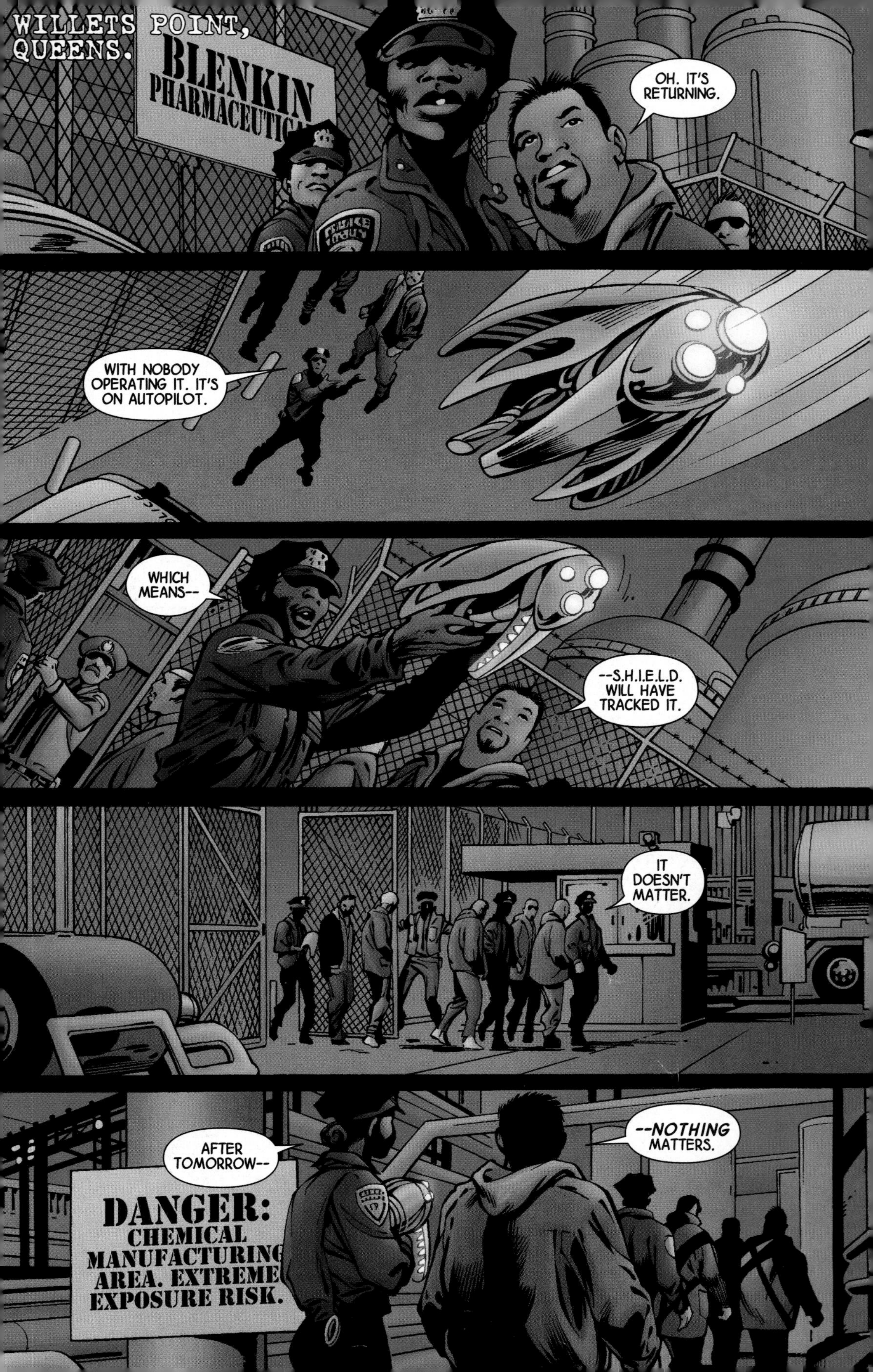
WILLETS POINT, QUEENS.
BLENKIN PHARMACEUTIC
OH. IT'S RETURNING.
WITH NOBODY OPERATING IT. IT'S ON AUTOPILOT.
WHICH MEANS--
--S.H.I.E.L.D. WILL HAVE TRACKED IT.
IT DOESN'T MATTER.
AFTER TOMORROW--
--*NOTHING* MATTERS.
DANGER:
CHEMICAL MANUFACTURING AREA. EXTREME EXPOSURE RISK.

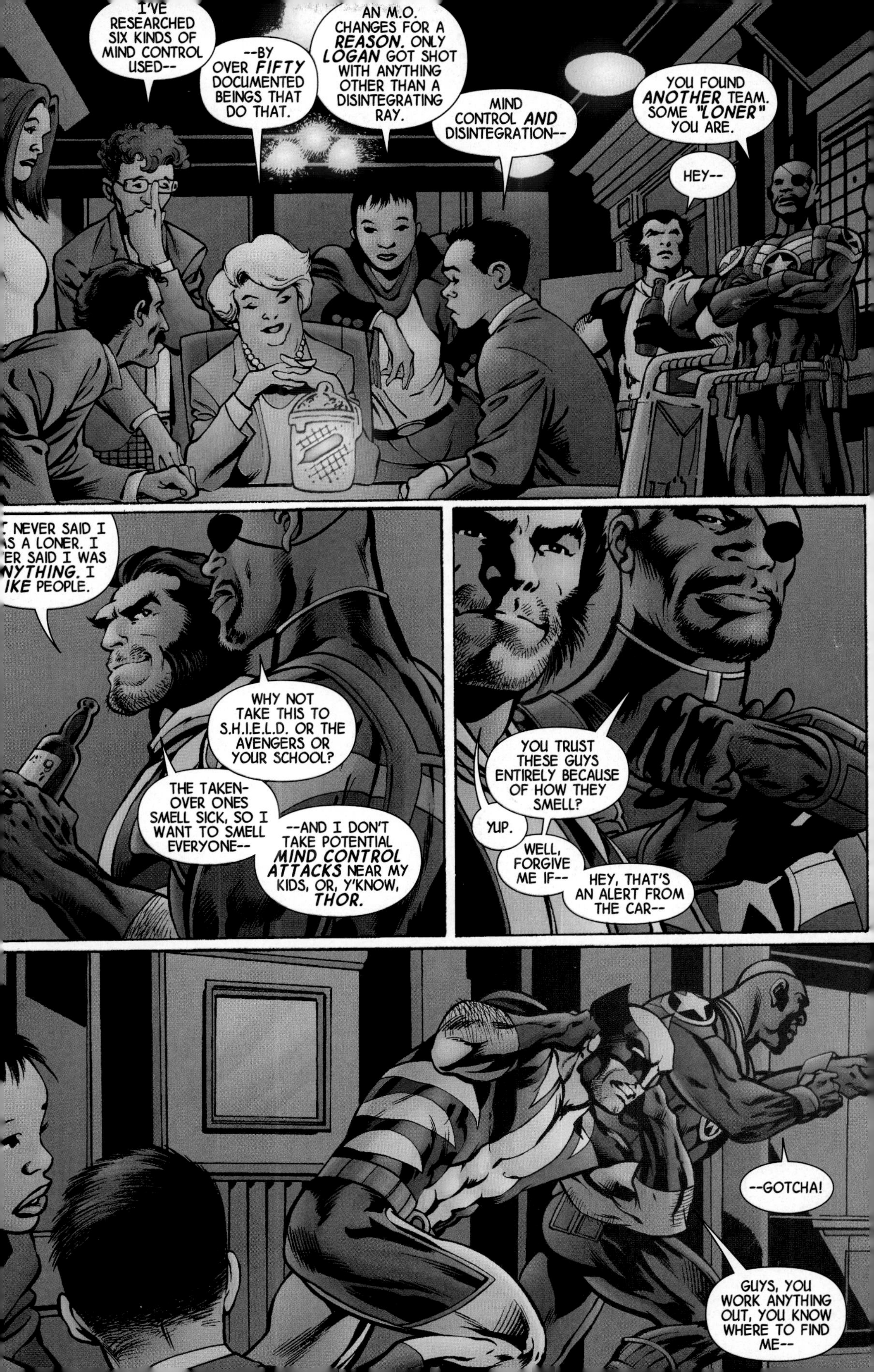
I'VE RESEARCHED SIX KINDS OF MIND CONTROL USED--
--BY OVER FIFTY DOCUMENTED BEINGS THAT DO THAT.
AN M.O. CHANGES FOR A REASON. ONLY LOGAN GOT SHOT WITH ANYTHING OTHER THAN A DISINTEGRATING RAY.
MIND CONTROL AND DISINTEGRATION--
YOU FOUND ANOTHER TEAM. SOME "LONER" YOU ARE.
HEY--
NEVER SAID I S A LONER. I ER SAID I WAS NYTHING. I IKE PEOPLE.
WHY NOT TAKE THIS TO S.H.I.E.L.D. OR THE AVENGERS OR YOUR SCHOOL?
THE TAKEN-OVER ONES SMELL SICK, SO I WANT TO SMELL EVERYONE--
--AND I DON'T TAKE POTENTIAL MIND CONTROL ATTACKS NEAR MY KIDS, OR, Y'KNOW, THOR.
YOU TRUST THESE GUYS ENTIRELY BECAUSE OF HOW THEY SMELL?
YUP.
WELL, FORGIVE ME IF--
HEY, THAT'S AN ALERT FROM THE CAR--
--GOTCHA!
GUYS, YOU WORK ANYTHING OUT, YOU KNOW WHERE TO FIND ME--

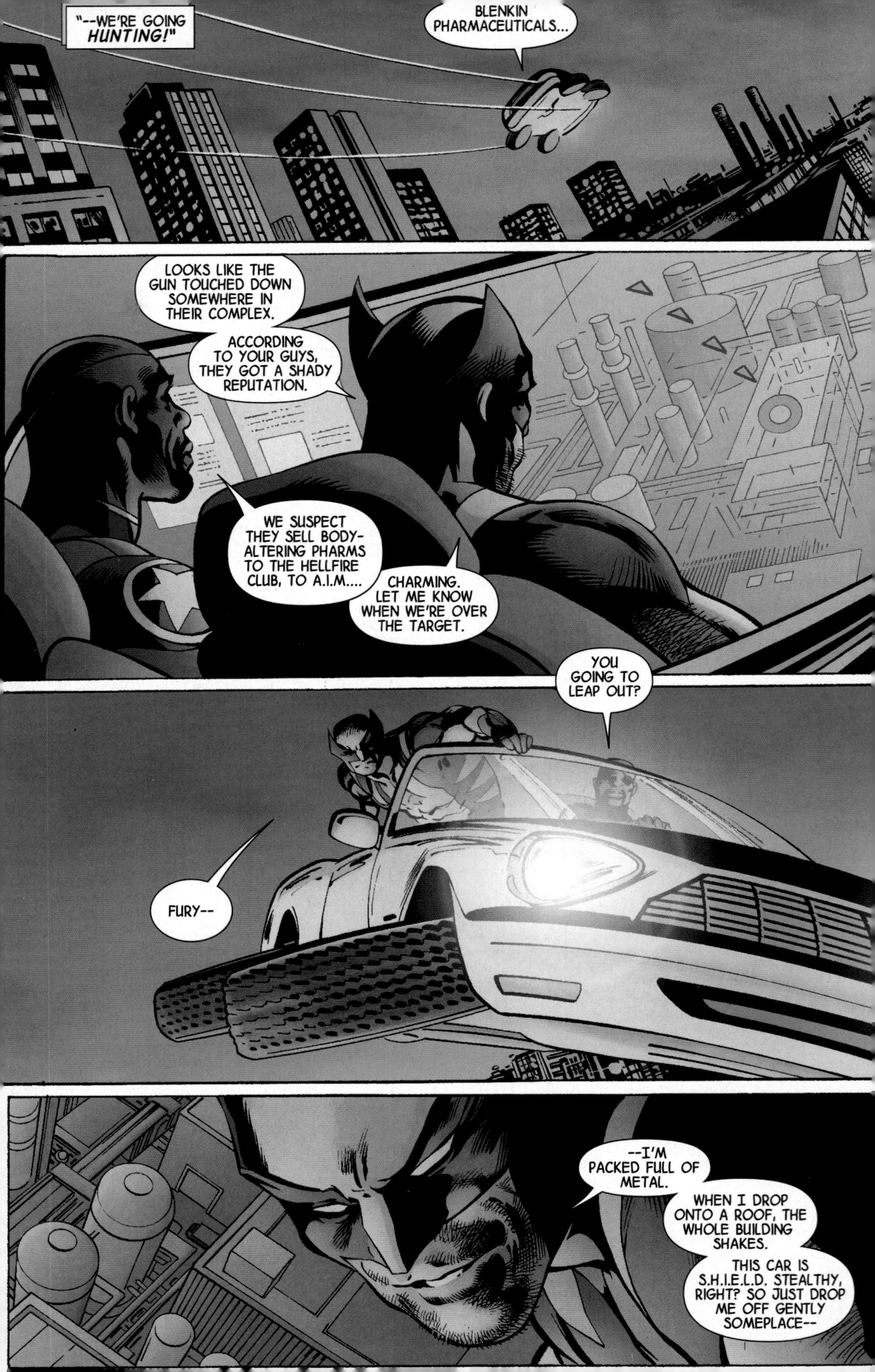
"--WE'RE GOING HUNTING!"
BLENKIN PHARMACEUTICALS...
LOOKS LIKE THE GUN TOUCHED DOWN SOMEWHERE IN THEIR COMPLEX.
ACCORDING TO YOUR GUYS, THEY GOT A SHADY REPUTATION.
WE SUSPECT THEY SELL BODY-ALTERING PHARMS TO THE HELLFIRE CLUB, TO A.I.M....
CHARMING. LET ME KNOW WHEN WE'RE OVER THE TARGET.
YOU GOING TO LEAP OUT?
FURY--
--I'M PACKED FULL OF METAL.
WHEN I DROP ONTO A ROOF, THE WHOLE BUILDING SHAKES.
THIS CAR IS S.H.I.E.L.D. STEALTHY, RIGHT? SO JUST DROP ME OFF GENTLY SOMEPLACE--

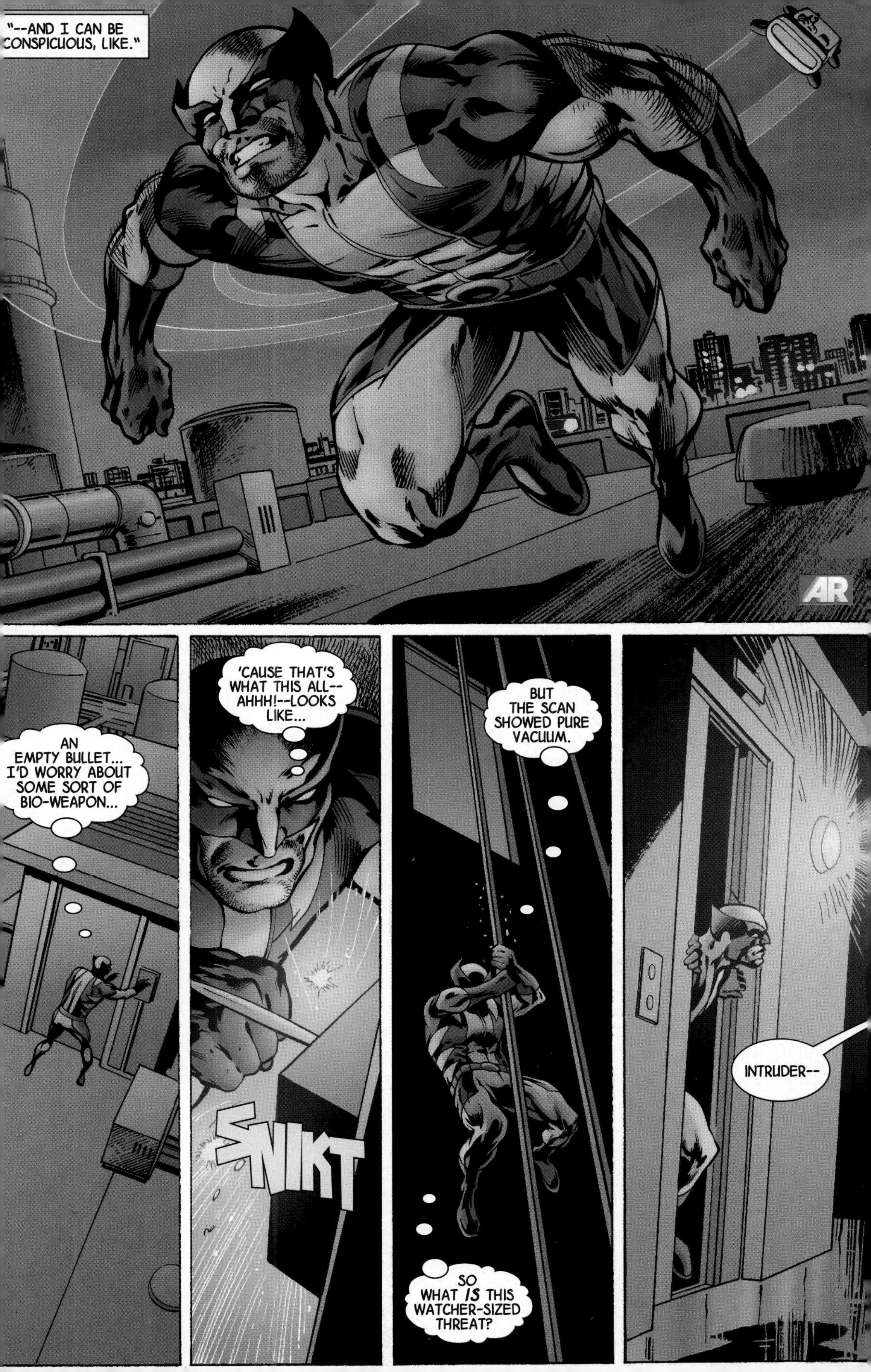
"--AND I CAN BE CONSPICUOUS, LIKE."
AR
AN EMPTY BULLET... I'D WORRY ABOUT SOME SORT OF BIO-WEAPON...
'CAUSE THAT'S WHAT THIS ALL--AHHH!--LOOKS LIKE...
SNIKT
BUT THE SCAN SHOWED PURE VACUUM.
SO WHAT IS THIS WATCHER-SIZED THREAT?
INTRUDER--

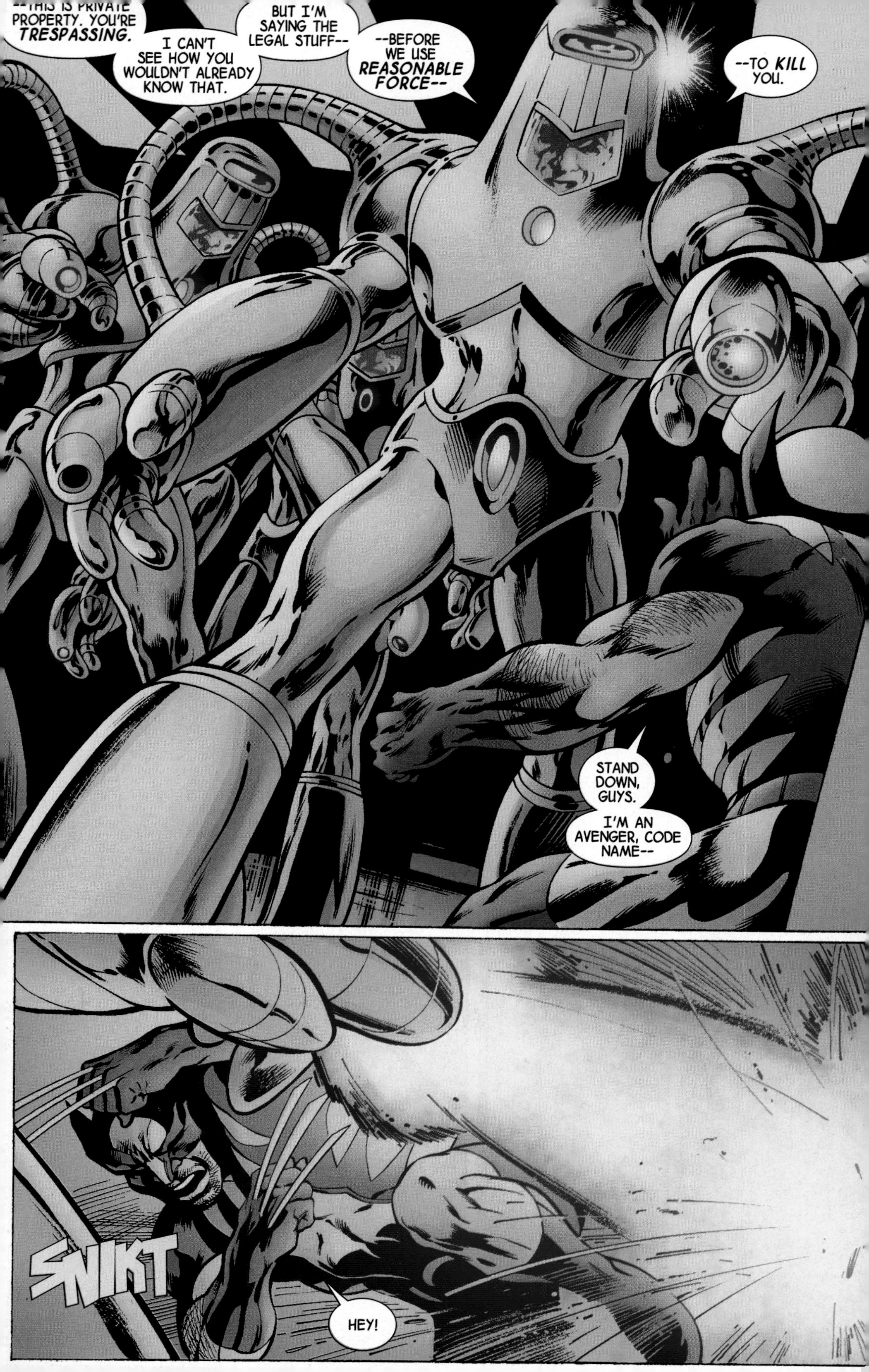
--THIS IS PRIVATE PROPERTY. YOU'RE TRESPASSING.
I CAN'T SEE HOW YOU WOULDN'T ALREADY KNOW THAT.
BUT I'M SAYING THE LEGAL STUFF--
--BEFORE WE USE REASONABLE FORCE--
--TO KILL YOU.
STAND DOWN, GUYS.
I'M AN AVENGER, CODE NAME--
SNIKT
HEY!

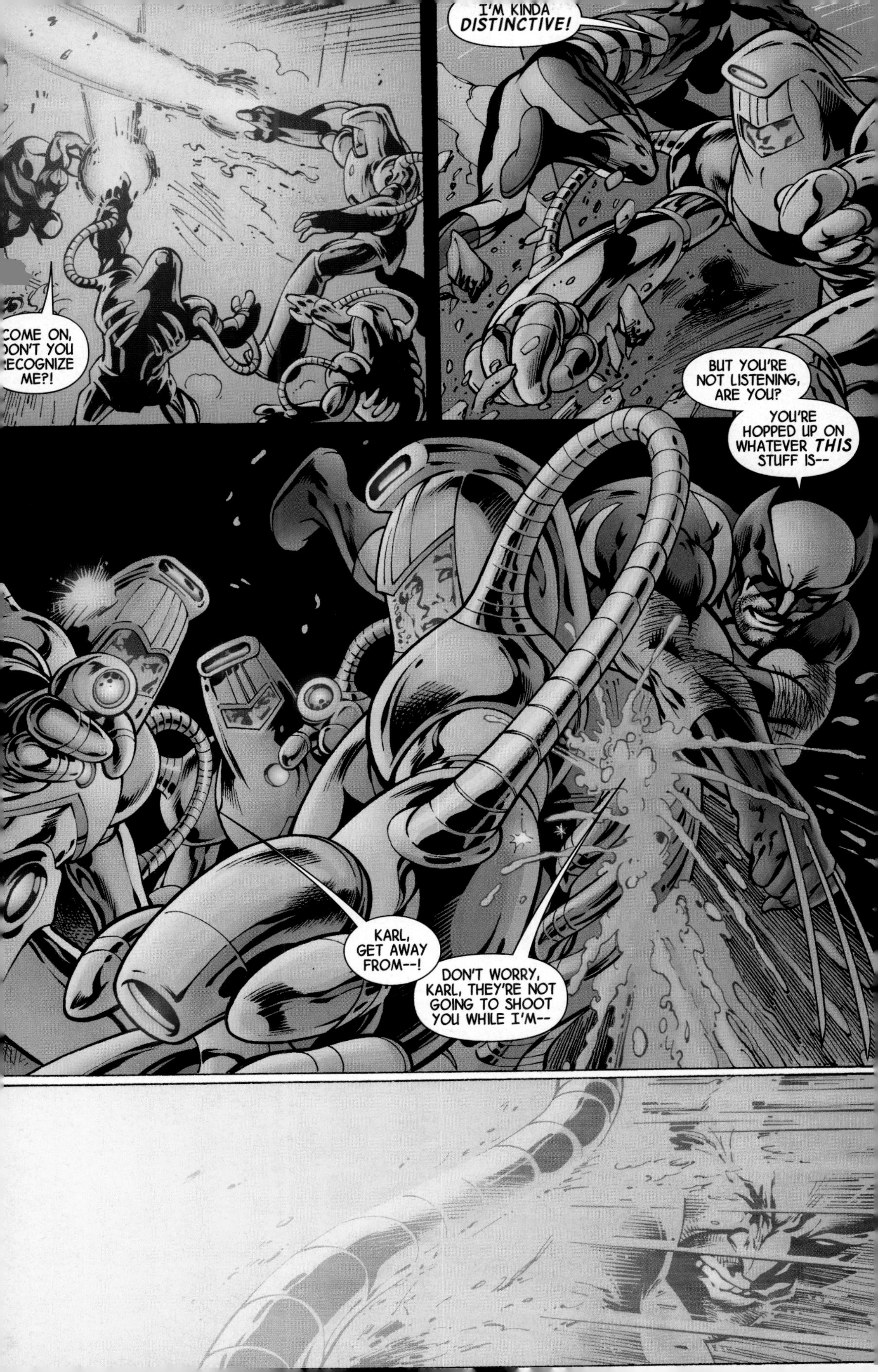
COME ON, DON'T YOU RECOGNIZE ME?!
I'M KINDA DISTINCTIVE!
BUT YOU'RE NOT LISTENING, ARE YOU?
YOU'RE HOPPED UP ON WHATEVER THIS STUFF IS--
KARL, GET AWAY FROM--!
DON'T WORRY, KARL, THEY'RE NOT GOING TO SHOOT YOU WHILE I'M--

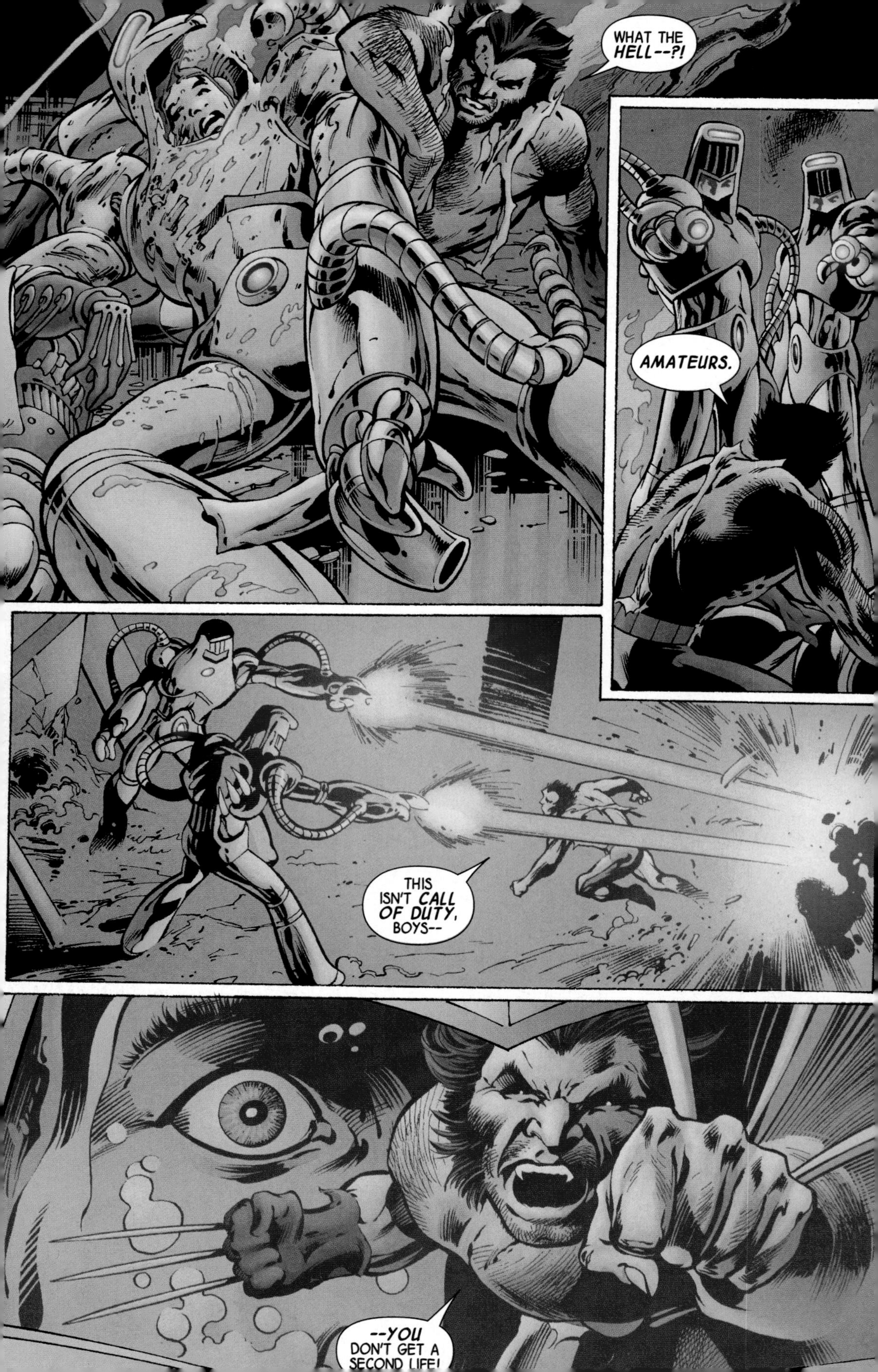
WHAT THE HELL--?!
AMATEURS.
THIS ISN'T CALL OF DUTY, BOYS--
--YOU DON'T GET A SECOND LIFE!

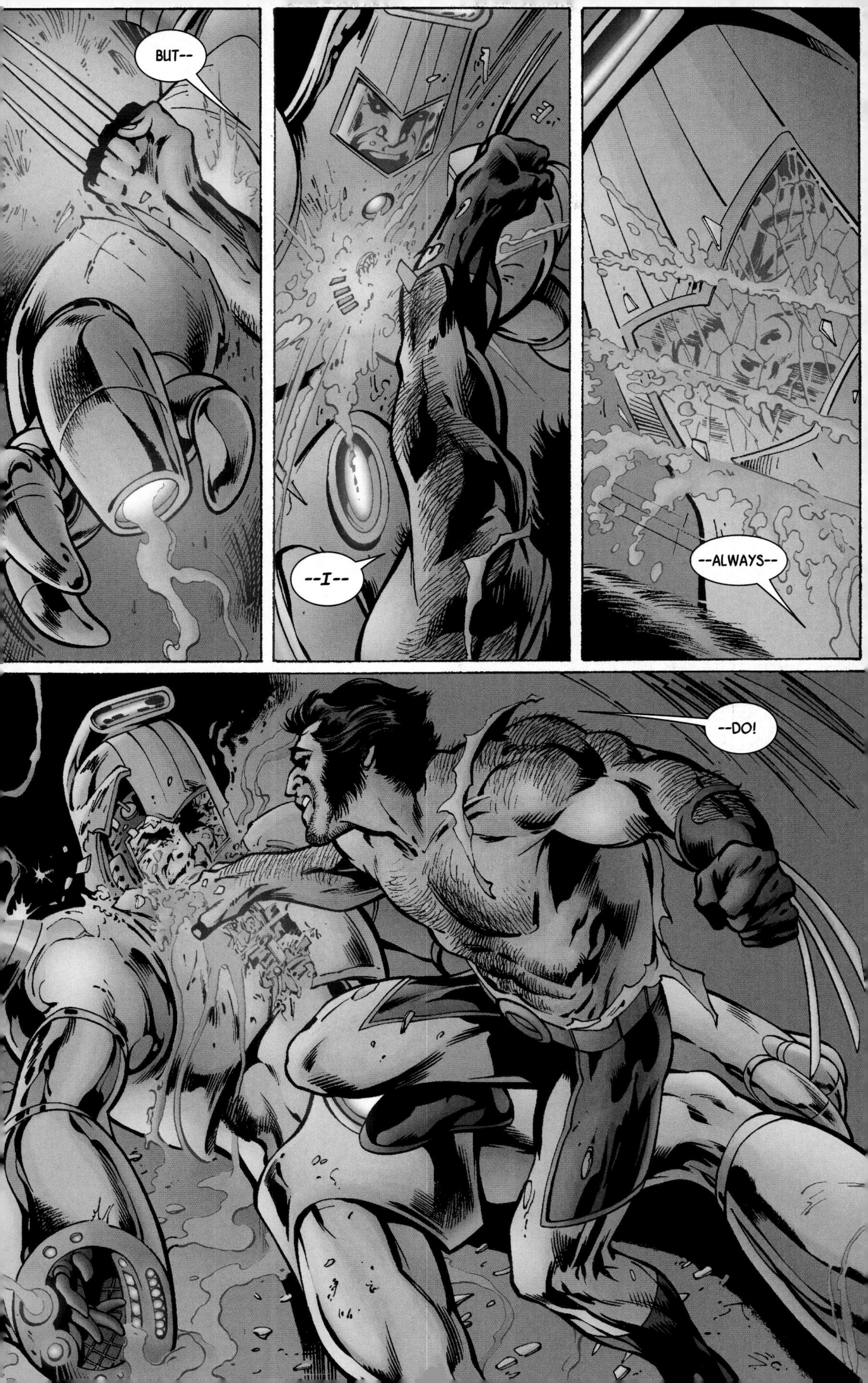
BUT--
--I--
--ALWAYS--
--DO!

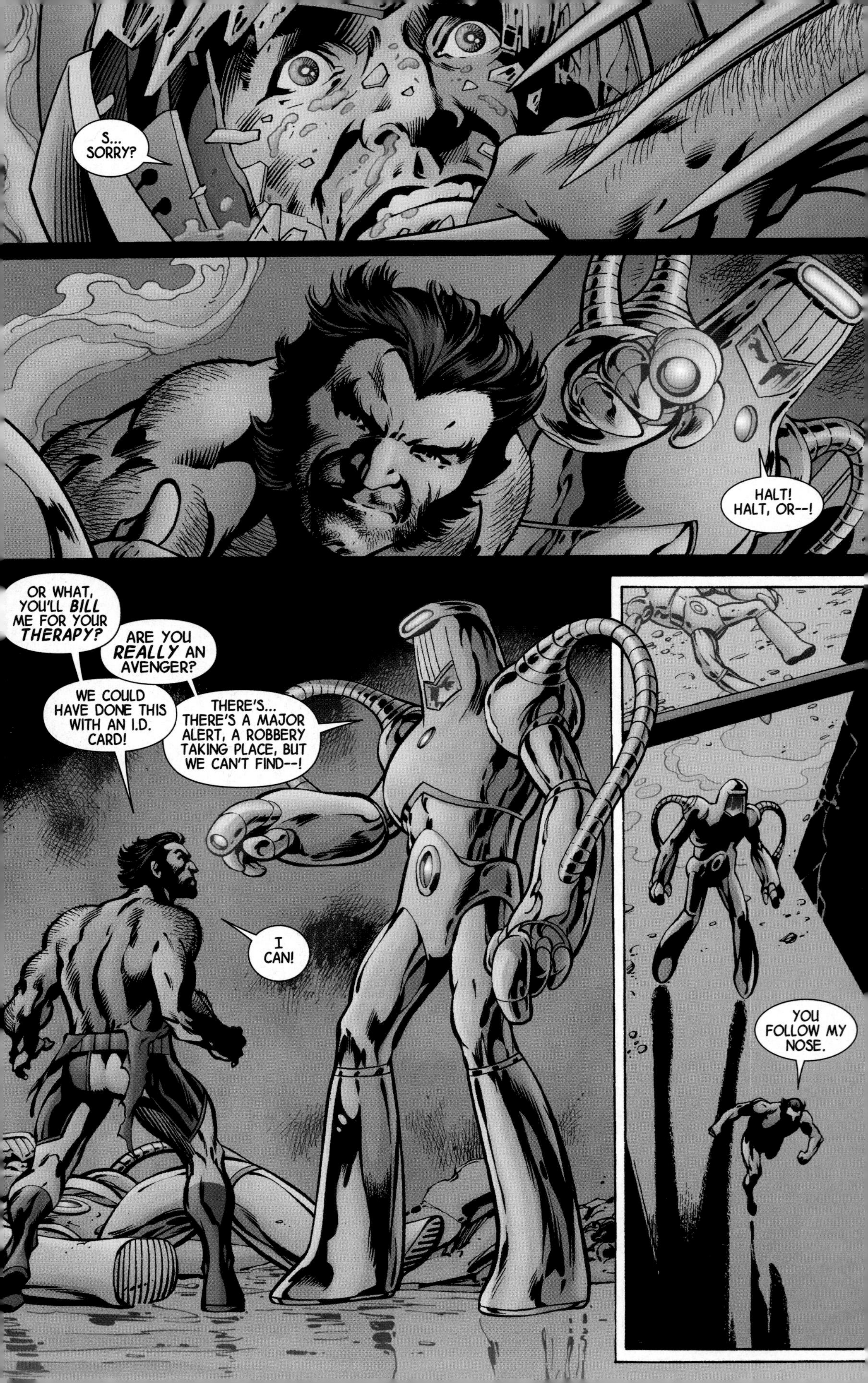
S... SORRY?
HALT! HALT, OR--!
OR WHAT, YOU'LL BILL ME FOR YOUR THERAPY?
ARE YOU REALLY AN AVENGER?
WE COULD HAVE DONE THIS WITH AN I.D. CARD!
THERE'S... THERE'S A MAJOR ALERT, A ROBBERY TAKING PLACE, BUT WE CAN'T FIND--!
I CAN!
YOU FOLLOW MY NOSE.

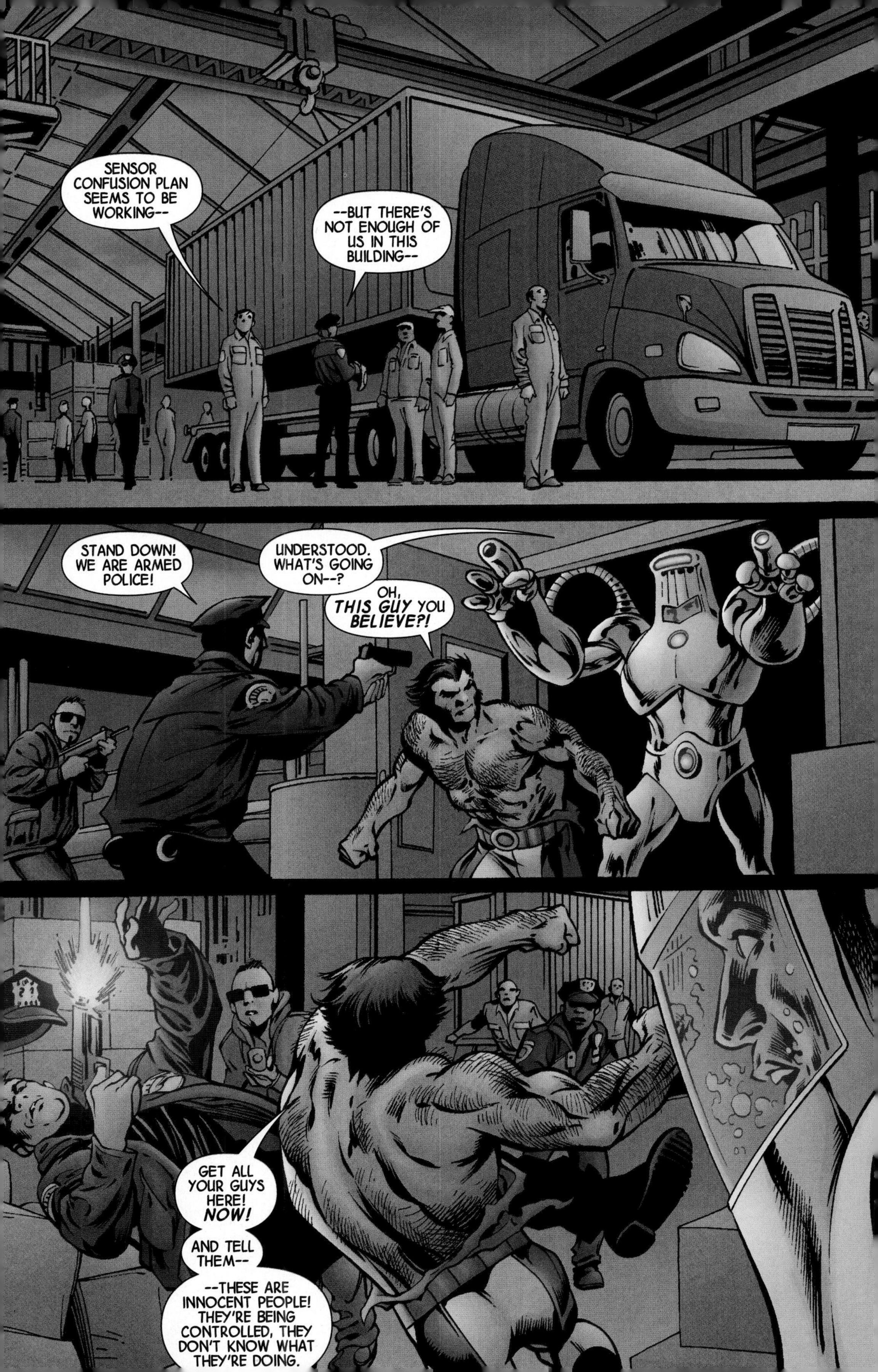
SENSOR CONFUSION PLAN SEEMS TO BE WORKING--
--BUT THERE'S NOT ENOUGH OF US IN THIS BUILDING--
STAND DOWN! WE ARE ARMED POLICE!
UNDERSTOOD. WHAT'S GOING ON--?
OH, THIS GUY YOU BELIEVE?!
GET ALL YOUR GUYS HERE! NOW!
AND TELL THEM--
--THESE ARE INNOCENT PEOPLE! THEY'RE BEING CONTROLLED, THEY DON'T KNOW WHAT THEY'RE DOING.

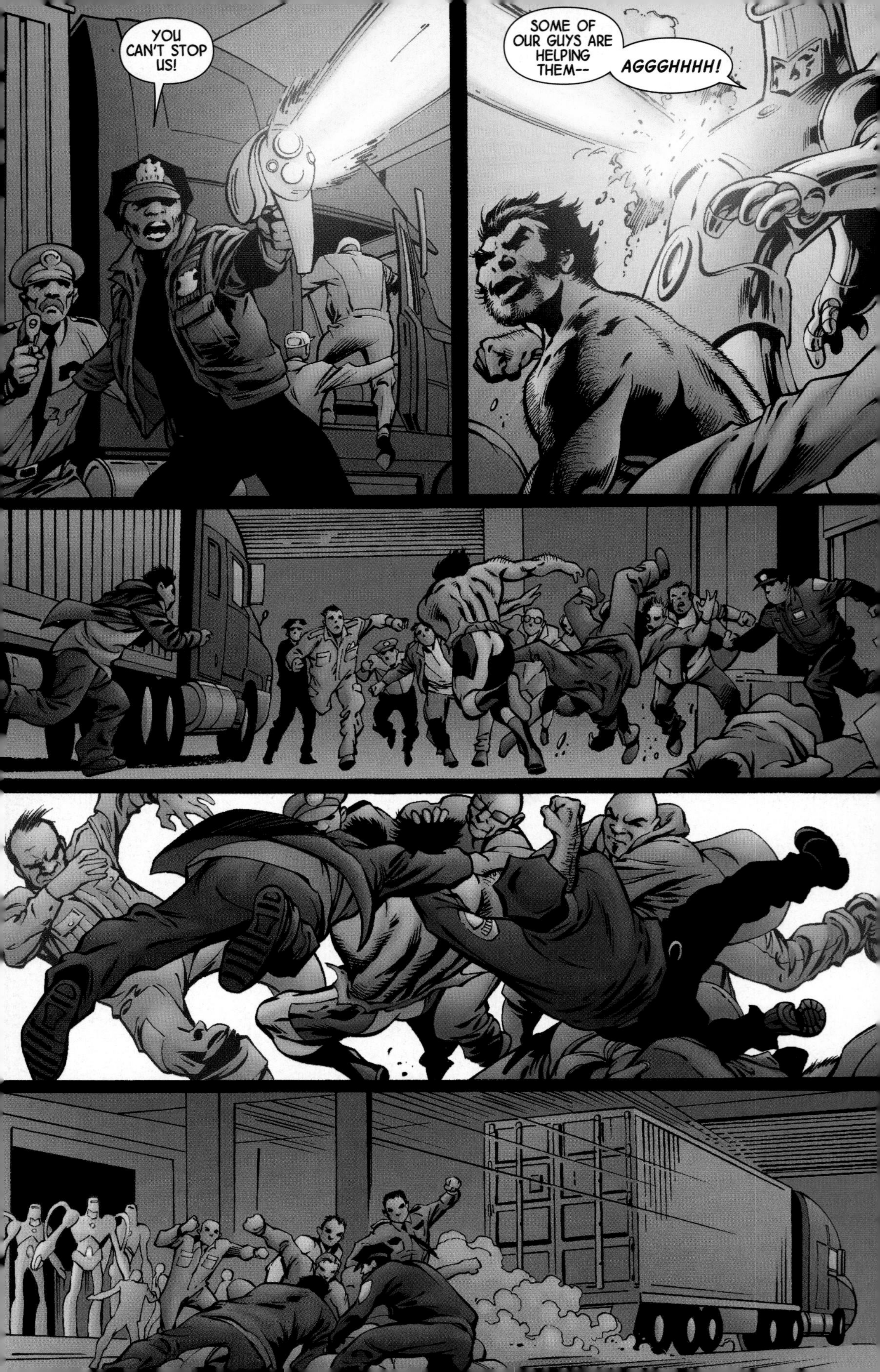
YOU CAN'T STOP US!
SOME OF OUR GUYS ARE HELPING THEM--
AGGGHHHH!

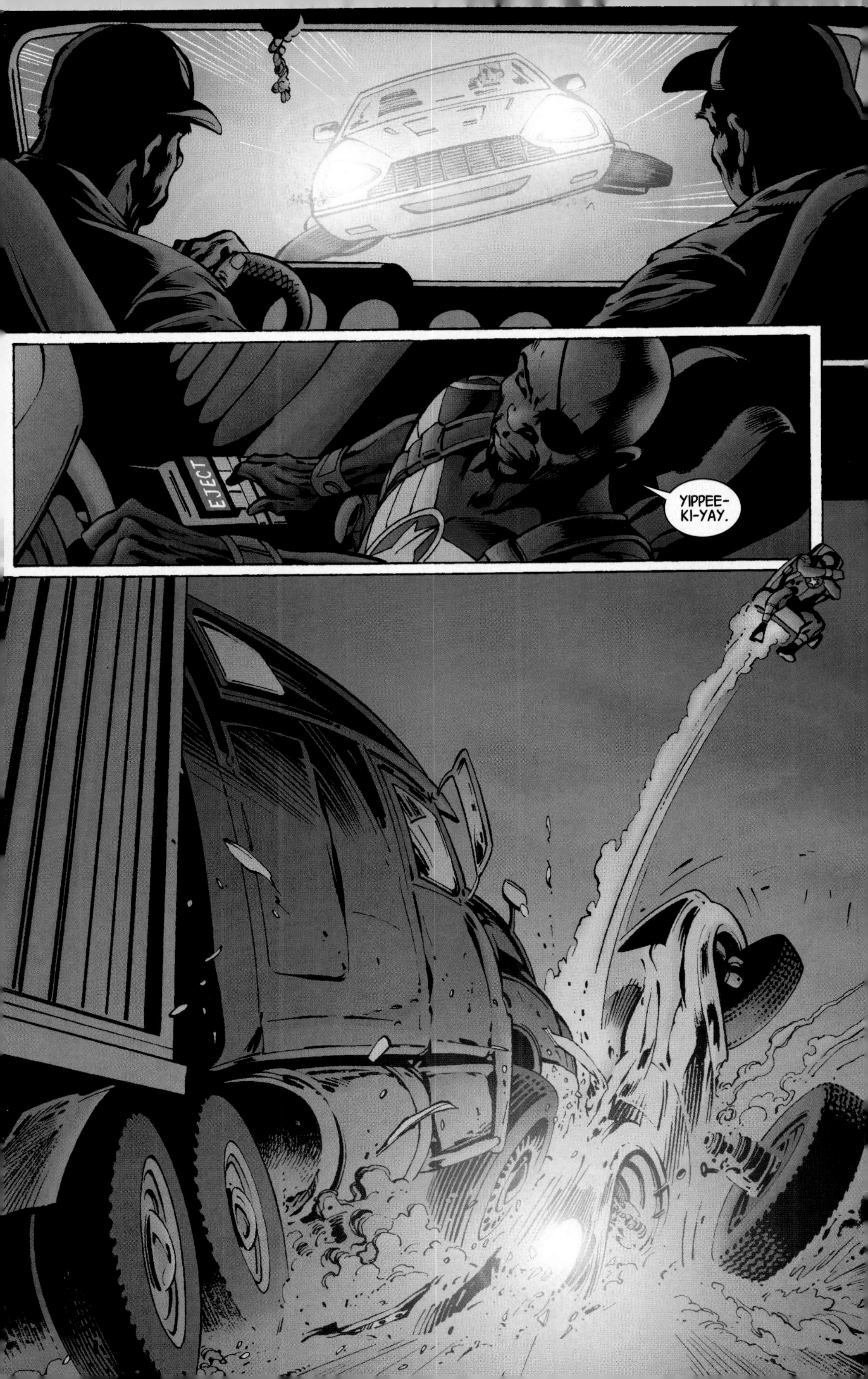
EJECT
YIPPEE-KI-YAY.

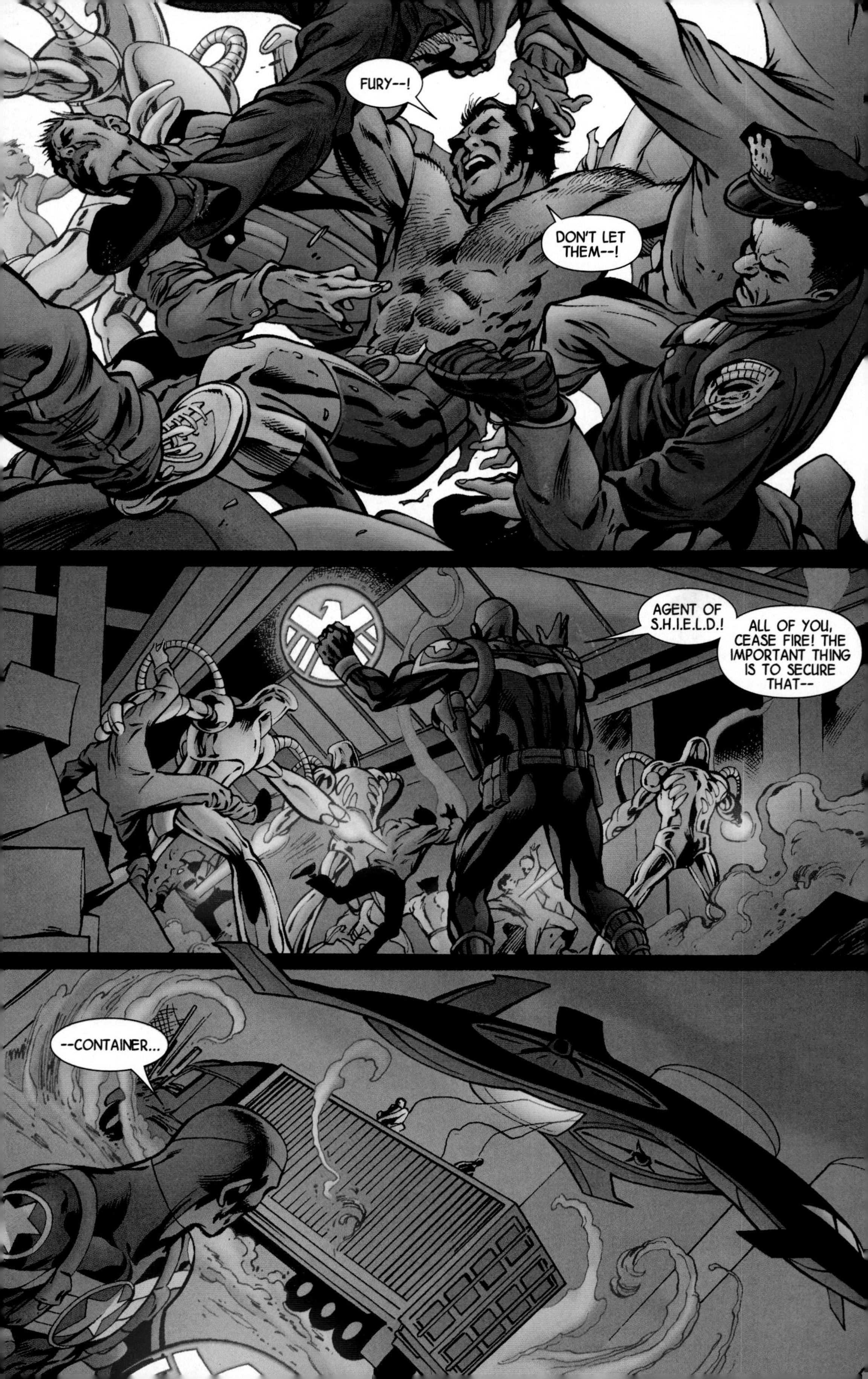
FURY--!
DON'T LET THEM--!
AGENT OF S.H.I.E.L.D.!
ALL OF YOU, CEASE FIRE! THE IMPORTANT THING IS TO SECURE THAT--
--CONTAINER...

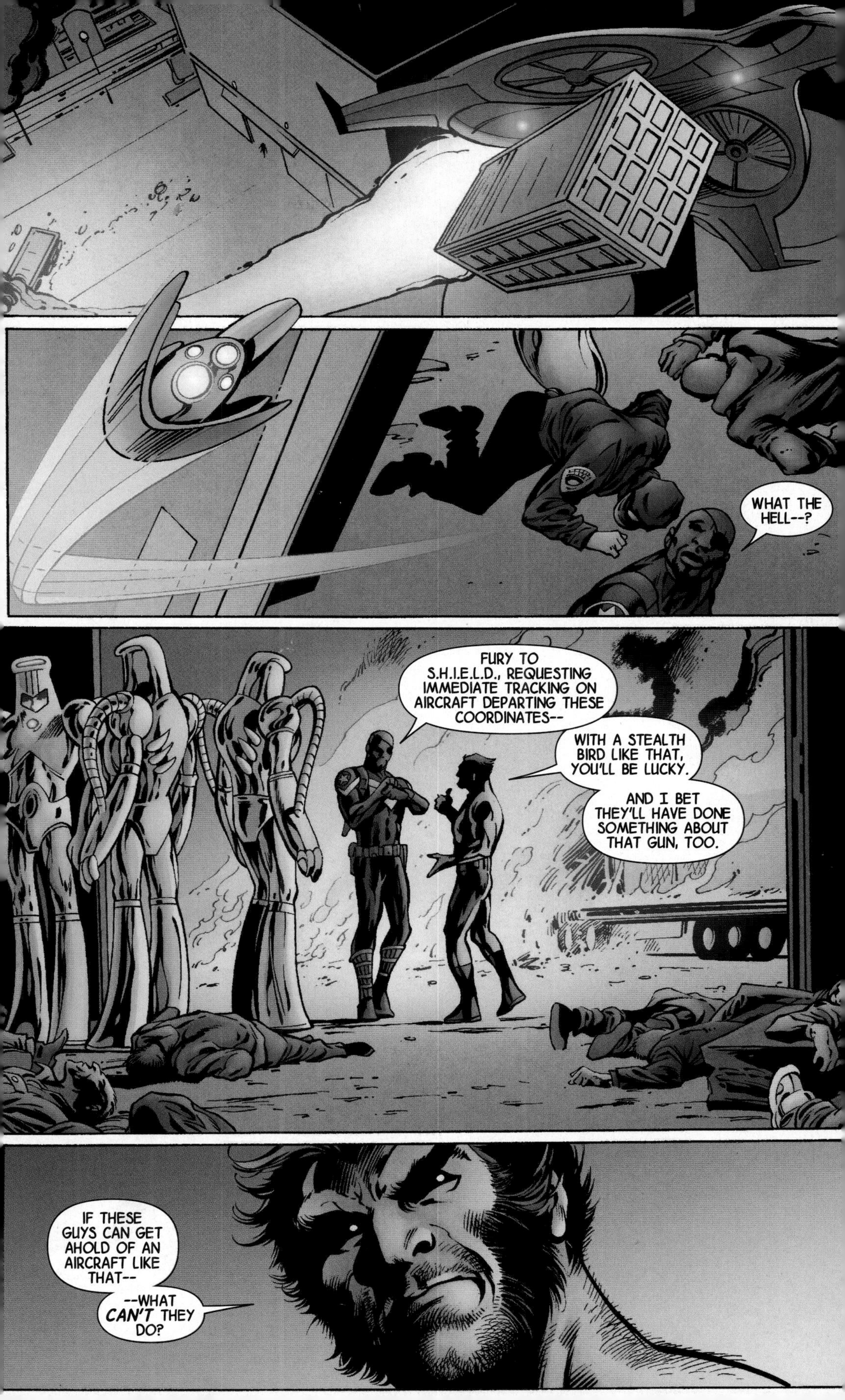
WHAT THE HELL--?
FURY TO S.H.I.E.L.D., REQUESTING IMMEDIATE TRACKING ON AIRCRAFT DEPARTING THESE COORDINATES--
WITH A STEALTH BIRD LIKE THAT, YOU'LL BE LUCKY.
AND I BET THEY'LL HAVE DONE SOMETHING ABOUT THAT GUN, TOO.
IF THESE GUYS CAN GET AHOLD OF AN AIRCRAFT LIKE THAT--
--WHAT *CAN'T* THEY DO?

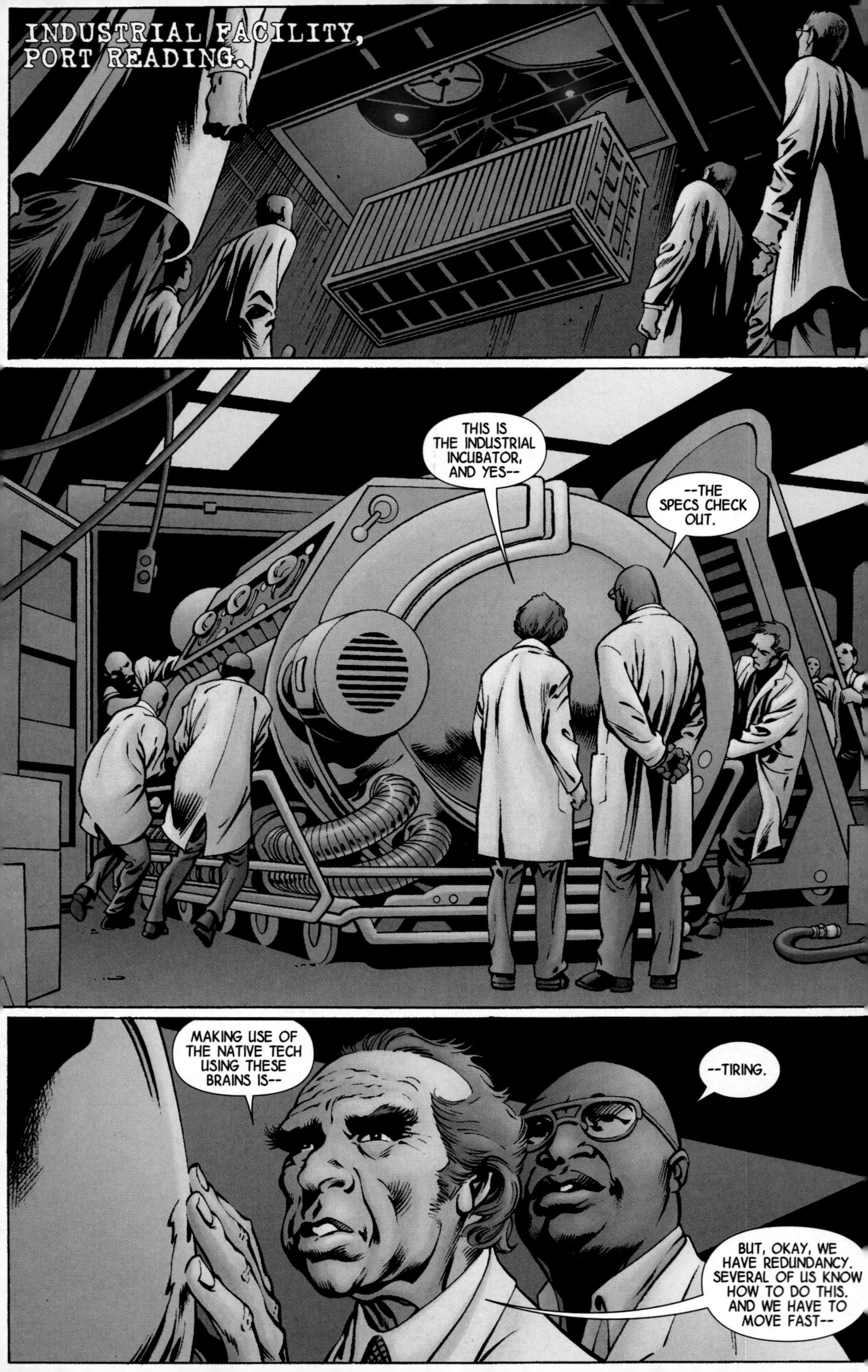
INDUSTRIAL FACILITY, PORT READING.
THIS IS THE INDUSTRIAL INCUBATOR, AND YES--
--THE SPECS CHECK OUT.
MAKING USE OF THE NATIVE TECH USING THESE BRAINS IS--
--TIRING.
BUT, OKAY, WE HAVE REDUNDANCY. SEVERAL OF US KNOW HOW TO DO THIS. AND WE HAVE TO MOVE FAST--

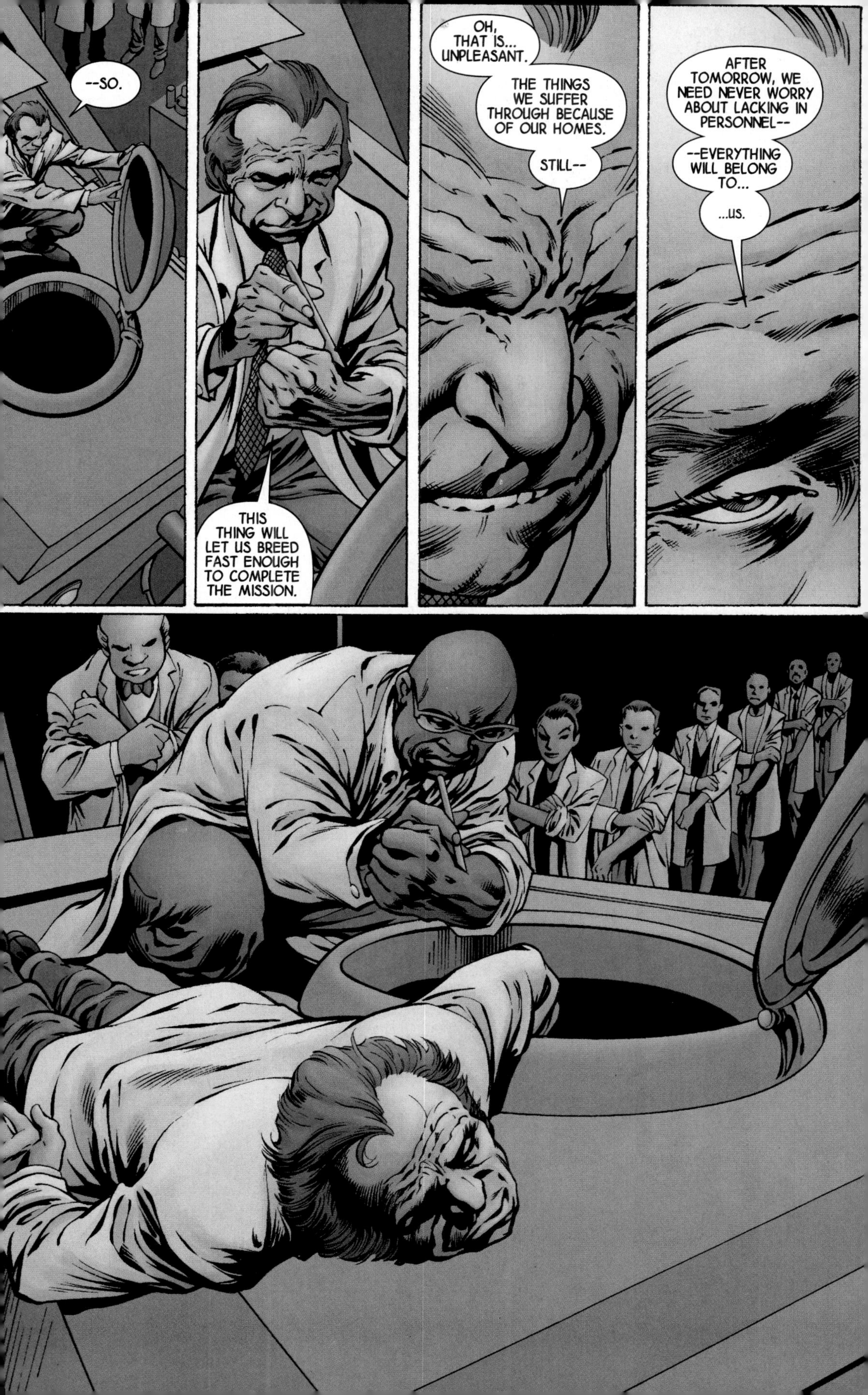
--SO.
THIS THING WILL LET US BREED FAST ENOUGH TO COMPLETE THE MISSION.
OH, THAT IS... UNPLEASANT.
THE THINGS WE SUFFER THROUGH BECAUSE OF OUR HOMES.
STILL--
AFTER TOMORROW, WE NEED NEVER WORRY ABOUT LACKING IN PERSONNEL--
--EVERYTHING WILL BELONG TO...
...US.

FOUR

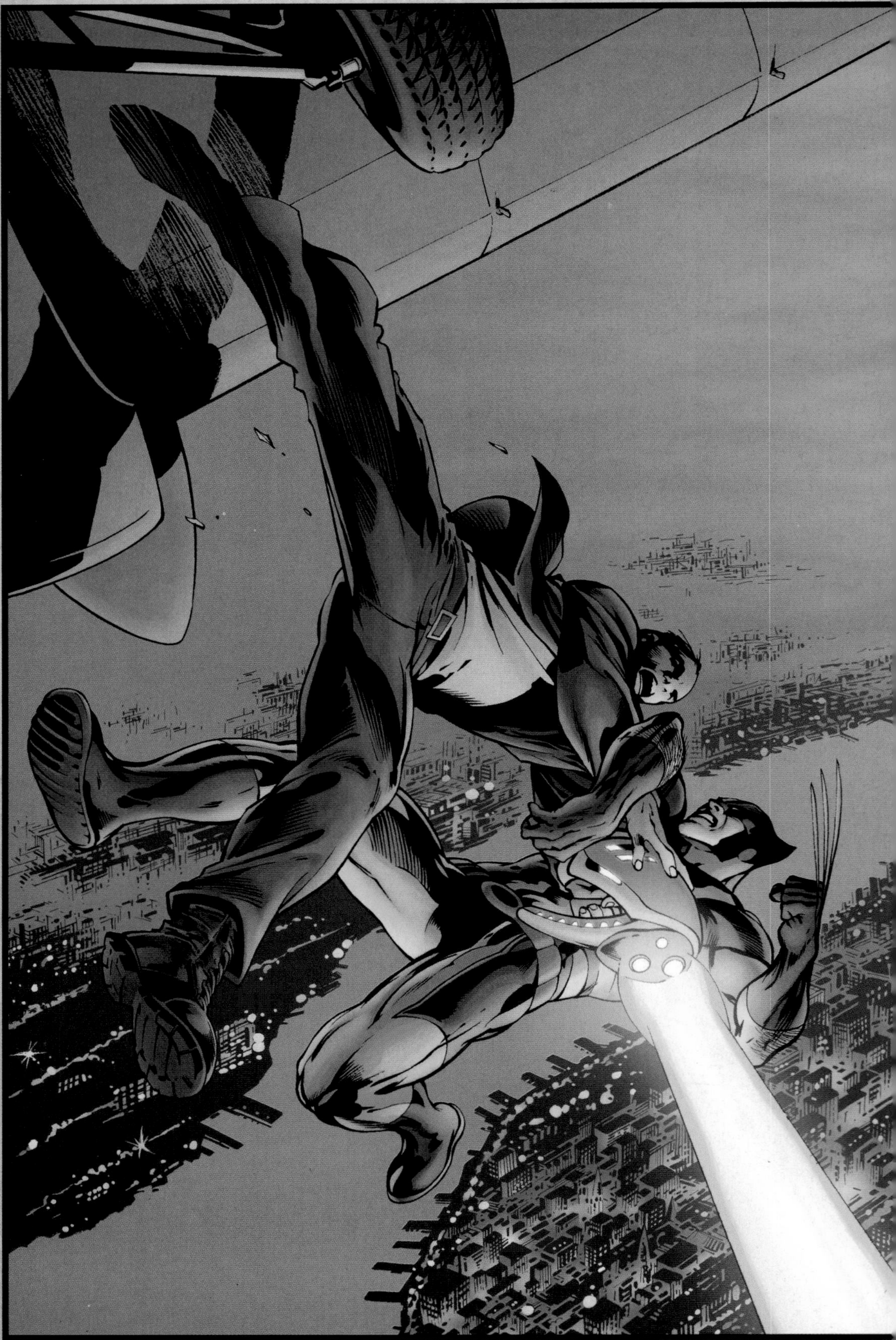

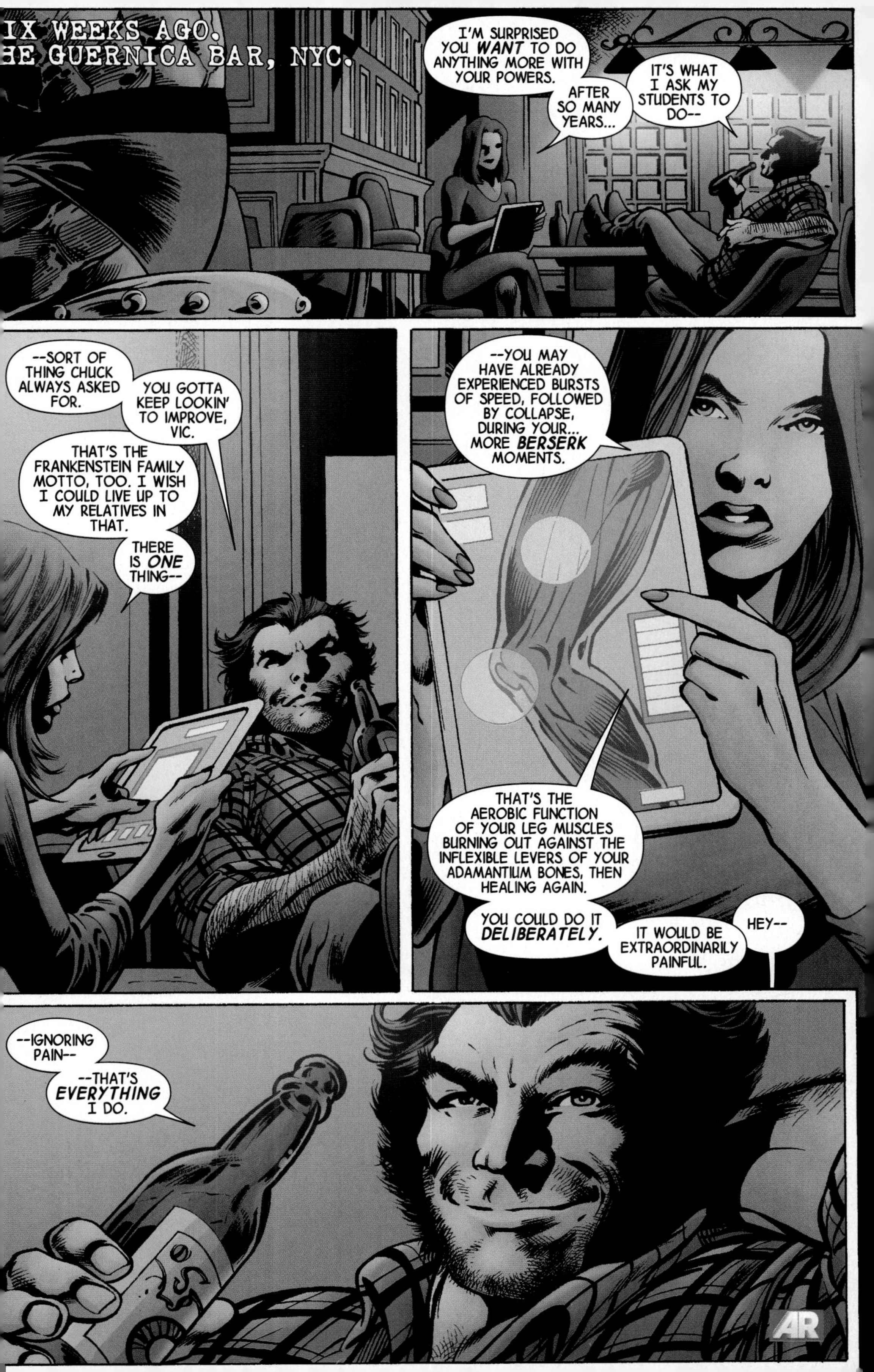
IX WEEKS AGO.
HE GUERNICA BAR, NYC.
I'M SURPRISED YOU WANT TO DO ANYTHING MORE WITH YOUR POWERS.
AFTER SO MANY YEARS...
IT'S WHAT I ASK MY STUDENTS TO DO--
--SORT OF THING CHUCK ALWAYS ASKED FOR.
YOU GOTTA KEEP LOOKIN' TO IMPROVE, VIC.
THAT'S THE FRANKENSTEIN FAMILY MOTTO, TOO. I WISH I COULD LIVE UP TO MY RELATIVES IN THAT.
THERE IS ONE THING--
--YOU MAY HAVE ALREADY EXPERIENCED BURSTS OF SPEED, FOLLOWED BY COLLAPSE, DURING YOUR... MORE BERSERK MOMENTS.
THAT'S THE AEROBIC FUNCTION OF YOUR LEG MUSCLES BURNING OUT AGAINST THE INFLEXIBLE LEVERS OF YOUR ADAMANTIUM BONES, THEN HEALING AGAIN.
YOU COULD DO IT DELIBERATELY.
IT WOULD BE EXTRAORDINARILY PAINFUL.
HEY--
--IGNORING PAIN--
--THAT'S EVERYTHING I DO.

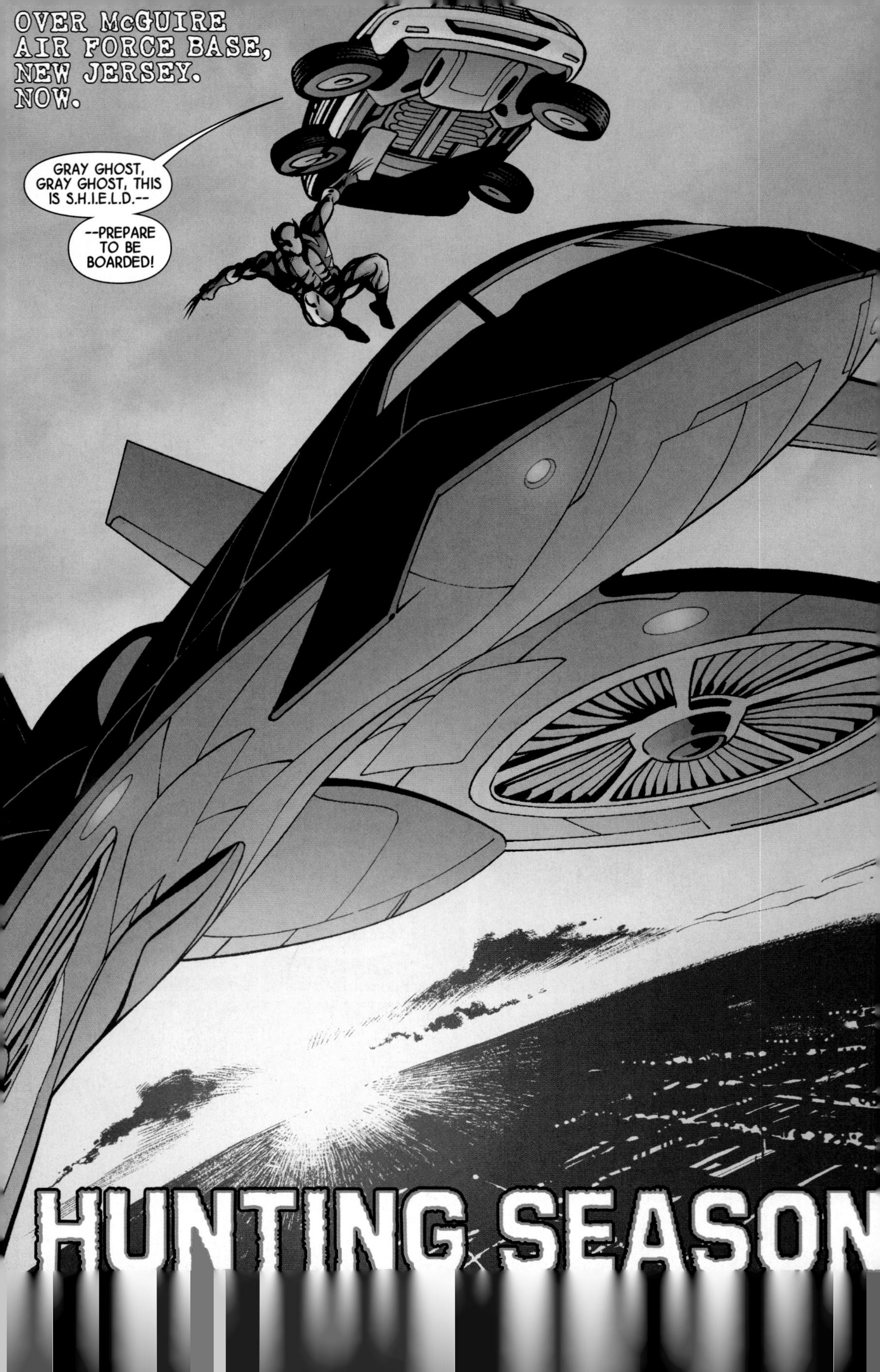
OVER McGUIRE AIR FORCE BASE, NEW JERSEY. NOW.
GRAY GHOST, GRAY GHOST, THIS IS S.H.I.E.L.D.--
--PREPARE TO BE BOARDED!
HUNTING SEASON

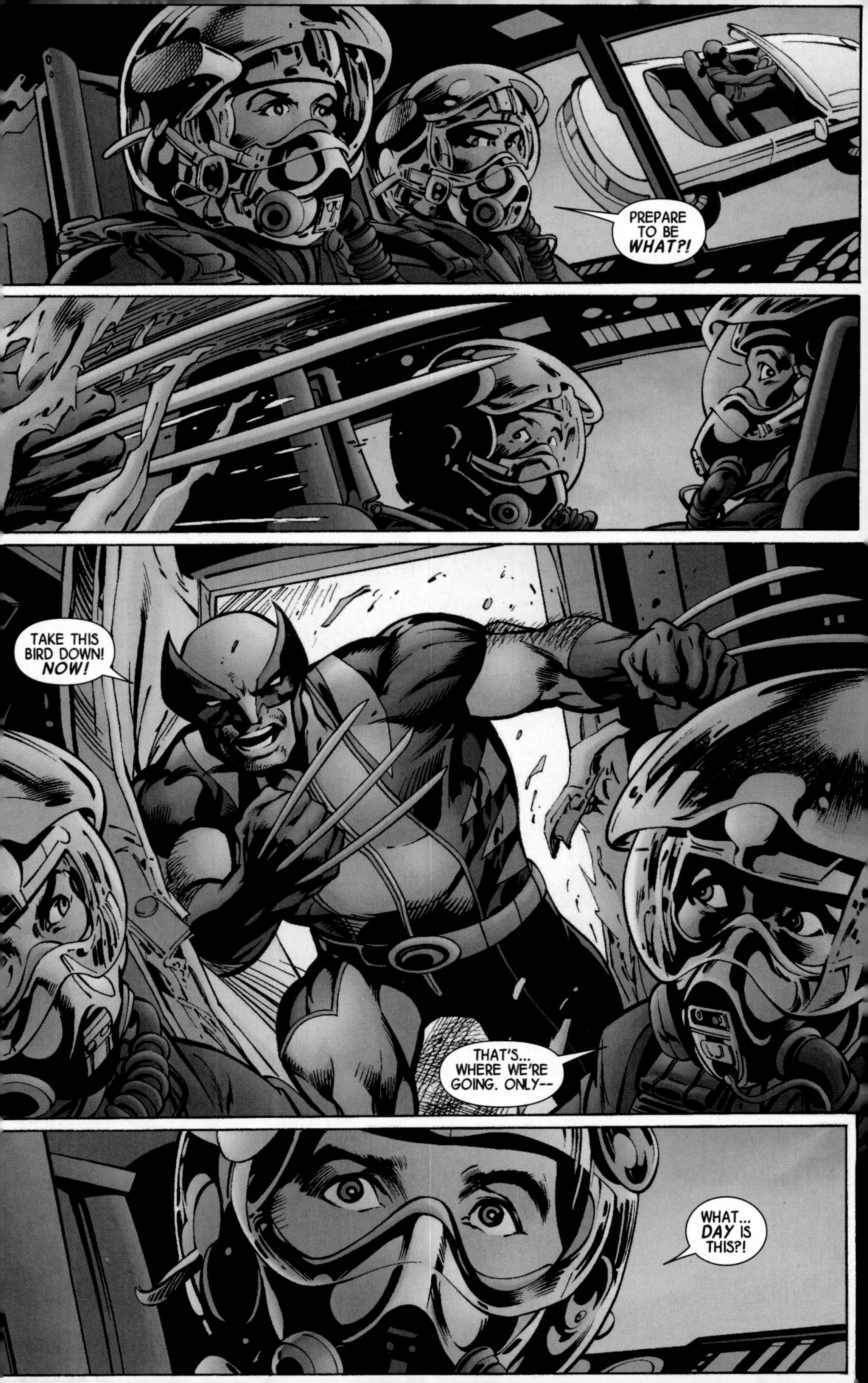
PREPARE TO BE WHAT?!
TAKE THIS BIRD DOWN! NOW!
THAT'S... WHERE WE'RE GOING. ONLY--
WHAT... DAY IS THIS?!

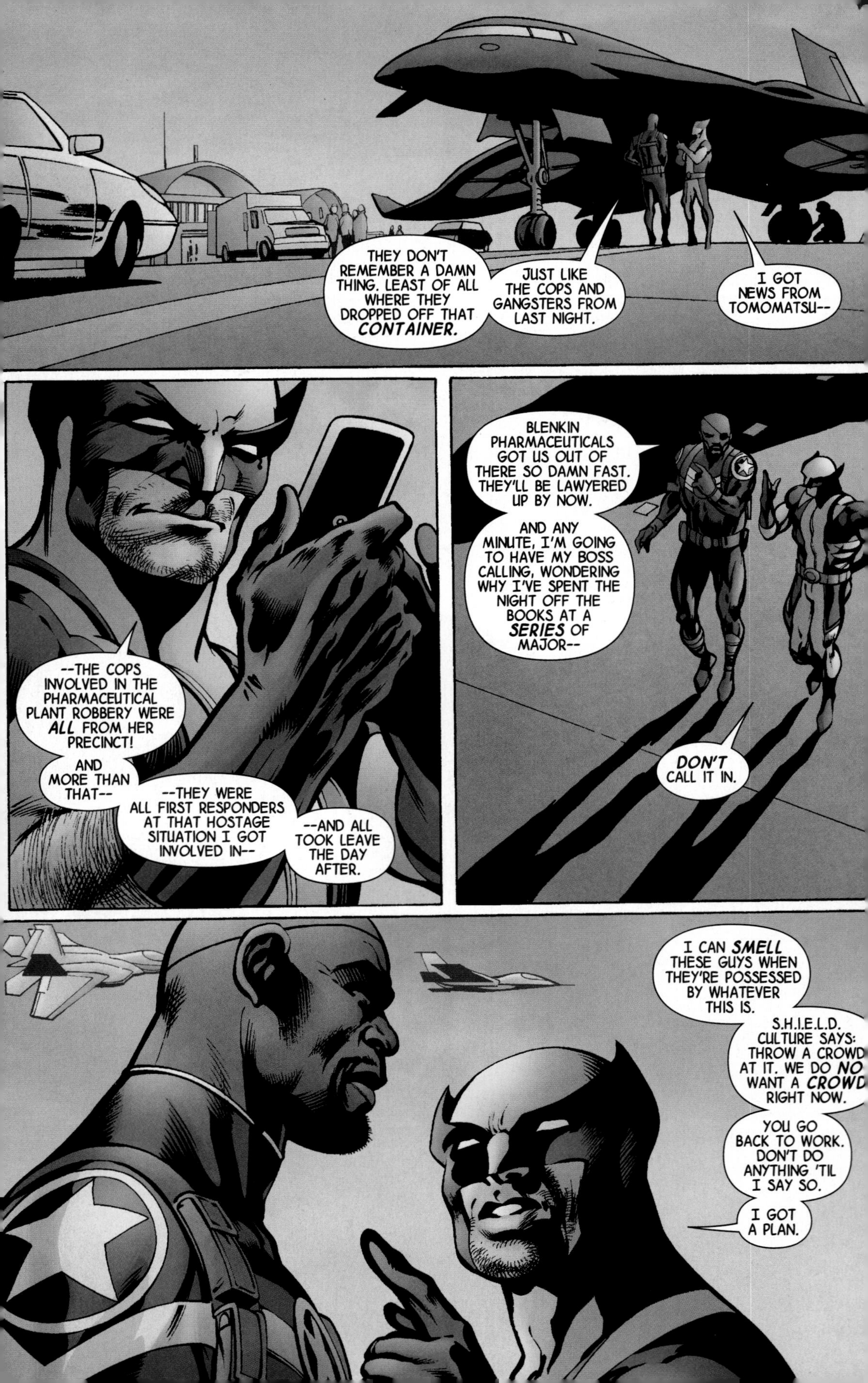
THEY DON'T REMEMBER A DAMN THING. LEAST OF ALL WHERE THEY DROPPED OFF THAT CONTAINER.
JUST LIKE THE COPS AND GANGSTERS FROM LAST NIGHT.
I GOT NEWS FROM TOMOMATSU--
--THE COPS INVOLVED IN THE PHARMACEUTICAL PLANT ROBBERY WERE ALL FROM HER PRECINCT!
AND MORE THAN THAT--
--THEY WERE ALL FIRST RESPONDERS AT THAT HOSTAGE SITUATION I GOT INVOLVED IN--
--AND ALL TOOK LEAVE THE DAY AFTER.
BLENKIN PHARMACEUTICALS GOT US OUT OF THERE SO DAMN FAST. THEY'LL BE LAWYERED UP BY NOW.
AND ANY MINUTE, I'M GOING TO HAVE MY BOSS CALLING, WONDERING WHY I'VE SPENT THE NIGHT OFF THE BOOKS AT A SERIES OF MAJOR--
DON'T CALL IT IN.
I CAN SMELL THESE GUYS WHEN THEY'RE POSSESSED BY WHATEVER THIS IS.
S.H.I.E.L.D. CULTURE SAYS: THROW A CROWD AT IT. WE DO NO WANT A CROWD RIGHT NOW.
YOU GO BACK TO WORK. DON'T DO ANYTHING 'TIL I SAY SO.
I GOT A PLAN.

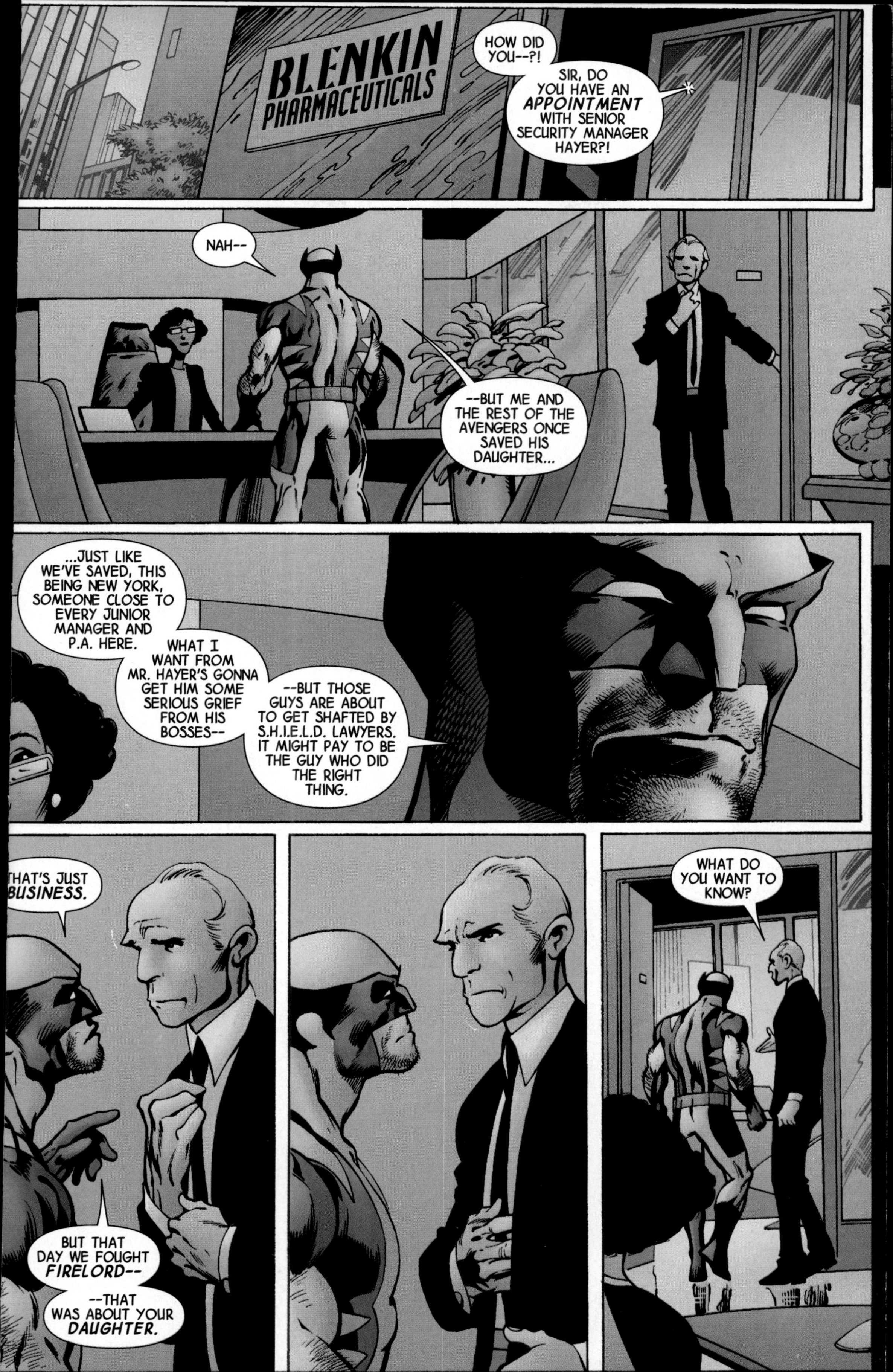
BLENKIN PHARMACEUTICALS
HOW DID YOU--?!
SIR, DO YOU HAVE AN APPOINTMENT WITH SENIOR SECURITY MANAGER HAYER?!
NAH--
--BUT ME AND THE REST OF THE AVENGERS ONCE SAVED HIS DAUGHTER...
...JUST LIKE WE'VE SAVED, THIS BEING NEW YORK, SOMEONE CLOSE TO EVERY JUNIOR MANAGER AND P.A. HERE.
WHAT I WANT FROM MR. HAYER'S GONNA GET HIM SOME SERIOUS GRIEF FROM HIS BOSSES--
--BUT THOSE GUYS ARE ABOUT TO GET SHAFTED BY S.H.I.E.L.D. LAWYERS. IT MIGHT PAY TO BE THE GUY WHO DID THE RIGHT THING.
THAT'S JUST BUSINESS.
BUT THAT DAY WE FOUGHT FIRELORD--
--THAT WAS ABOUT YOUR DAUGHTER.
WHAT DO YOU WANT TO KNOW?

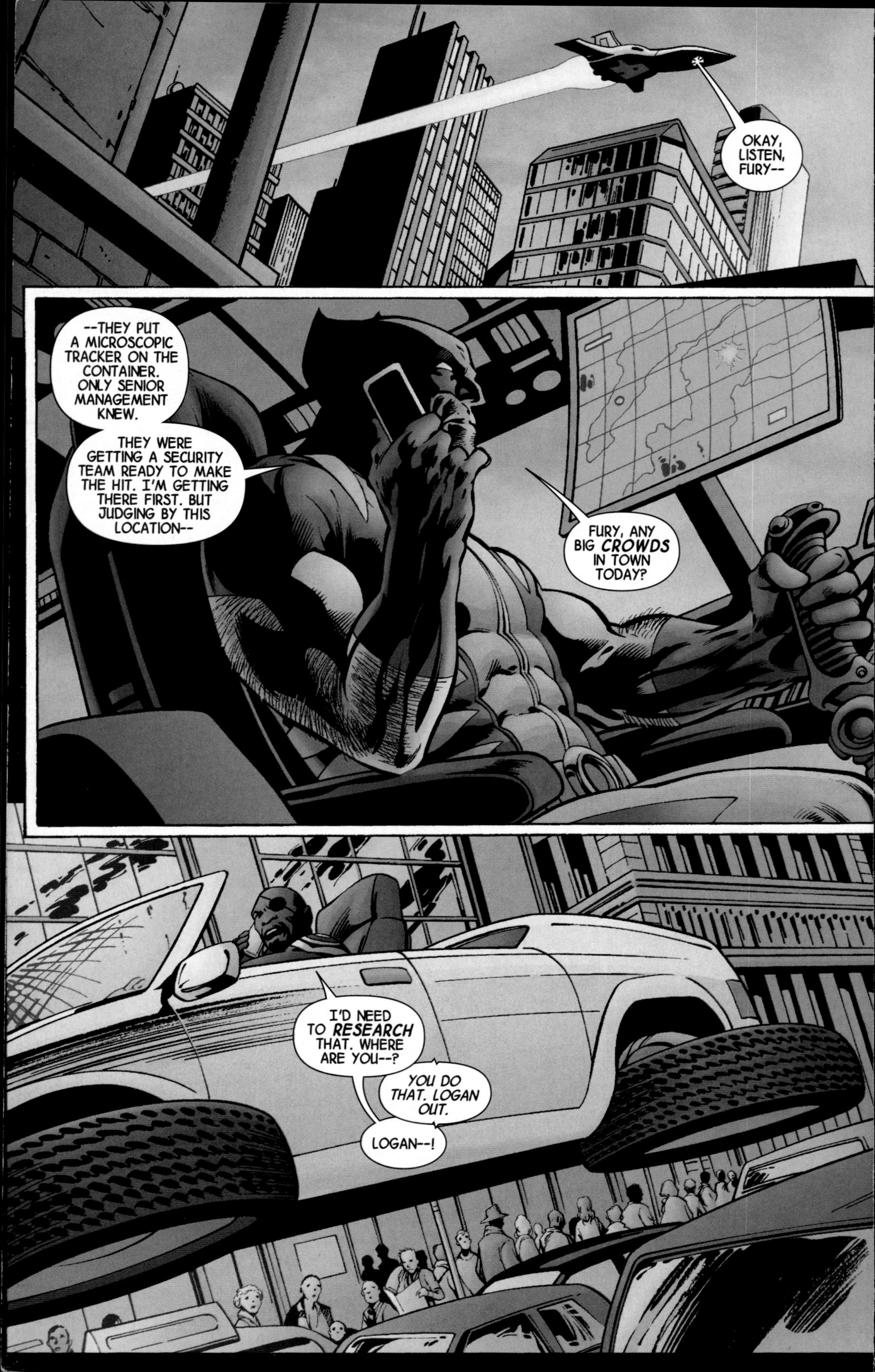
OKAY, LISTEN, FURY--
--THEY PUT A MICROSCOPIC TRACKER ON THE CONTAINER. ONLY SENIOR MANAGEMENT KNEW.
THEY WERE GETTING A SECURITY TEAM READY TO MAKE THE HIT. I'M GETTING THERE FIRST. BUT JUDGING BY THIS LOCATION--
FURY, ANY BIG CROWDS IN TOWN TODAY?
I'D NEED TO RESEARCH THAT. WHERE ARE YOU--?
YOU DO THAT. LOGAN OUT.
LOGAN--!

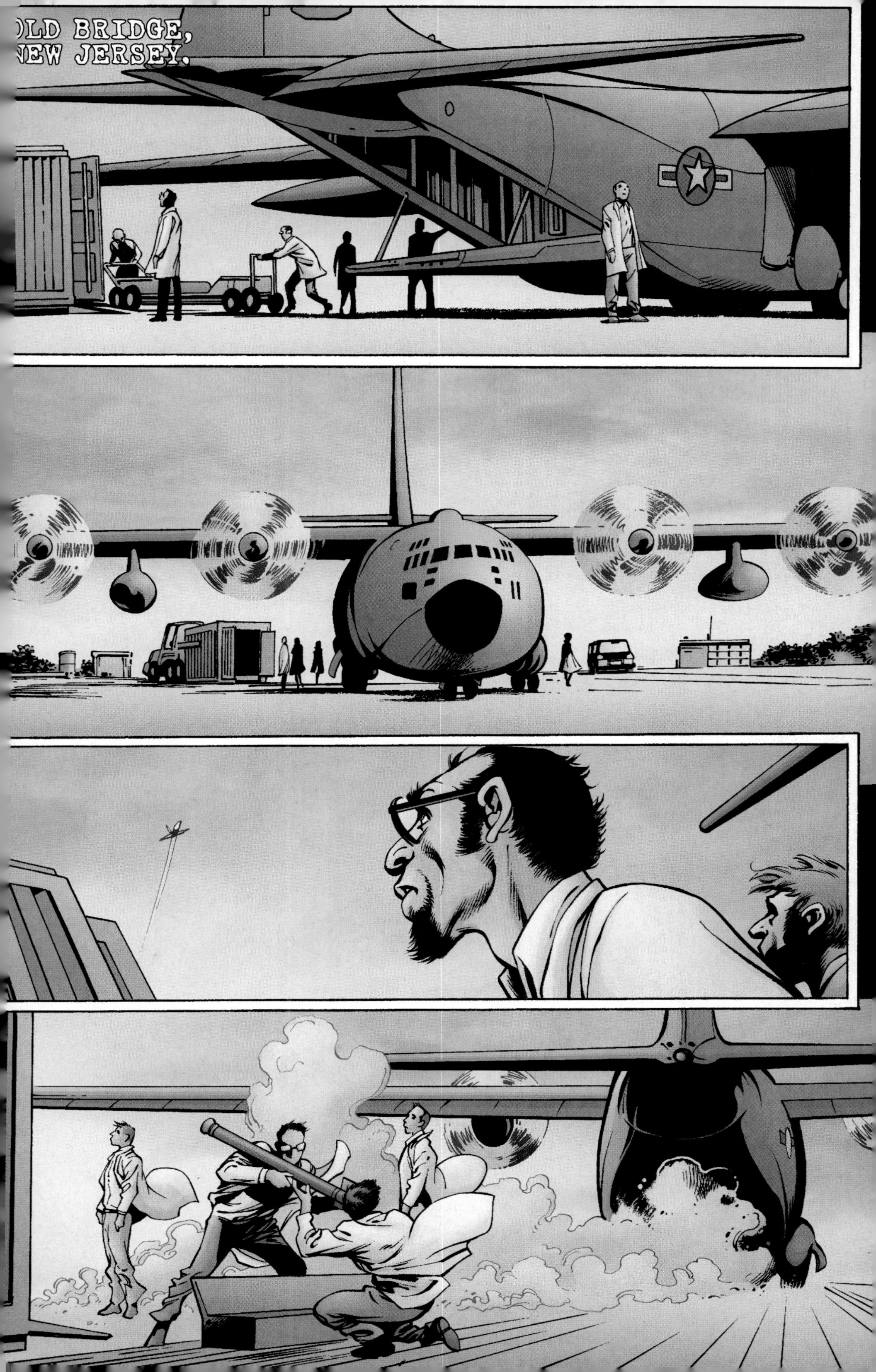
OLD BRIDGE, NEW JERSEY.

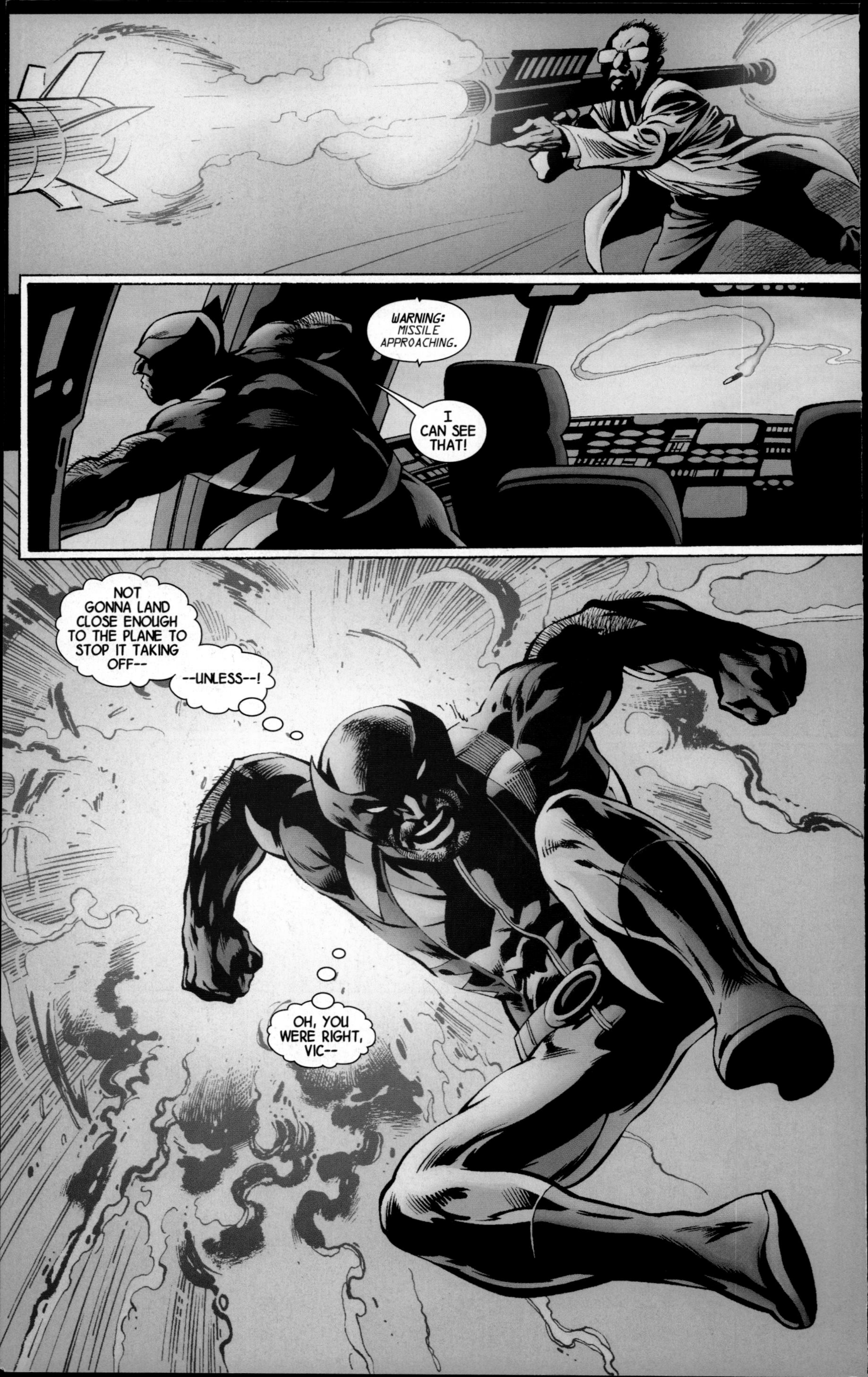
WARNING: MISSILE APPROACHING.
I CAN SEE THAT!
NOT GONNA LAND CLOSE ENOUGH TO THE PLANE TO STOP IT TAKING OFF--
--UNLESS--!
OH, YOU WERE RIGHT, VIC--

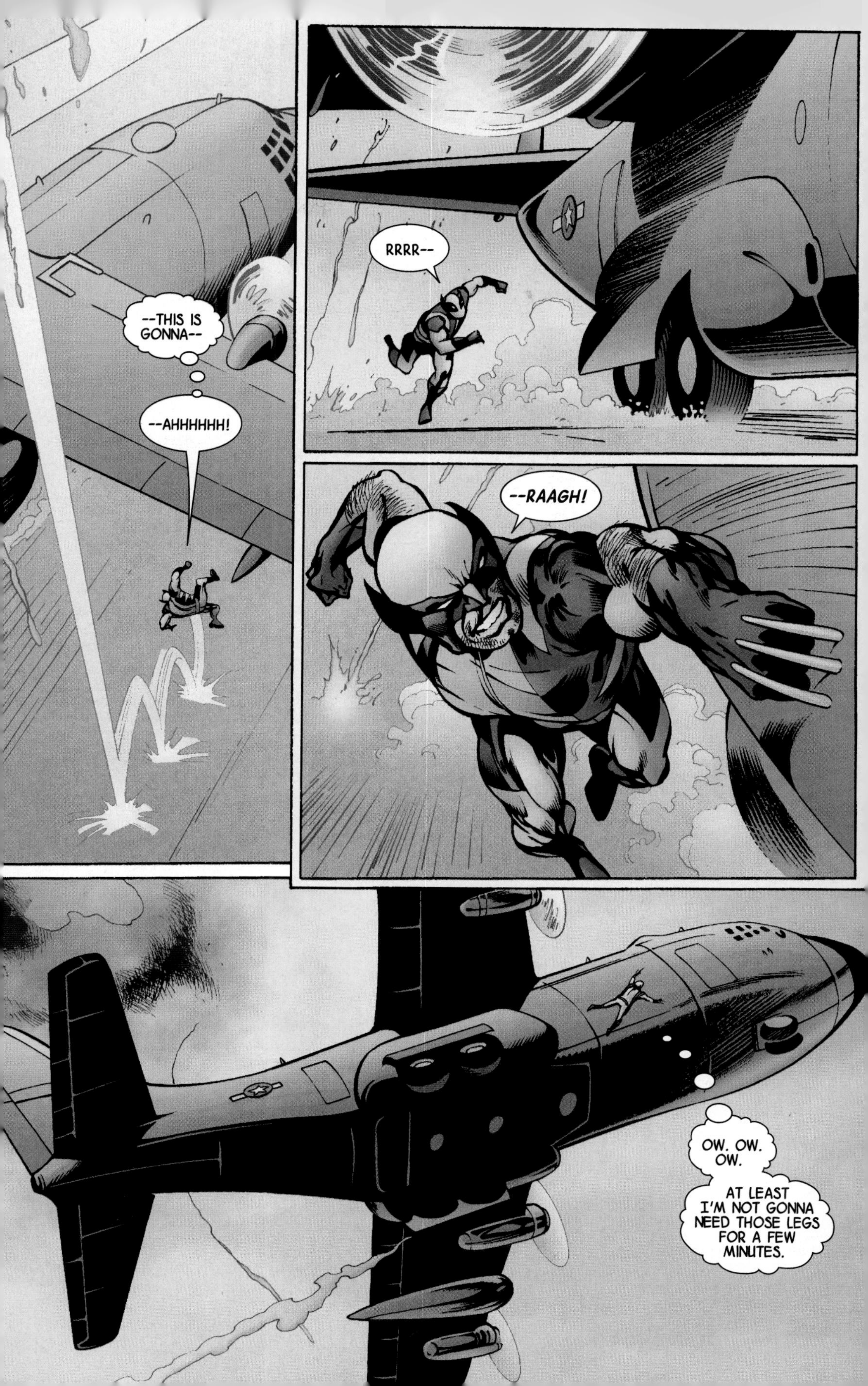
--THIS IS GONNA--
--AHHHHHH!
RRRR--
--RAAGH!
OW. OW. OW.
AT LEAST I'M NOT GONNA NEED THOSE LEGS FOR A FEW MINUTES.

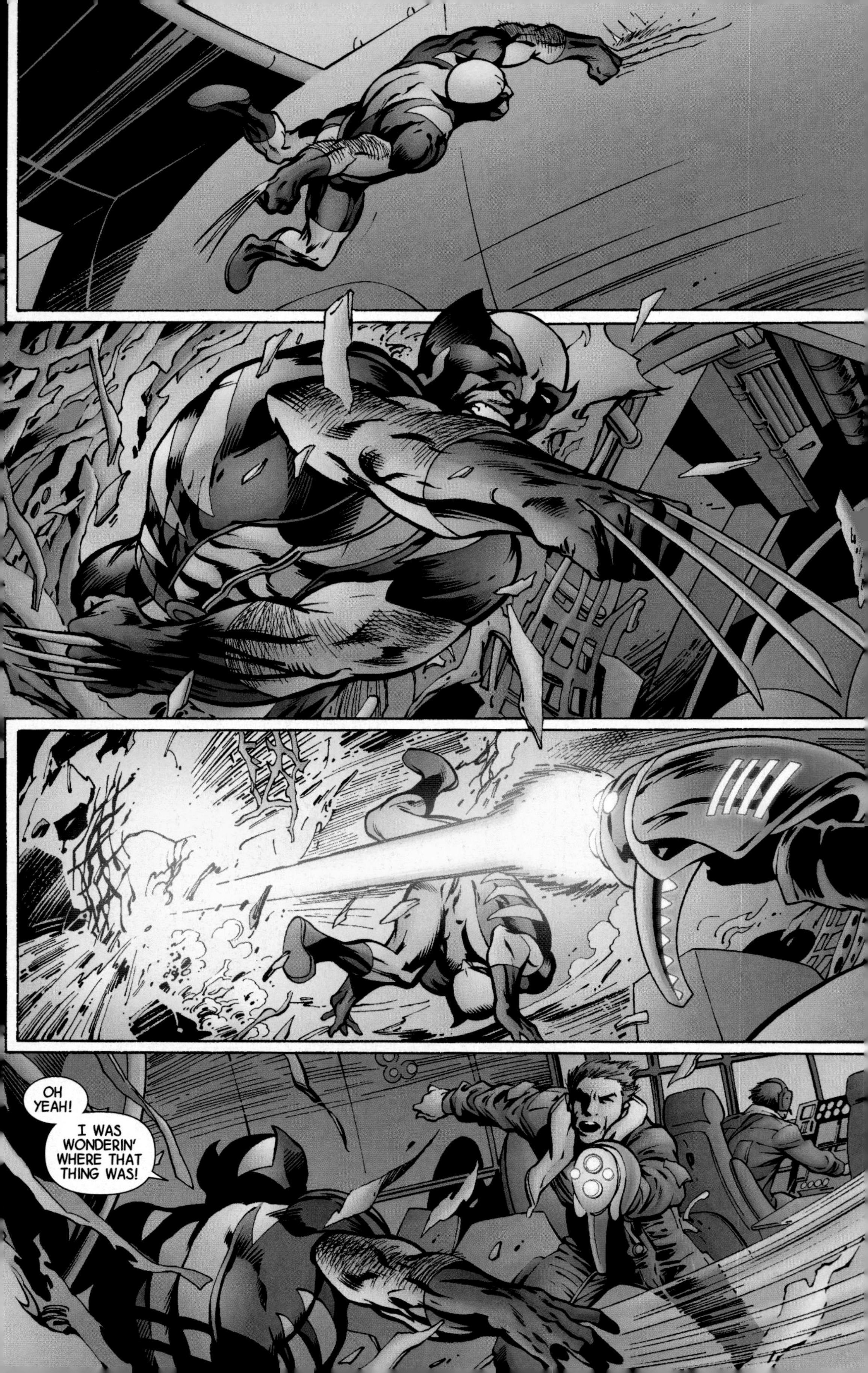
OH YEAH!
I WAS WONDERIN' WHERE THAT THING WAS!

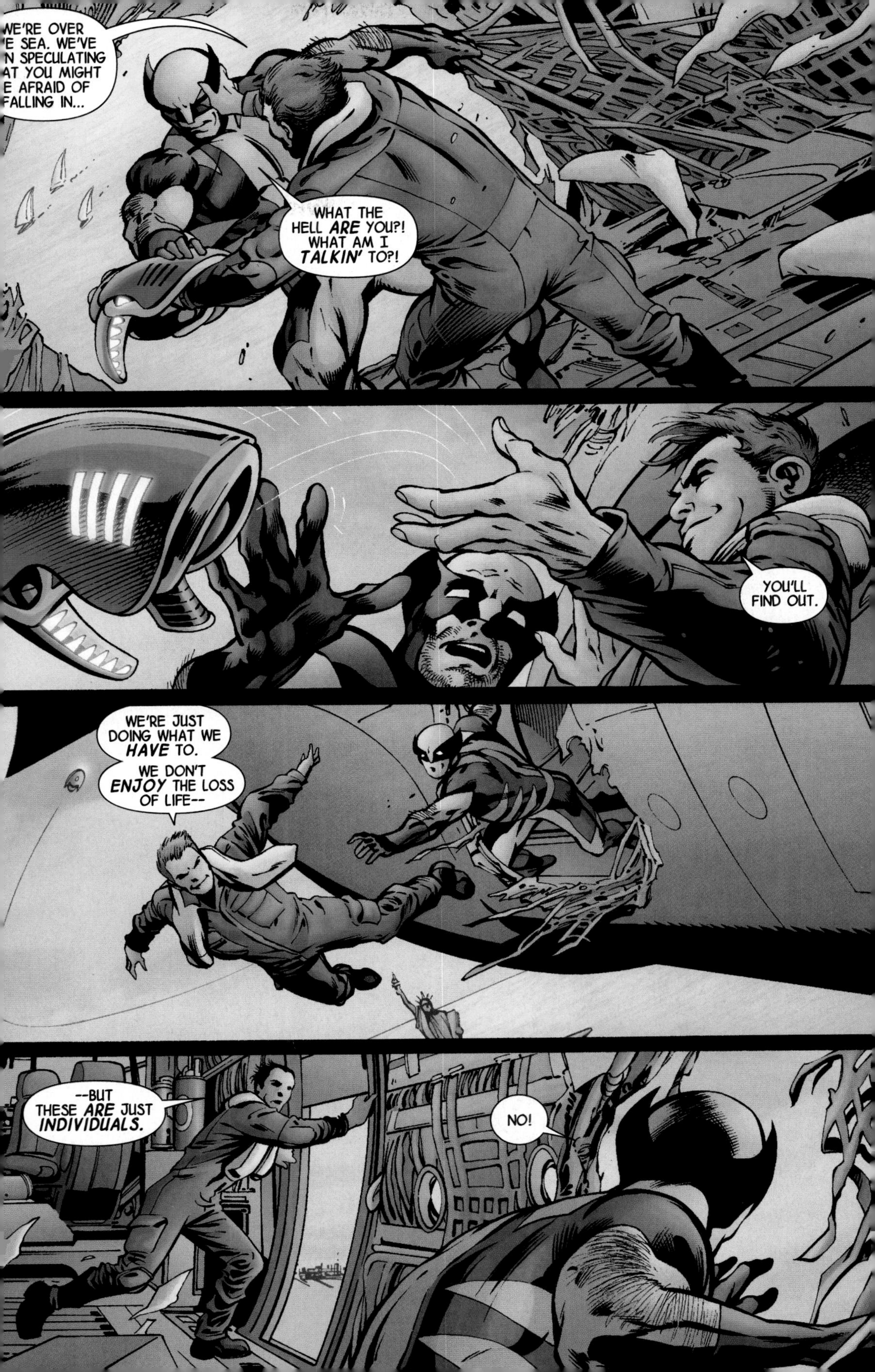
WE'RE OVER
'E SEA. WE'VE
N SPECULATING
AT YOU MIGHT
E AFRAID OF
FALLING IN...
WHAT THE HELL ARE YOU?! WHAT AM I TALKIN' TO?!
YOU'LL FIND OUT.
WE'RE JUST DOING WHAT WE HAVE TO.
WE DON'T ENJOY THE LOSS OF LIFE--
--BUT THESE ARE JUST INDIVIDUALS.
NO!

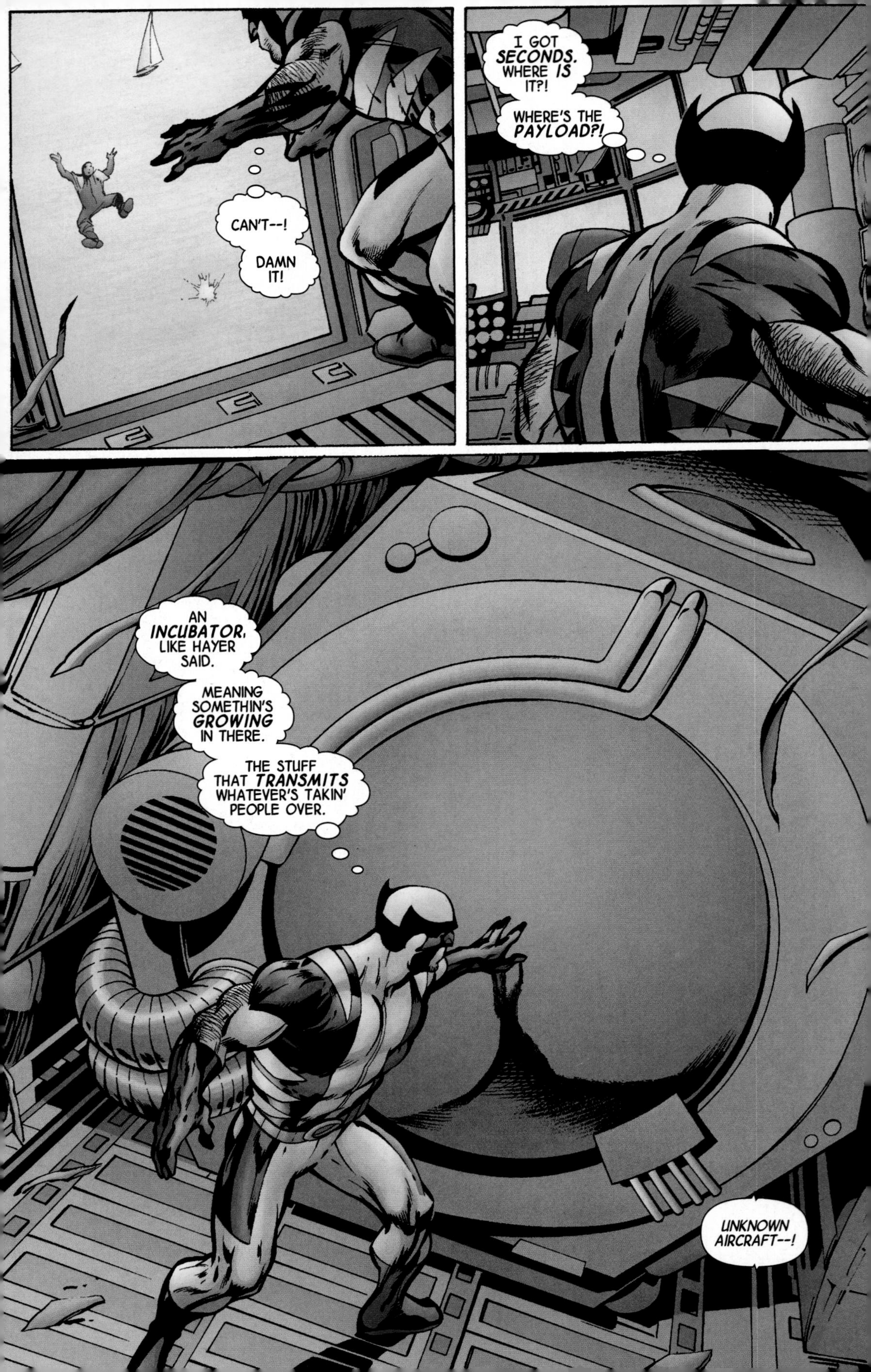
CAN'T--!
DAMN IT!
I GOT SECONDS. WHERE IS IT?!
WHERE'S THE PAYLOAD?!
AN INCUBATOR, LIKE HAYER SAID.
MEANING SOMETHIN'S GROWING IN THERE.
THE STUFF THAT TRANSMITS WHATEVER'S TAKIN' PEOPLE OVER.
UNKNOWN AIRCRAFT--!

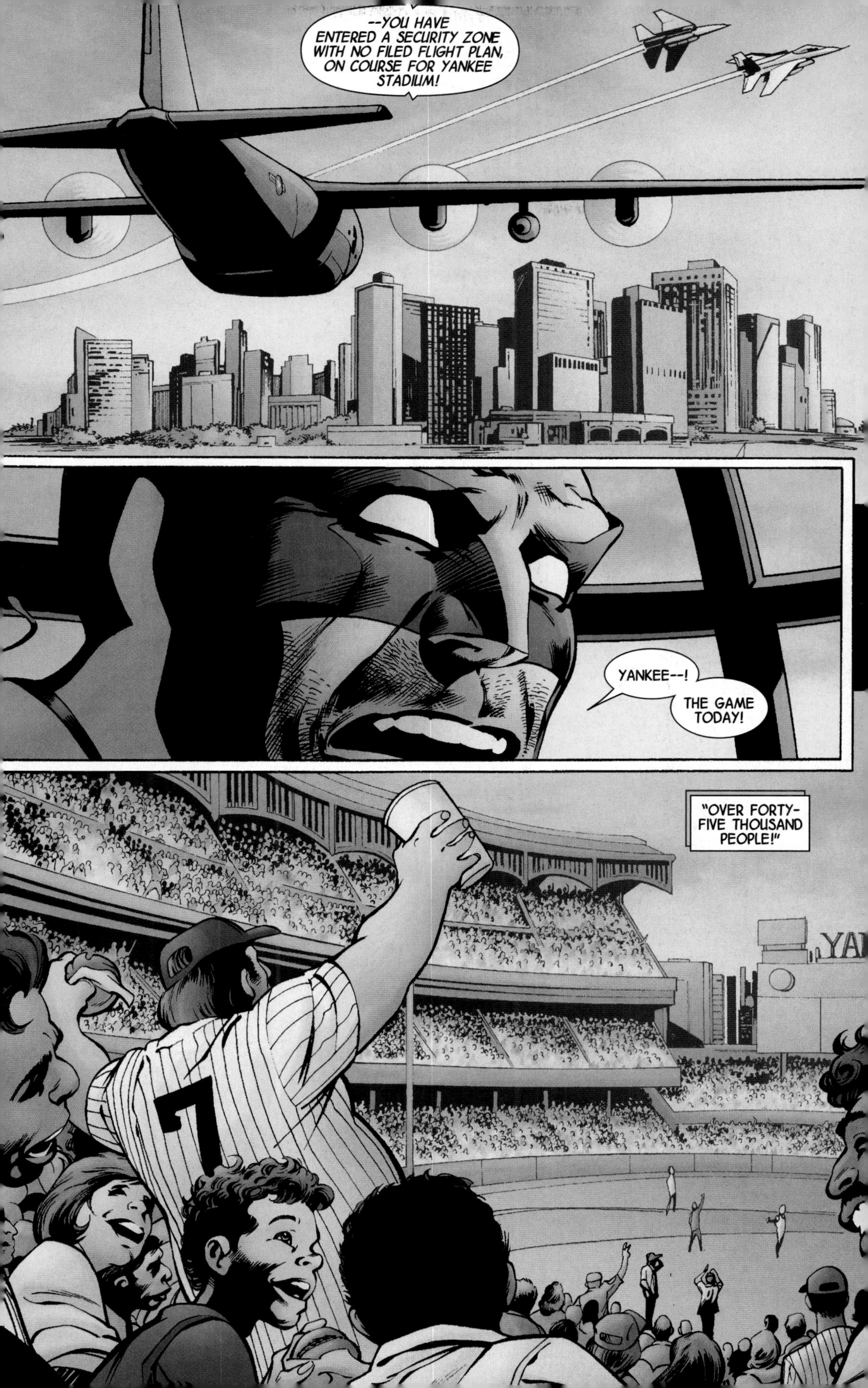
--YOU HAVE ENTERED A SECURITY ZONE WITH NO FILED FLIGHT PLAN, ON COURSE FOR YANKEE STADIUM!
YANKEE--!
THE GAME TODAY!
"OVER FORTY-FIVE THOUSAND PEOPLE!"
7

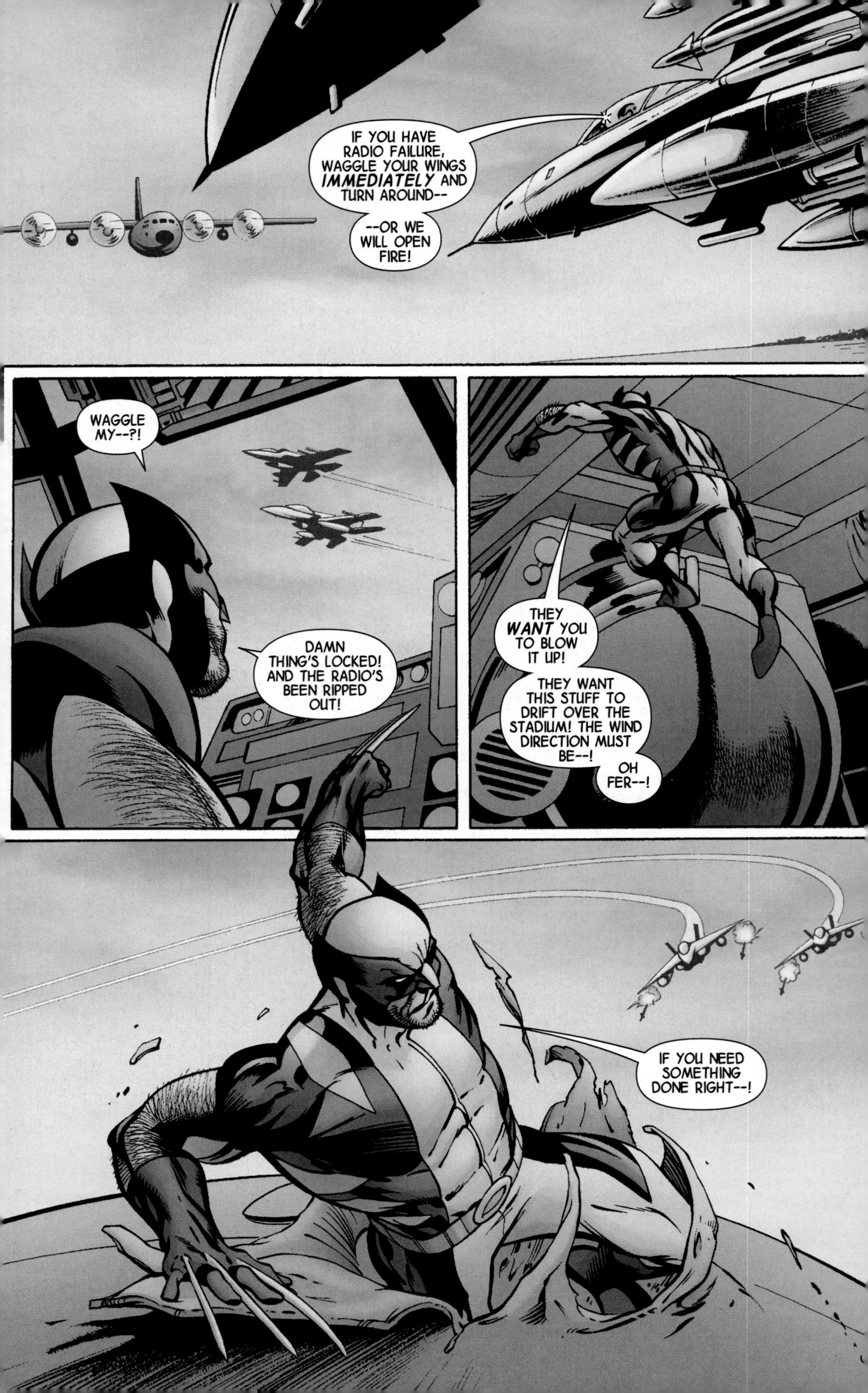
IF YOU HAVE RADIO FAILURE, WAGGLE YOUR WINGS *IMMEDIATELY* AND TURN AROUND--
--OR WE WILL OPEN FIRE!
WAGGLE MY--?!
DAMN THING'S LOCKED! AND THE RADIO'S BEEN RIPPED OUT!
THEY *WANT* YOU TO BLOW IT UP!
THEY WANT THIS STUFF TO DRIFT OVER THE STADIUM! THE WIND DIRECTION MUST BE--!
OH FER--!
IF YOU NEED SOMETHING DONE RIGHT--!

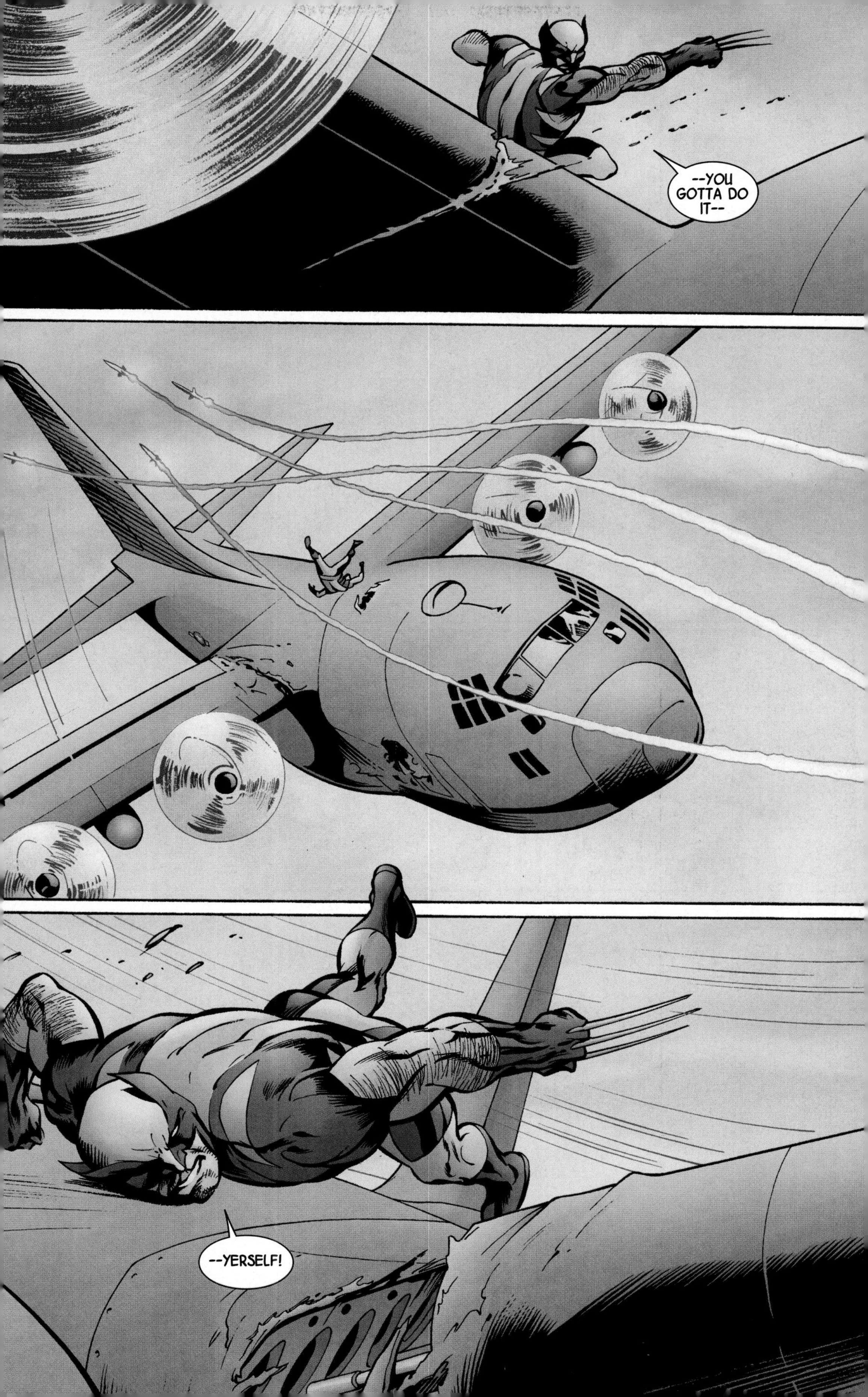
--YOU GOTTA DO IT--
--YERSELF!

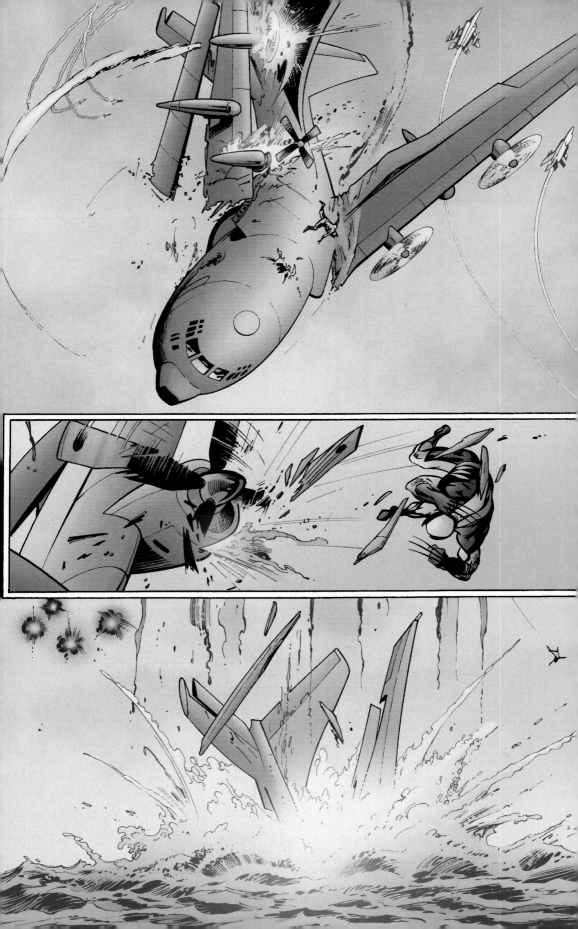

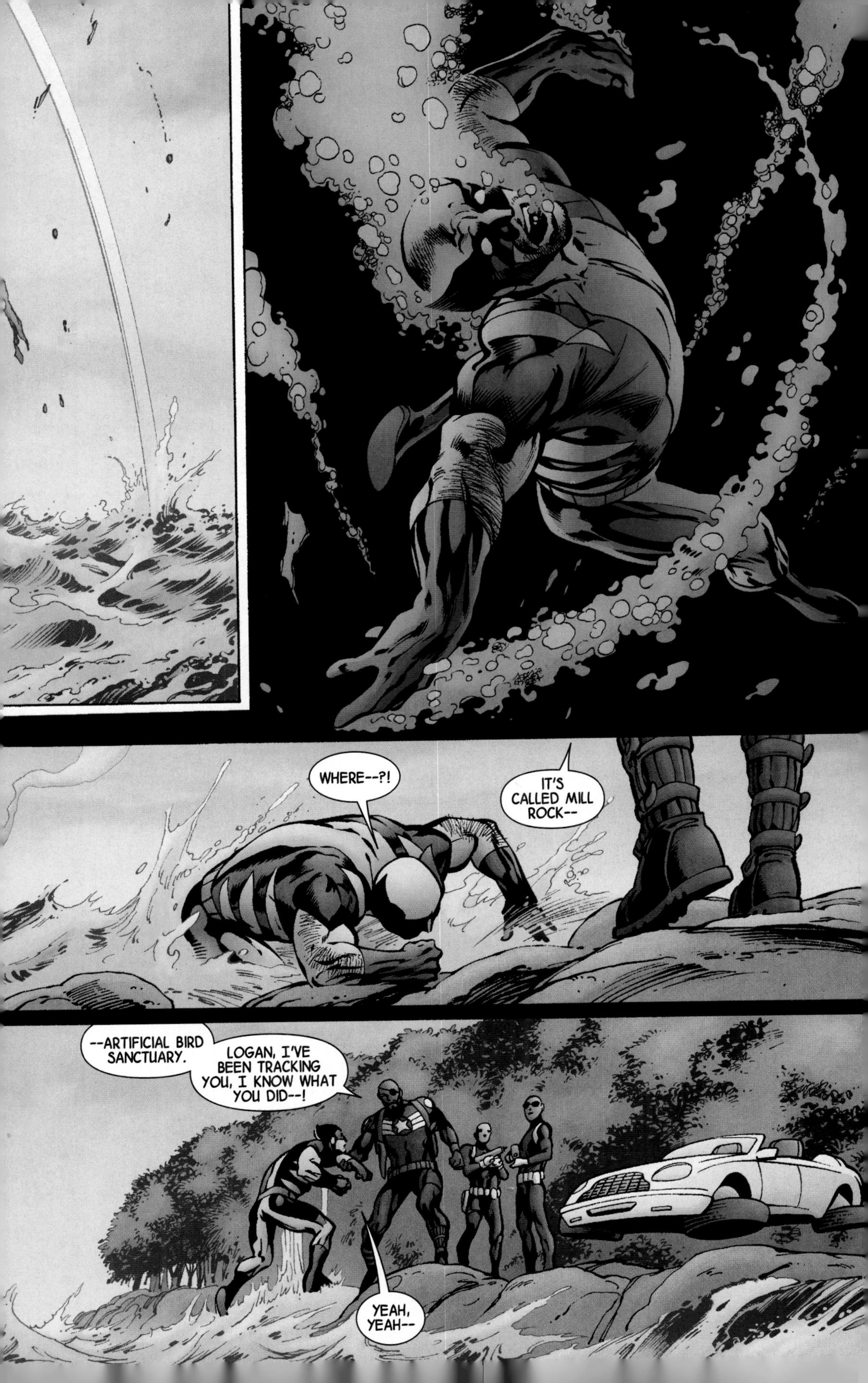
WHERE--?!
IT'S CALLED MILL ROCK--
--ARTIFICIAL BIRD SANCTUARY.
LOGAN, I'VE BEEN TRACKING YOU, I KNOW WHAT YOU DID--!
YEAH, YEAH--

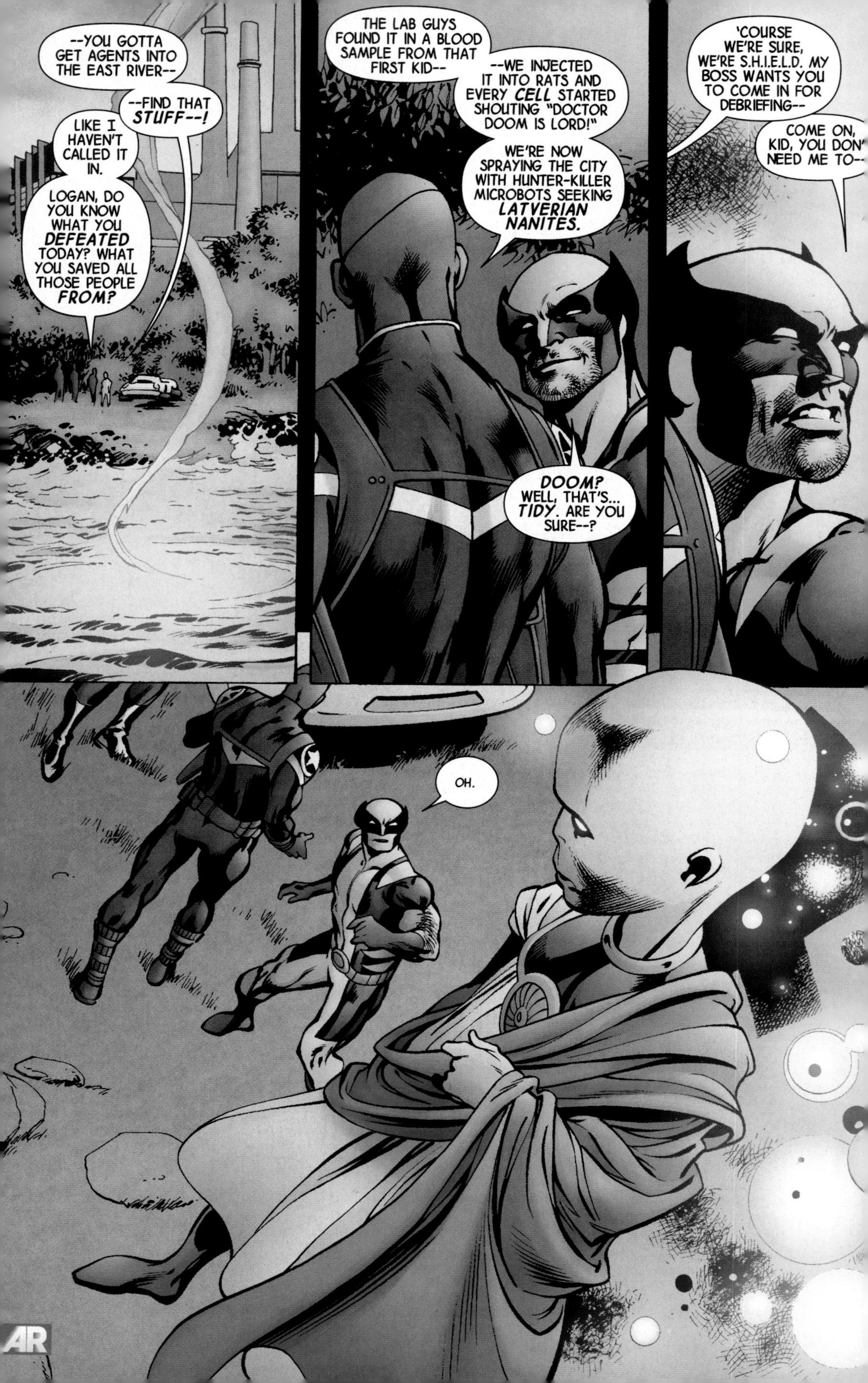
--YOU GOTTA GET AGENTS INTO THE EAST RIVER--
--FIND THAT STUFF--!
LIKE I HAVEN'T CALLED IT IN.
LOGAN, DO YOU KNOW WHAT YOU DEFEATED TODAY? WHAT YOU SAVED ALL THOSE PEOPLE FROM?
THE LAB GUYS FOUND IT IN A BLOOD SAMPLE FROM THAT FIRST KID--
--WE INJECTED IT INTO RATS AND EVERY CELL STARTED SHOUTING "DOCTOR DOOM IS LORD!"
WE'RE NOW SPRAYING THE CITY WITH HUNTER-KILLER MICROBOTS SEEKING LATVERIAN NANITES.
DOOM? WELL, THAT'S... TIDY. ARE YOU SURE--?
'COURSE WE'RE SURE, WE'RE S.H.I.E.L.D. MY BOSS WANTS YOU TO COME IN FOR DEBRIEFING--
COME ON, KID, YOU DON' NEED ME TO--
OH.

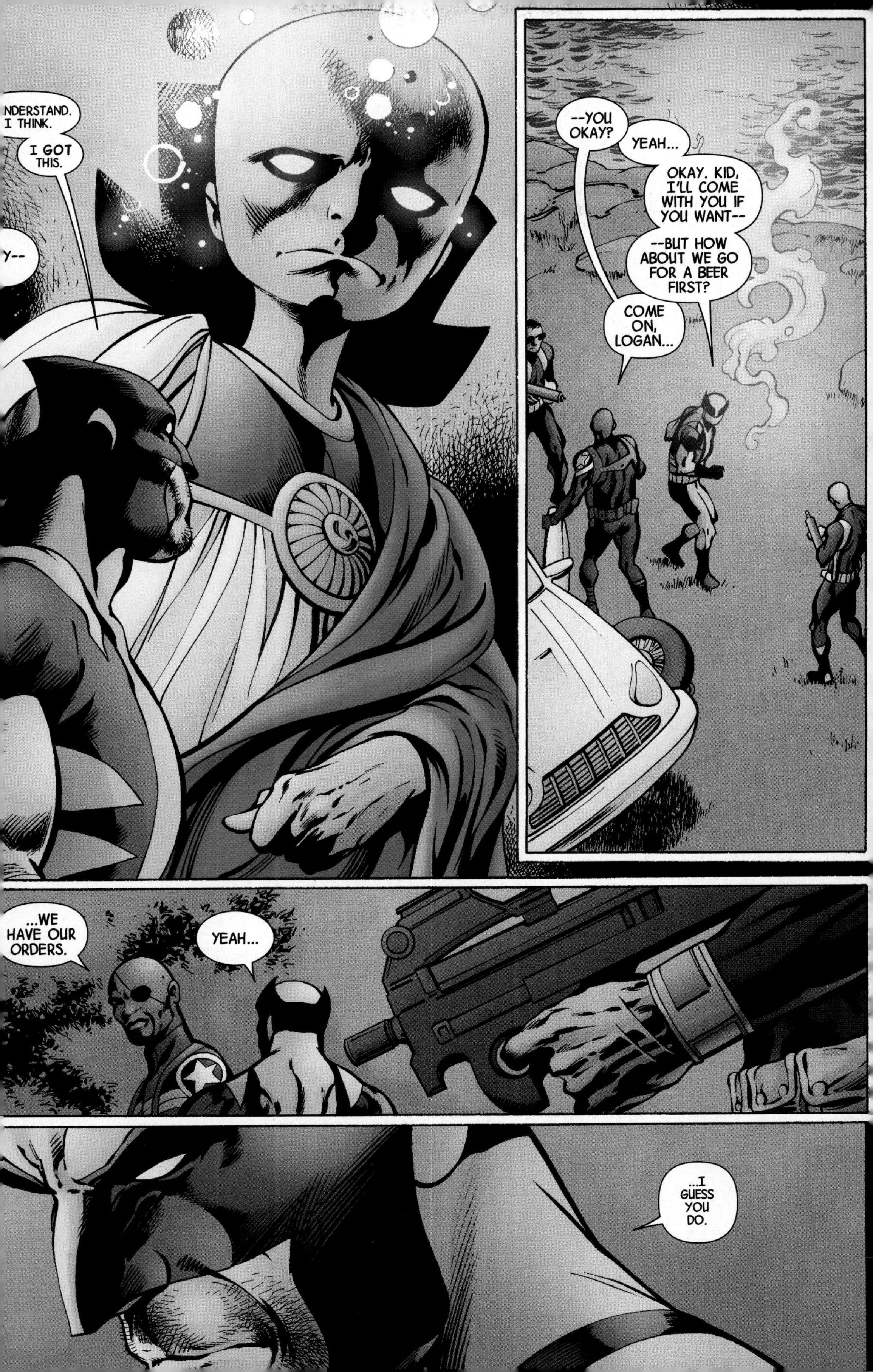
NDERSTAND. I THINK.
I GOT THIS.
Y--
--YOU OKAY?
YEAH...
OKAY. KID, I'LL COME WITH YOU IF YOU WANT--
--BUT HOW ABOUT WE GO FOR A BEER FIRST?
COME ON, LOGAN...
...WE HAVE OUR ORDERS.
YEAH...
...I GUESS YOU DO.

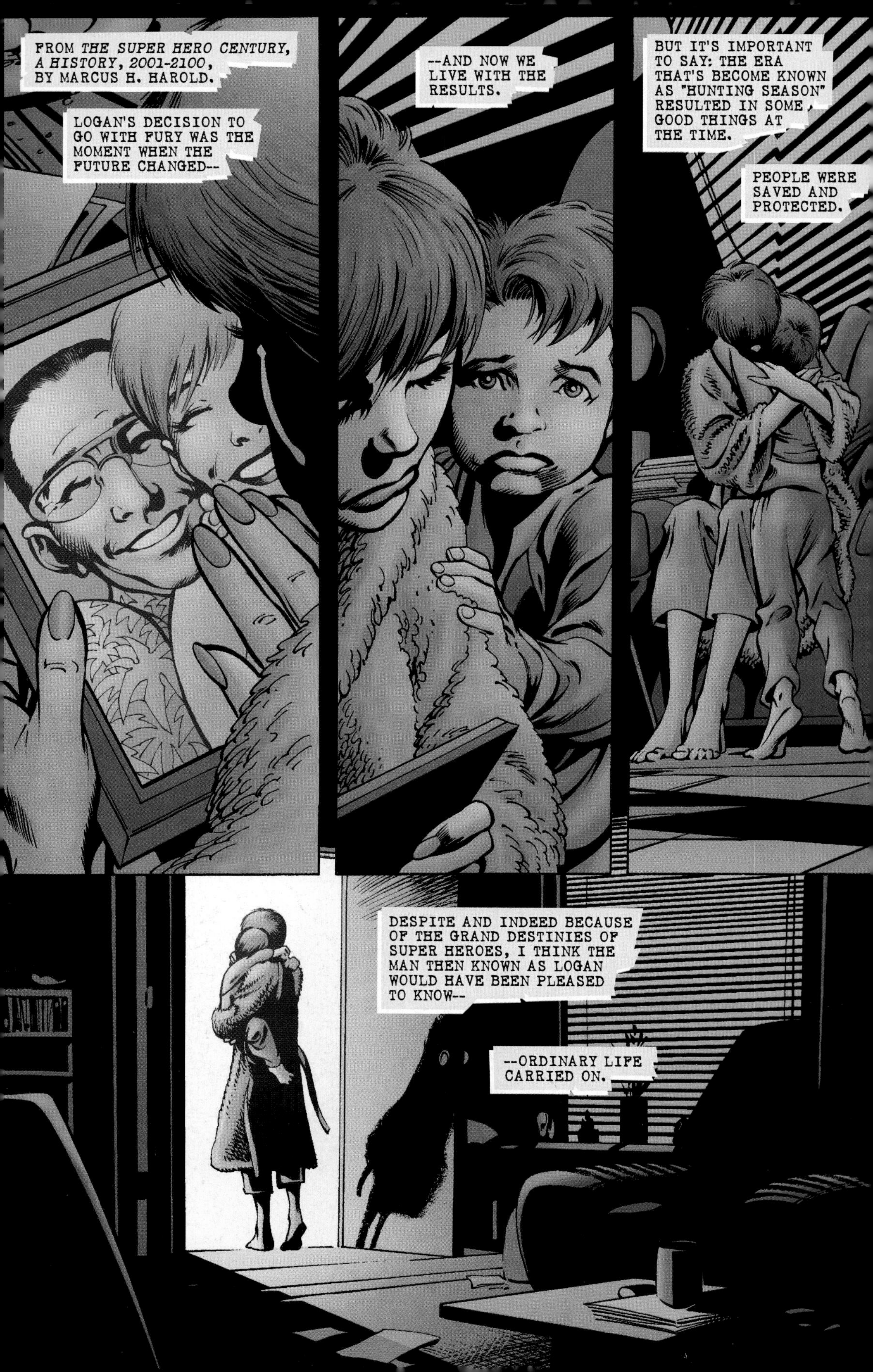
FROM *THE SUPER HERO CENTURY, A HISTORY, 2001-2100*, BY MARCUS H. HAROLD.
LOGAN'S DECISION TO GO WITH FURY WAS THE MOMENT WHEN THE FUTURE CHANGED--
--AND NOW WE LIVE WITH THE RESULTS.
BUT IT'S IMPORTANT TO SAY: THE ERA THAT'S BECOME KNOWN AS "HUNTING SEASON" RESULTED IN SOME GOOD THINGS AT THE TIME.
PEOPLE WERE SAVED AND PROTECTED.
DESPITE AND INDEED BECAUSE OF THE GRAND DESTINIES OF SUPER HEROES, I THINK THE MAN THEN KNOWN AS LOGAN WOULD HAVE BEEN PLEASED TO KNOW--
--ORDINARY LIFE CARRIED ON.

FIVE

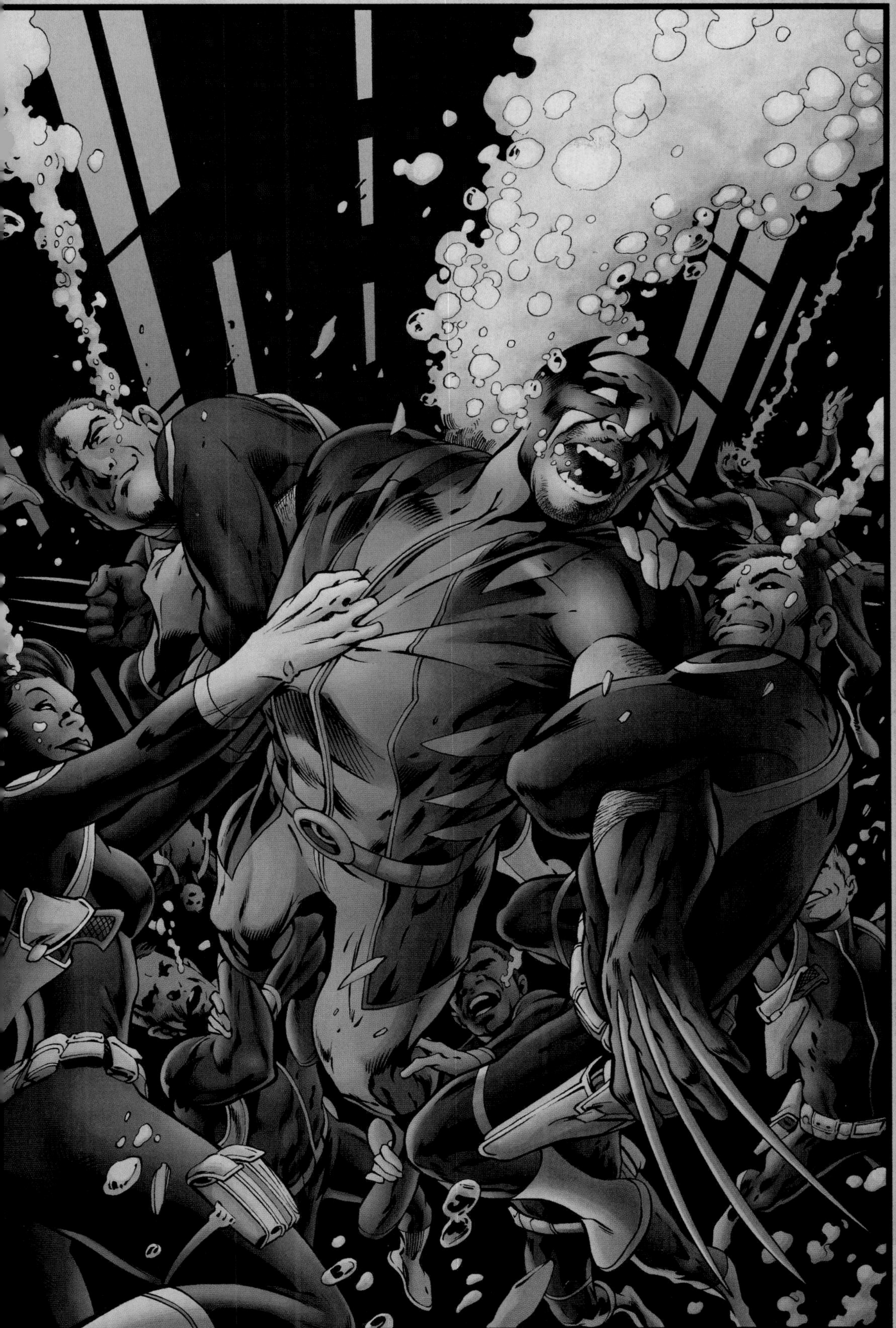

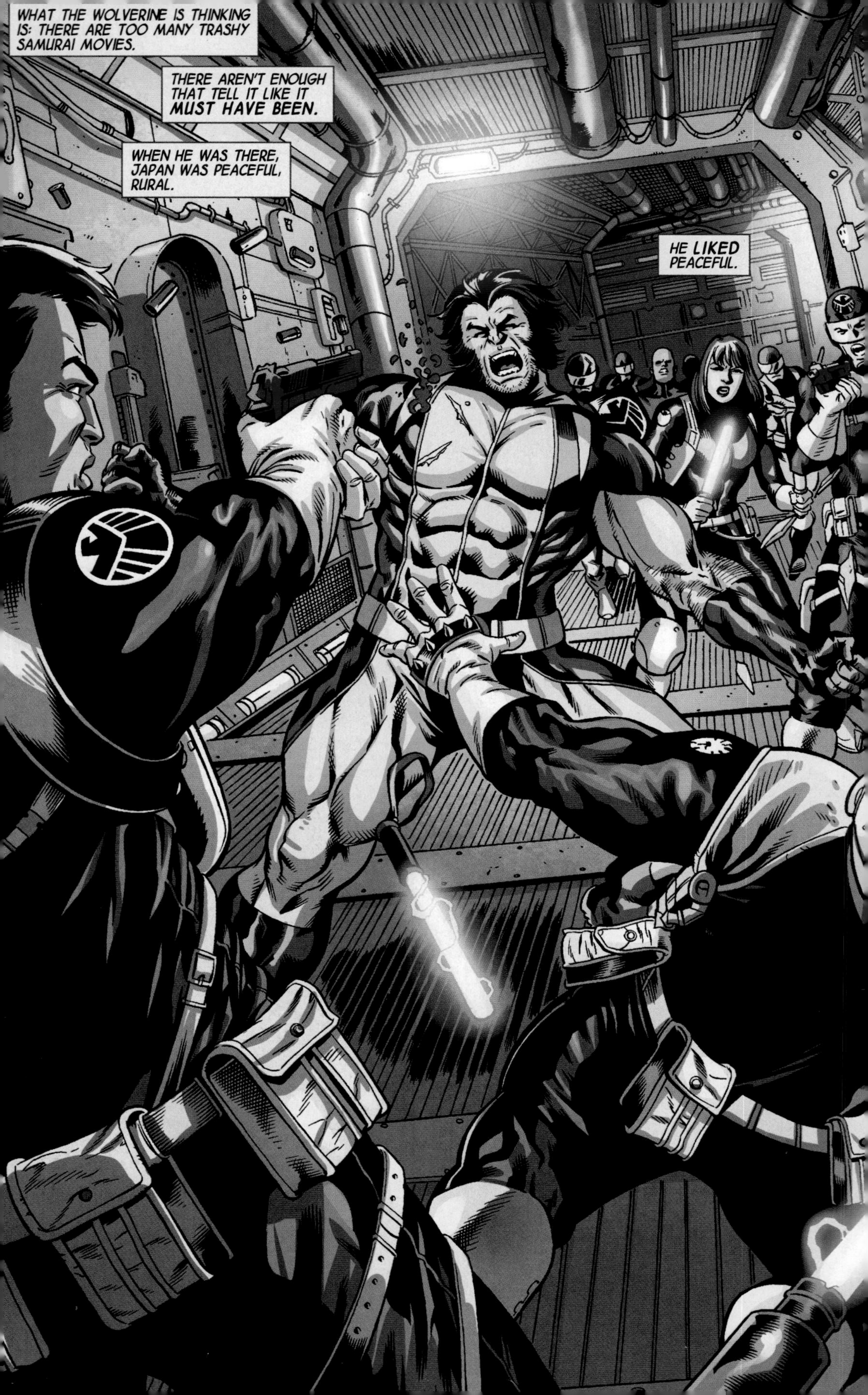
WHAT THE WOLVERINE IS THINKING IS: THERE ARE TOO MANY TRASHY SAMURAI MOVIES.
THERE AREN'T ENOUGH THAT TELL IT LIKE IT MUST HAVE BEEN.
WHEN HE WAS THERE, JAPAN WAS PEACEFUL, RURAL.
HE LIKED PEACEFUL.

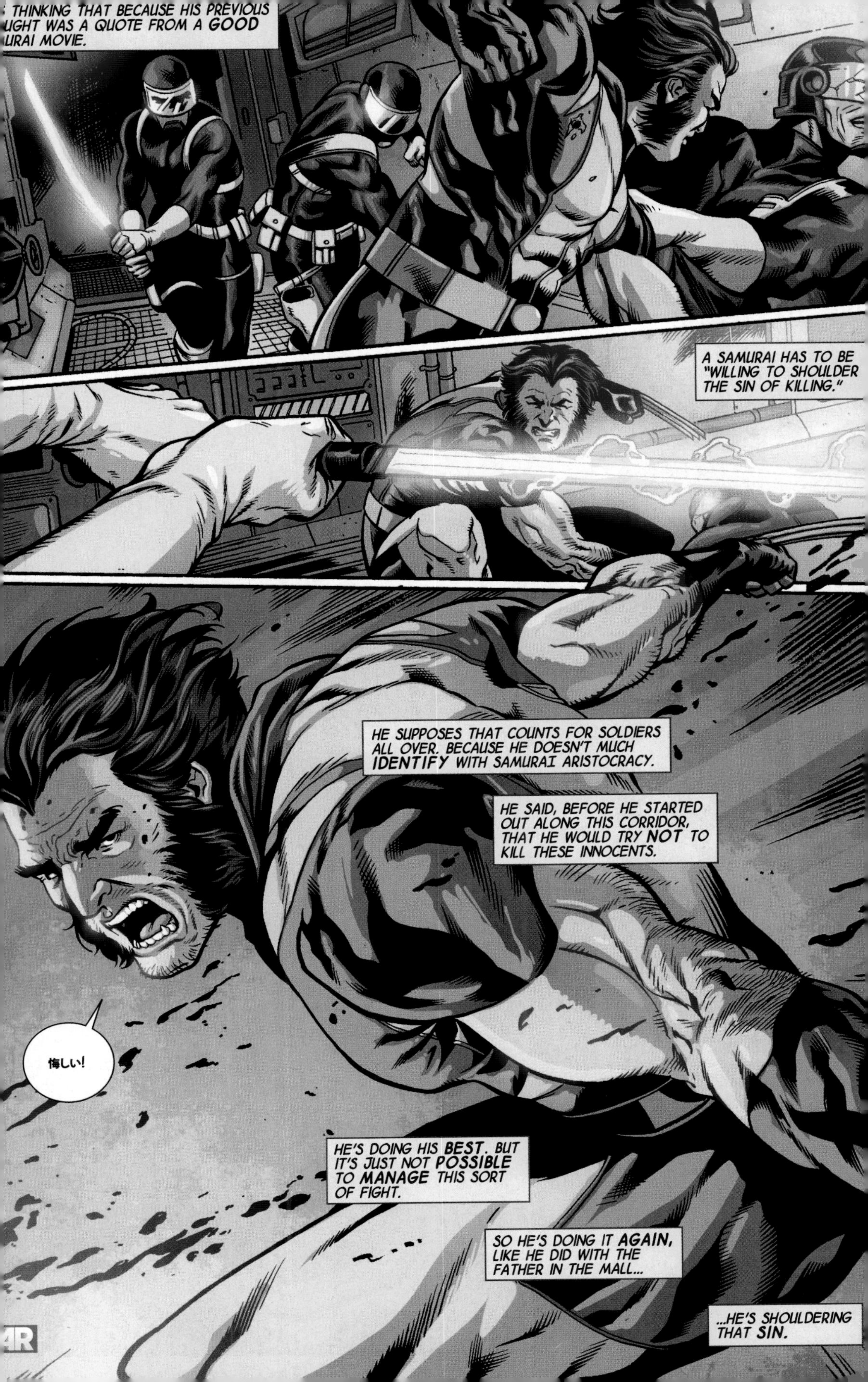

S THINKING THAT BECAUSE HIS PREVIOUS UGHT WAS A QUOTE FROM A GOOD URAI MOVIE.
A SAMURAI HAS TO BE "WILLING TO SHOULDER THE SIN OF KILLING."
HE SUPPOSES THAT COUNTS FOR SOLDIERS ALL OVER. BECAUSE HE DOESN'T MUCH IDENTIFY WITH SAMURAI ARISTOCRACY.
HE SAID, BEFORE HE STARTED OUT ALONG THIS CORRIDOR, THAT HE WOULD TRY NOT TO KILL THESE INNOCENTS.
悔しい!
HE'S DOING HIS BEST. BUT IT'S JUST NOT POSSIBLE TO MANAGE THIS SORT OF FIGHT.
SO HE'S DOING IT AGAIN, LIKE HE DID WITH THE FATHER IN THE MALL...
...HE'S SHOULDERING THAT SIN.

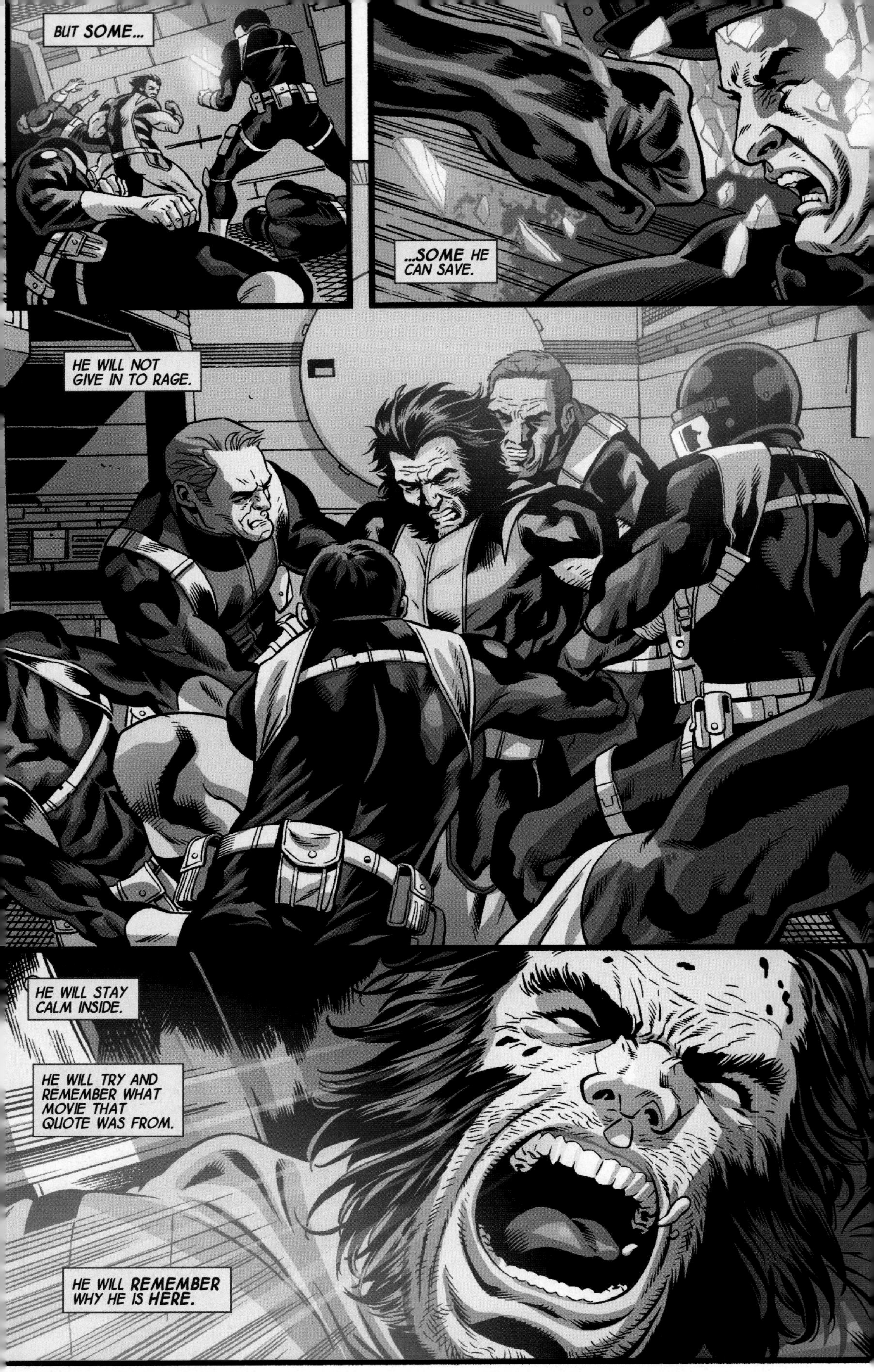
BUT SOME...
...SOME HE CAN SAVE.
HE WILL NOT GIVE IN TO RAGE.
HE WILL STAY CALM INSIDE.
HE WILL TRY AND REMEMBER WHAT MOVIE THAT QUOTE WAS FROM.
HE WILL REMEMBER WHY HE IS HERE.

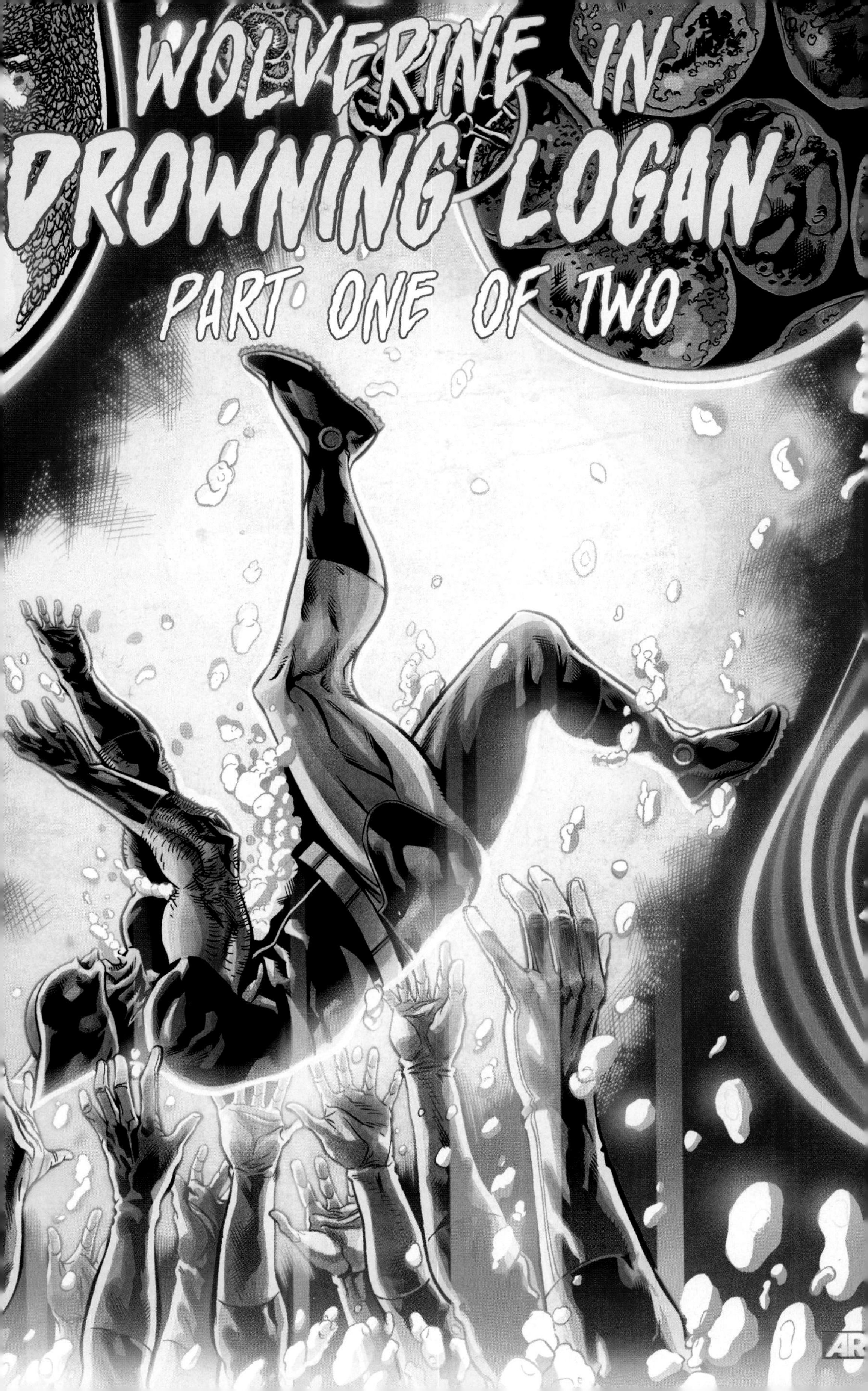
WOLVERINE IN
DROWNING LOGAN
PART ONE OF TWO

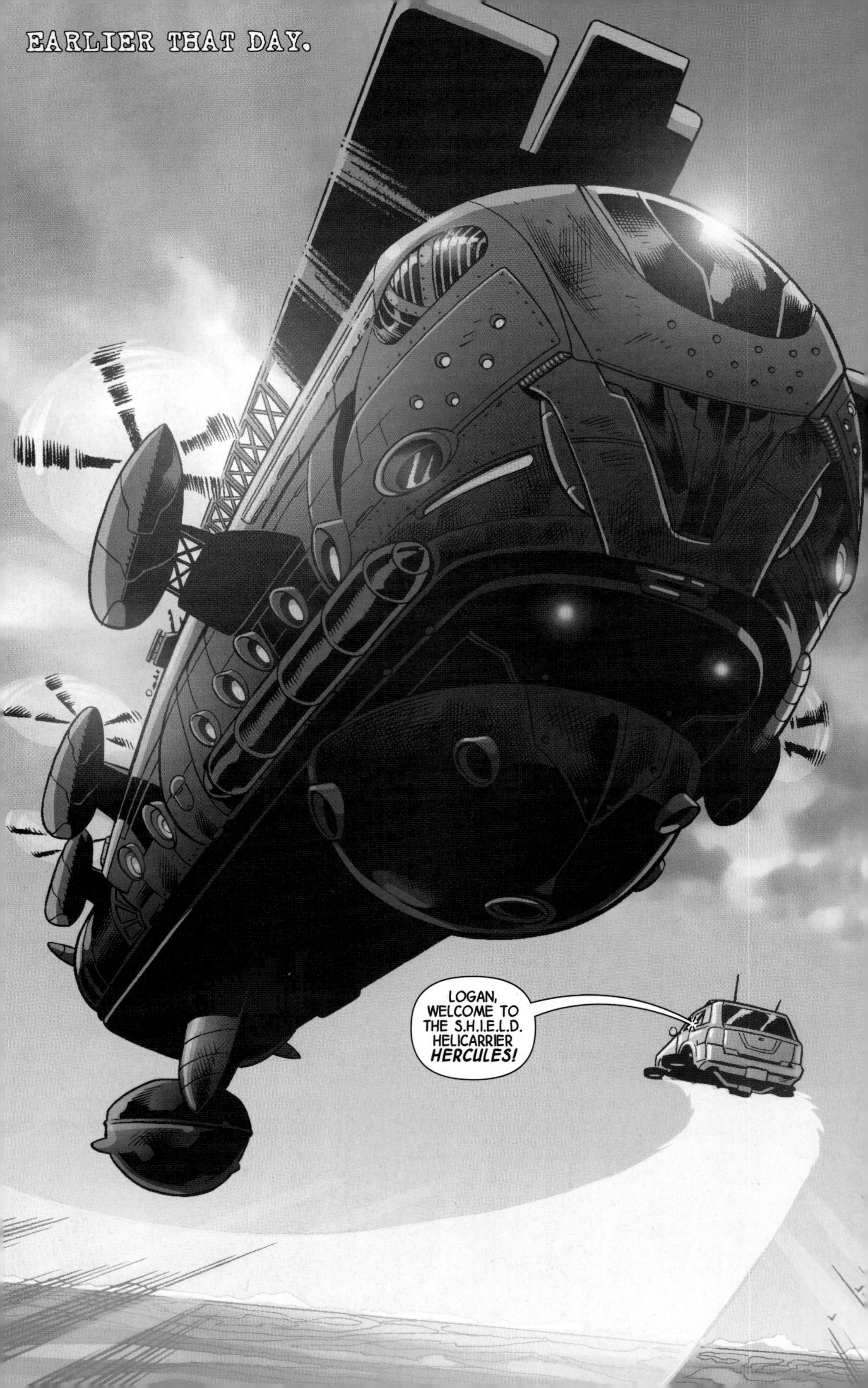
EARLIER THAT DAY.
LOGAN, WELCOME TO THE S.H.I.E.L.D. HELICARRIER HERCULES!

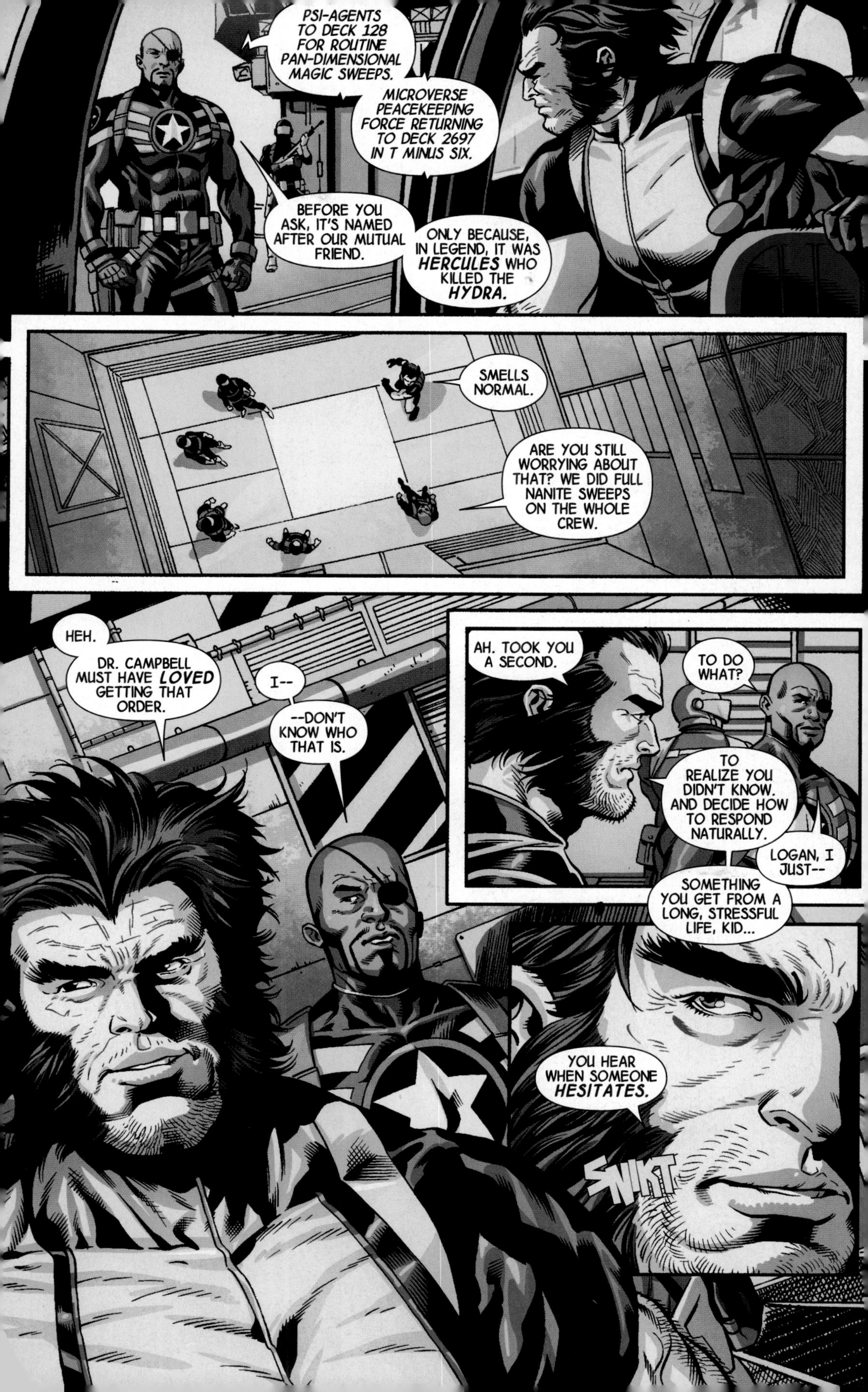
PSI-AGENTS TO DECK 128 FOR ROUTINE PAN-DIMENSIONAL MAGIC SWEEPS.
MICROVERSE PEACEKEEPING FORCE RETURNING TO DECK 2697 IN T MINUS SIX.
BEFORE YOU ASK, IT'S NAMED AFTER OUR MUTUAL FRIEND.
ONLY BECAUSE, IN LEGEND, IT WAS HERCULES WHO KILLED THE HYDRA.
SMELLS NORMAL.
ARE YOU STILL WORRYING ABOUT THAT? WE DID FULL NANITE SWEEPS ON THE WHOLE CREW.
HEH.
DR. CAMPBELL MUST HAVE LOVED GETTING THAT ORDER.
I--
--DON'T KNOW WHO THAT IS.
AH. TOOK YOU A SECOND.
TO DO WHAT?
TO REALIZE YOU DIDN'T KNOW. AND DECIDE HOW TO RESPOND NATURALLY.
LOGAN, I JUST--
SOMETHING YOU GET FROM A LONG, STRESSFUL LIFE, KID...
YOU HEAR WHEN SOMEONE HESITATES.
SNIKT

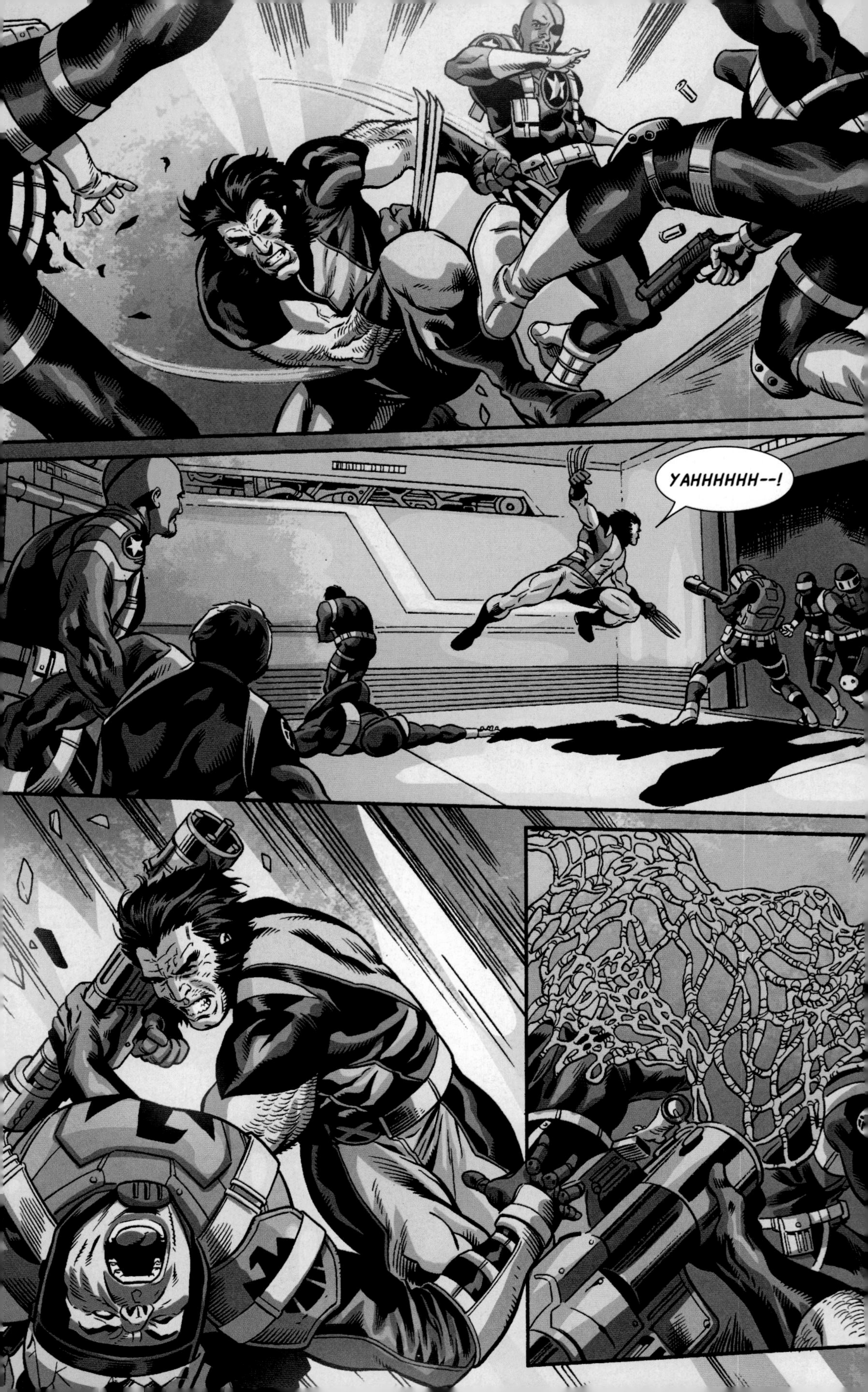
YAHHHHHH--!

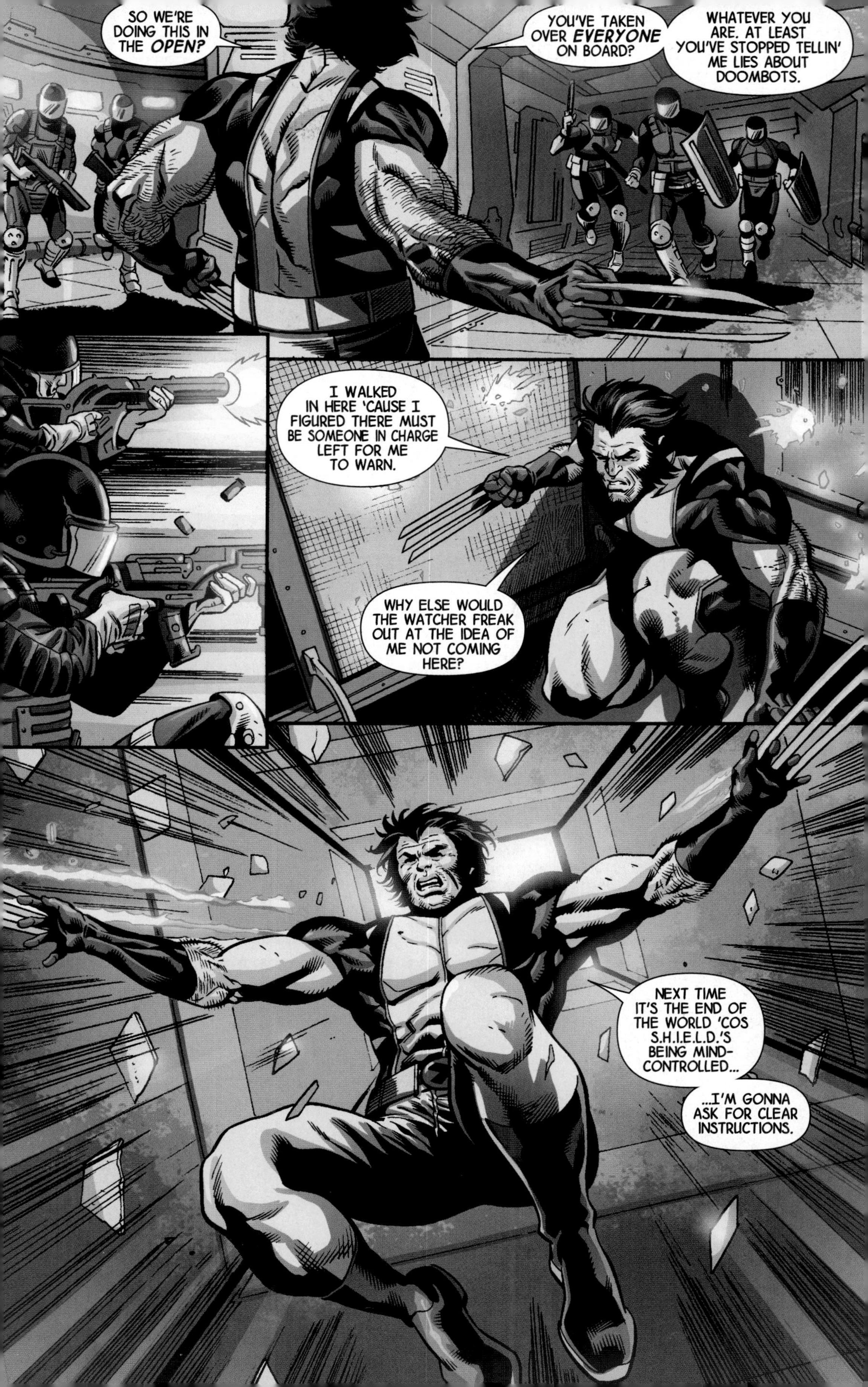
SO WE'RE DOING THIS IN THE *OPEN?*
YOU'VE TAKEN OVER *EVERYONE* ON BOARD?
WHATEVER YOU ARE. AT LEAST YOU'VE STOPPED TELLIN' ME LIES ABOUT DOOMBOTS.
I WALKED IN HERE 'CAUSE I FIGURED THERE MUST BE SOMEONE IN CHARGE LEFT FOR ME TO WARN.
WHY ELSE WOULD THE WATCHER FREAK OUT AT THE IDEA OF ME NOT COMING HERE?
NEXT TIME IT'S THE END OF THE WORLD 'COS S.H.I.E.L.D.'S BEING MIND-CONTROLLED...
...I'M GONNA ASK FOR CLEAR INSTRUCTIONS.

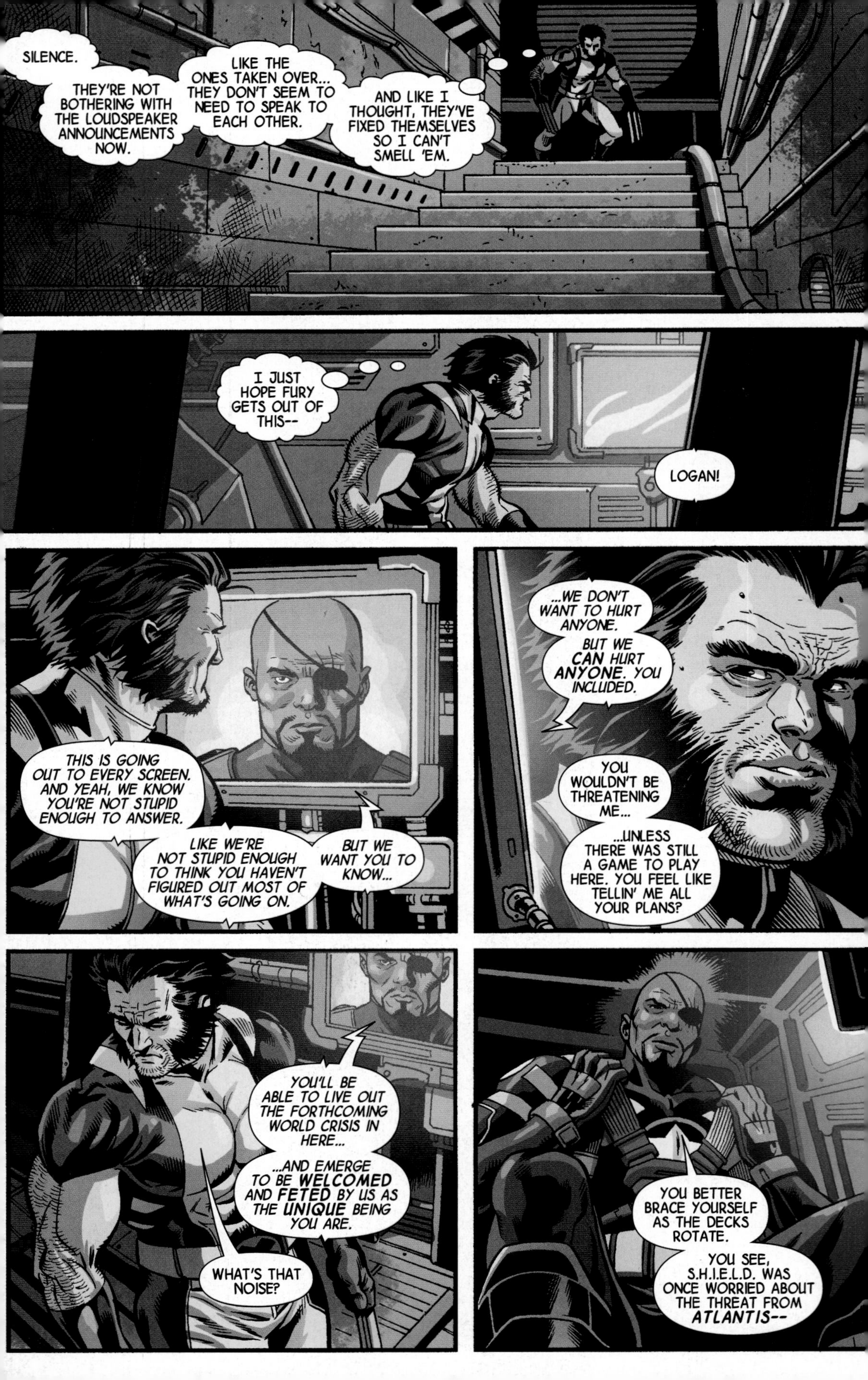
SILENCE.
THEY'RE NOT BOTHERING WITH THE LOUDSPEAKER ANNOUNCEMENTS NOW.
LIKE THE ONES TAKEN OVER... THEY DON'T SEEM TO NEED TO SPEAK TO EACH OTHER.
AND LIKE I THOUGHT, THEY'VE FIXED THEMSELVES SO I CAN'T SMELL 'EM.
I JUST HOPE FURY GETS OUT OF THIS--
LOGAN!
THIS IS GOING OUT TO EVERY SCREEN. AND YEAH, WE KNOW YOU'RE NOT STUPID ENOUGH TO ANSWER.
LIKE WE'RE NOT STUPID ENOUGH TO THINK YOU HAVEN'T FIGURED OUT MOST OF WHAT'S GOING ON.
BUT WE WANT YOU TO KNOW...
...WE DON'T WANT TO HURT ANYONE.
BUT WE CAN HURT ANYONE. YOU INCLUDED.
YOU WOULDN'T BE THREATENING ME...
...UNLESS THERE WAS STILL A GAME TO PLAY HERE. YOU FEEL LIKE TELLIN' ME ALL YOUR PLANS?
YOU'LL BE ABLE TO LIVE OUT THE FORTHCOMING WORLD CRISIS IN HERE...
...AND EMERGE TO BE WELCOMED AND FETED BY US AS THE UNIQUE BEING YOU ARE.
WHAT'S THAT NOISE?
YOU BETTER BRACE YOURSELF AS THE DECKS ROTATE.
YOU SEE, S.H.I.E.L.D. WAS ONCE WORRIED ABOUT THE THREAT FROM ATLANTIS--

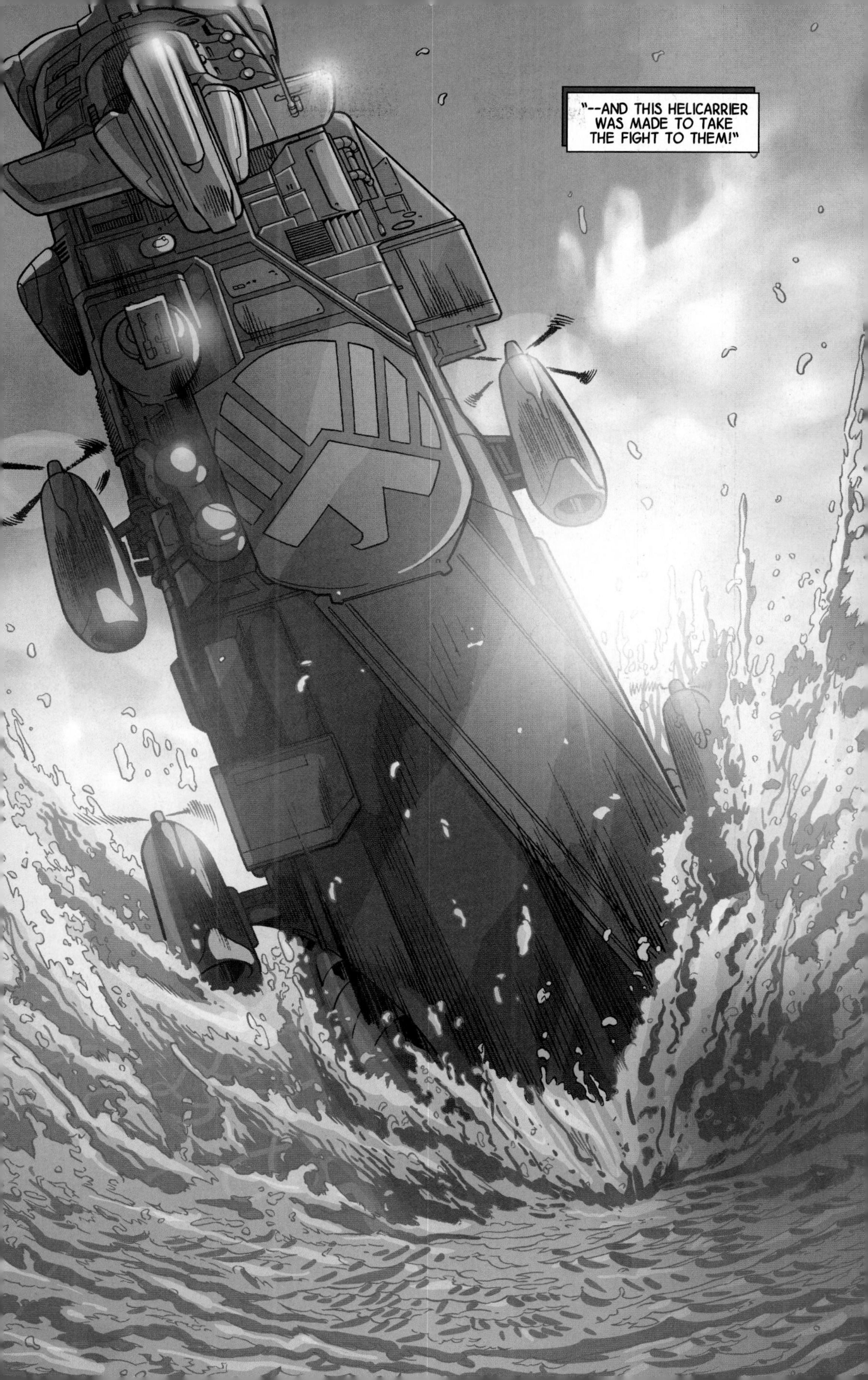
"--AND THIS HELICARRIER WAS MADE TO TAKE THE FIGHT TO THEM!"

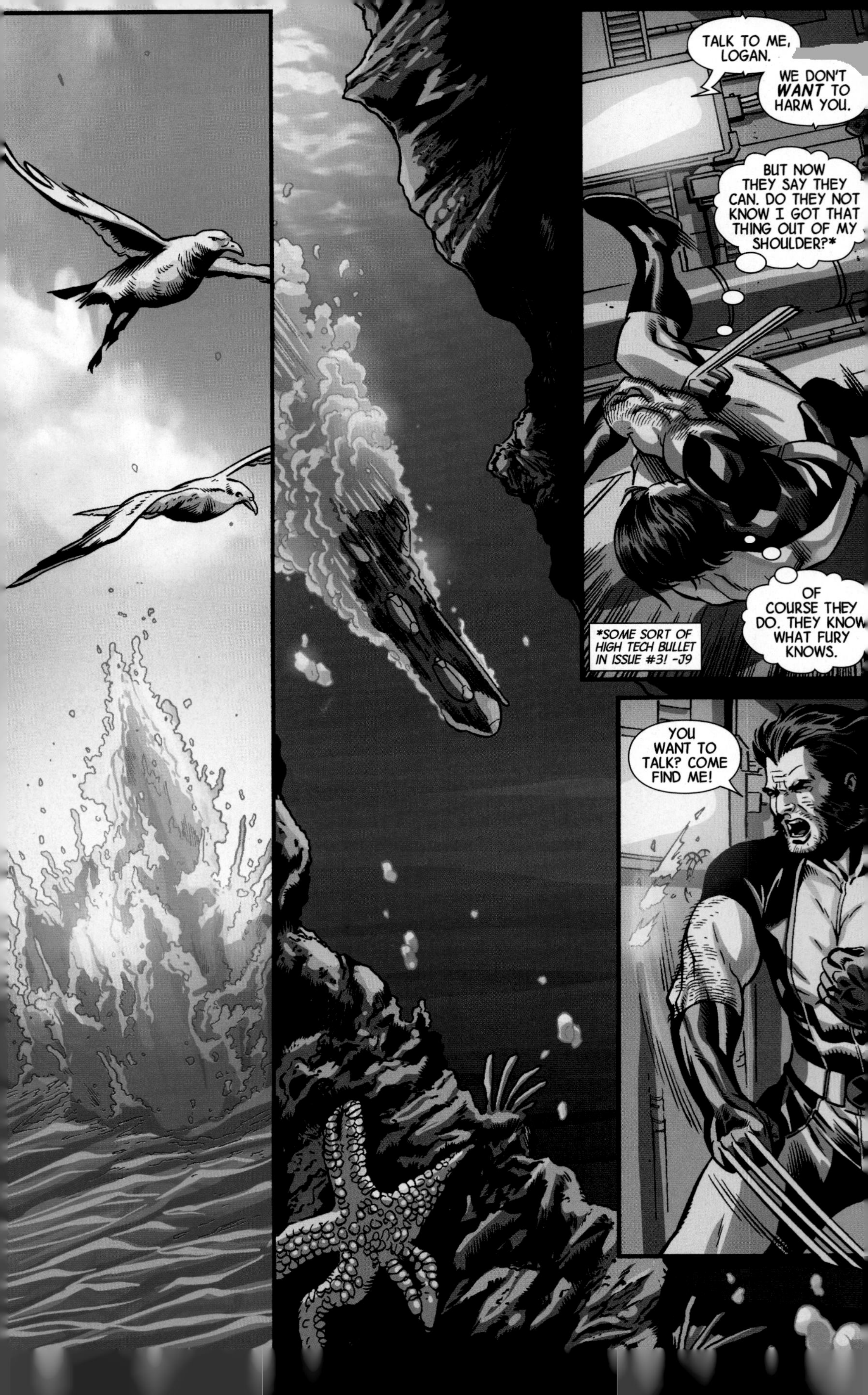
TALK TO ME, LOGAN.
WE DON'T *WANT* TO HARM YOU.
BUT NOW THEY SAY THEY CAN. DO THEY NOT KNOW I GOT THAT THING OUT OF MY SHOULDER?*
OF COURSE THEY DO. THEY KNOW WHAT FURY KNOWS.
*SOME SORT OF HIGH TECH BULLET IN ISSUE #3! -J9
YOU WANT TO TALK? COME FIND ME!

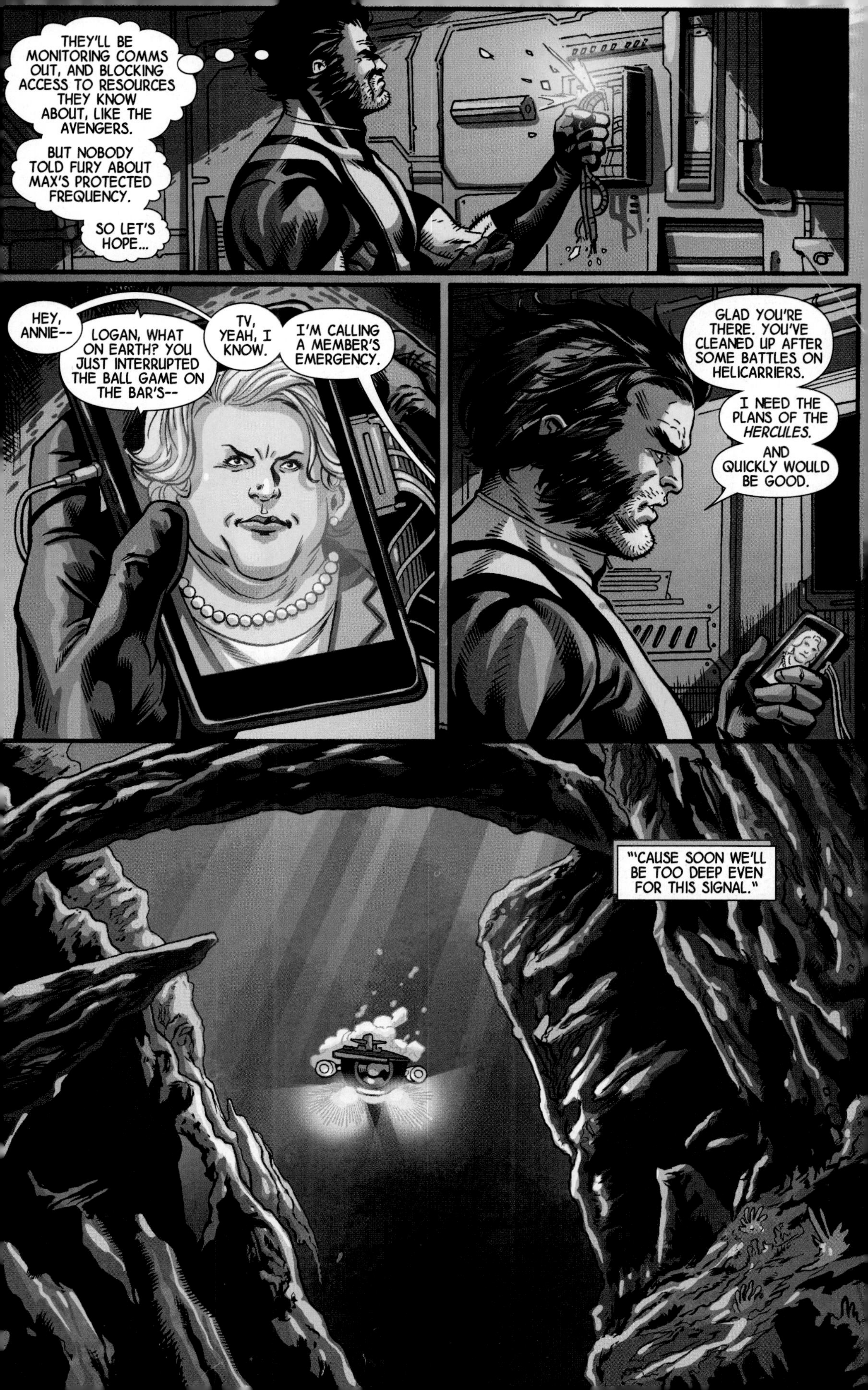
THEY'LL BE MONITORING COMMS OUT, AND BLOCKING ACCESS TO RESOURCES THEY KNOW ABOUT, LIKE THE AVENGERS.
BUT NOBODY TOLD FURY ABOUT MAX'S PROTECTED FREQUENCY.
SO LET'S HOPE...
HEY, ANNIE--
LOGAN, WHAT ON EARTH? YOU JUST INTERRUPTED THE BALL GAME ON THE BAR'S--
TV, YEAH, I KNOW.
I'M CALLING A MEMBER'S EMERGENCY.
GLAD YOU'RE THERE. YOU'VE CLEANED UP AFTER SOME BATTLES ON HELICARRIERS.
I NEED THE PLANS OF THE *HERCULES.*
AND QUICKLY WOULD BE GOOD.
"'CAUSE SOON WE'LL BE TOO DEEP EVEN FOR THIS SIGNAL."

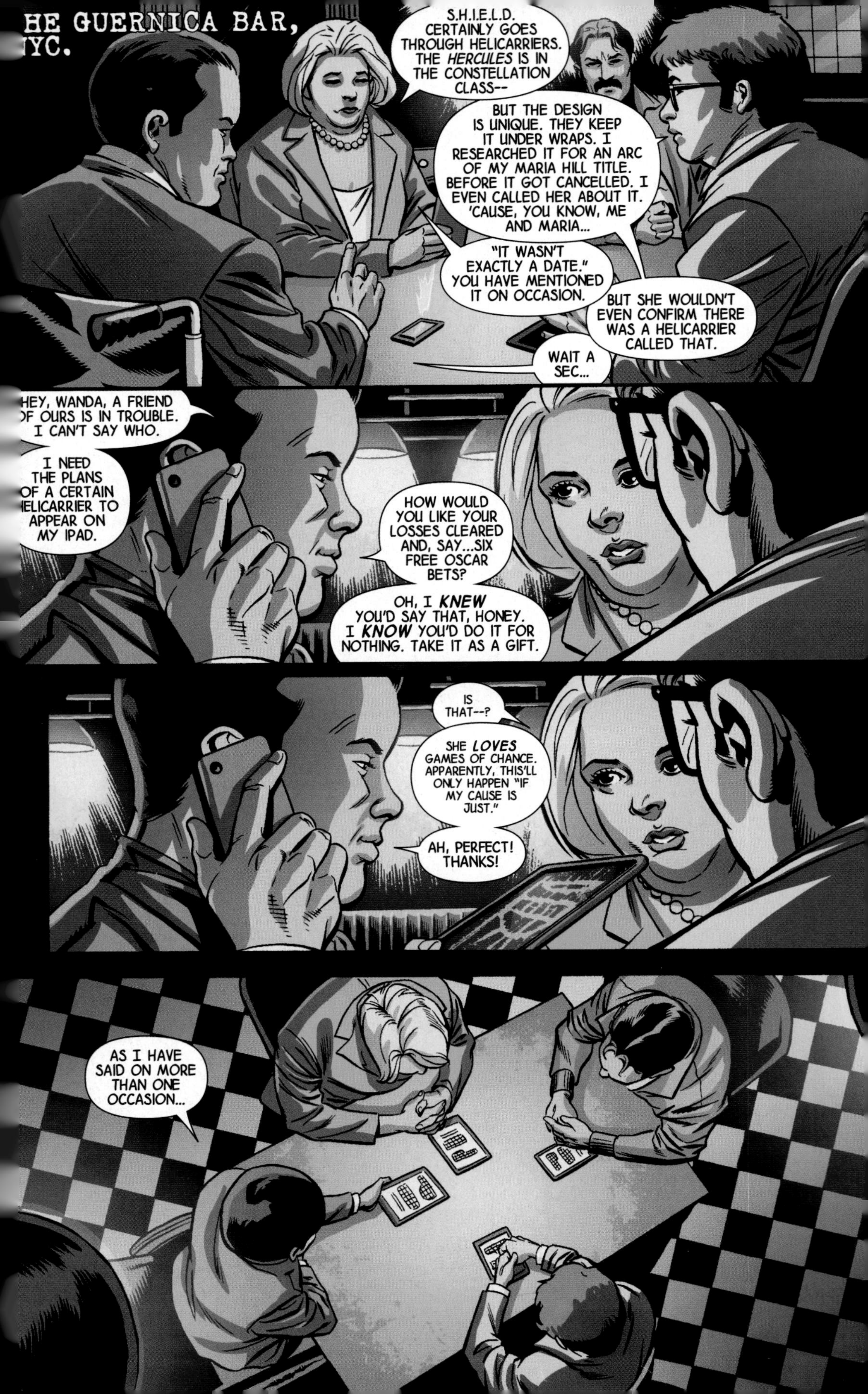
HE GUERNICA BAR, NYC.
S.H.I.E.L.D. CERTAINLY GOES THROUGH HELICARRIERS. THE *HERCULES* IS IN THE CONSTELLATION CLASS--
BUT THE DESIGN IS UNIQUE. THEY KEEP IT UNDER WRAPS. I RESEARCHED IT FOR AN ARC OF MY MARIA HILL TITLE. BEFORE IT GOT CANCELLED. I EVEN CALLED HER ABOUT IT. 'CAUSE, YOU KNOW, ME AND MARIA...
"IT WASN'T EXACTLY A DATE." YOU HAVE MENTIONED IT ON OCCASION.
BUT SHE WOULDN'T EVEN CONFIRM THERE WAS A HELICARRIER CALLED THAT.
WAIT A SEC...
HEY, WANDA, A FRIEND OF OURS IS IN TROUBLE. I CAN'T SAY WHO.
I NEED THE PLANS OF A CERTAIN HELICARRIER TO APPEAR ON MY IPAD.
HOW WOULD YOU LIKE YOUR LOSSES CLEARED AND, SAY...SIX FREE OSCAR BETS?
OH, I ***KNEW*** YOU'D SAY THAT, HONEY. I ***KNOW*** YOU'D DO IT FOR NOTHING. TAKE IT AS A GIFT.
IS THAT--?
SHE ***LOVES*** GAMES OF CHANCE. APPARENTLY, THIS'LL ONLY HAPPEN "IF MY CAUSE IS JUST."
AH, PERFECT! THANKS!
AS I HAVE SAID ON MORE THAN ONE OCCASION...

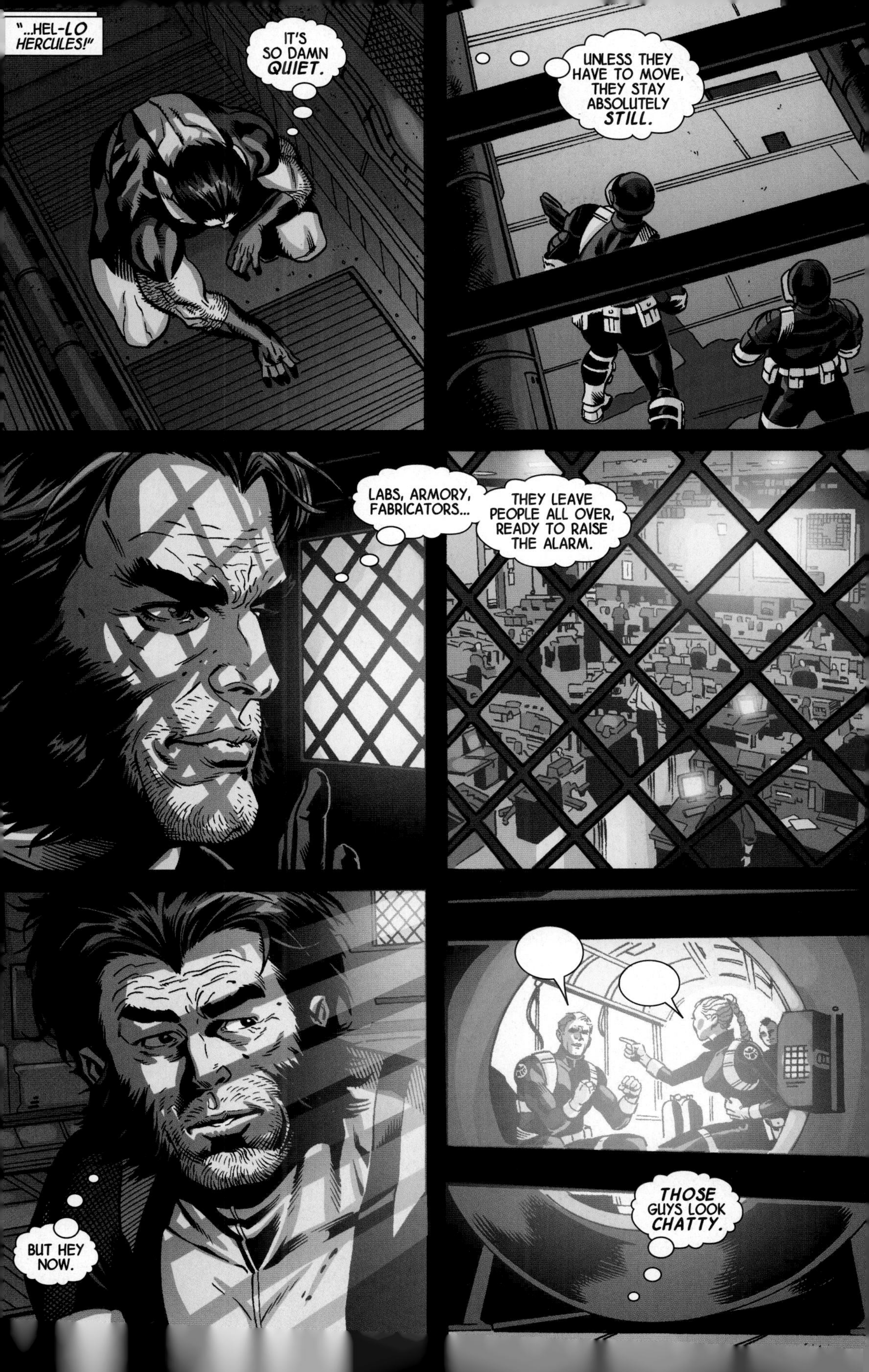
"...HEL-LO HERCULES!"
IT'S SO DAMN QUIET.
UNLESS THEY HAVE TO MOVE, THEY STAY ABSOLUTELY STILL.
LABS, ARMORY, FABRICATORS...
THEY LEAVE PEOPLE ALL OVER, READY TO RAISE THE ALARM.
BUT HEY NOW.
THOSE GUYS LOOK CHATTY.

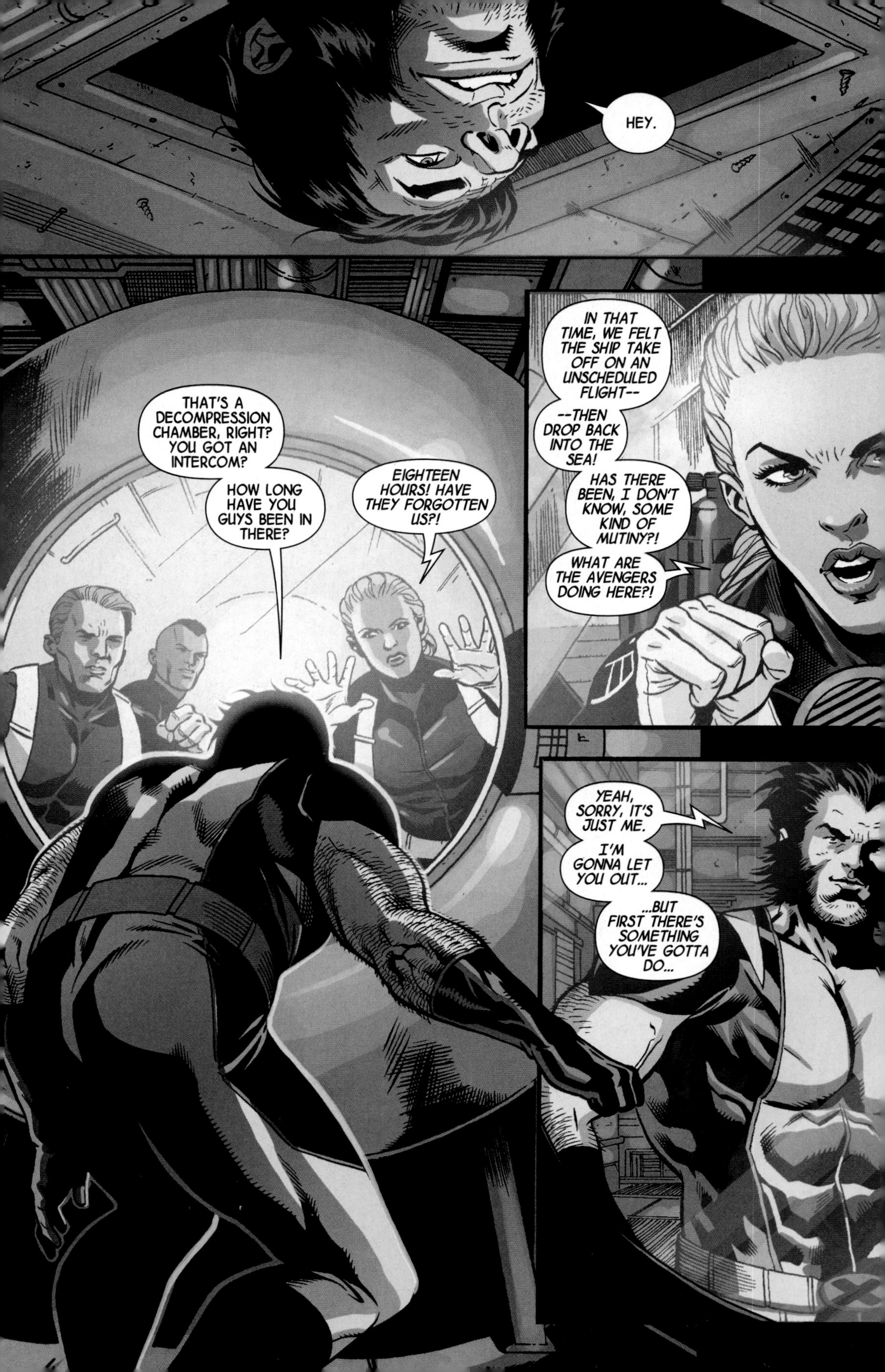
HEY.
THAT'S A DECOMPRESSION CHAMBER, RIGHT? YOU GOT AN INTERCOM?
HOW LONG HAVE YOU GUYS BEEN IN THERE?
EIGHTEEN HOURS! HAVE THEY FORGOTTEN US?!
IN THAT TIME, WE FELT THE SHIP TAKE OFF ON AN UNSCHEDULED FLIGHT--
--THEN DROP BACK INTO THE SEA!
HAS THERE BEEN, I DON'T KNOW, SOME KIND OF MUTINY?!
WHAT ARE THE AVENGERS DOING HERE?!
YEAH, SORRY, IT'S JUST ME.
I'M GONNA LET YOU OUT...
...BUT FIRST THERE'S SOMETHING YOU'VE GOTTA DO...

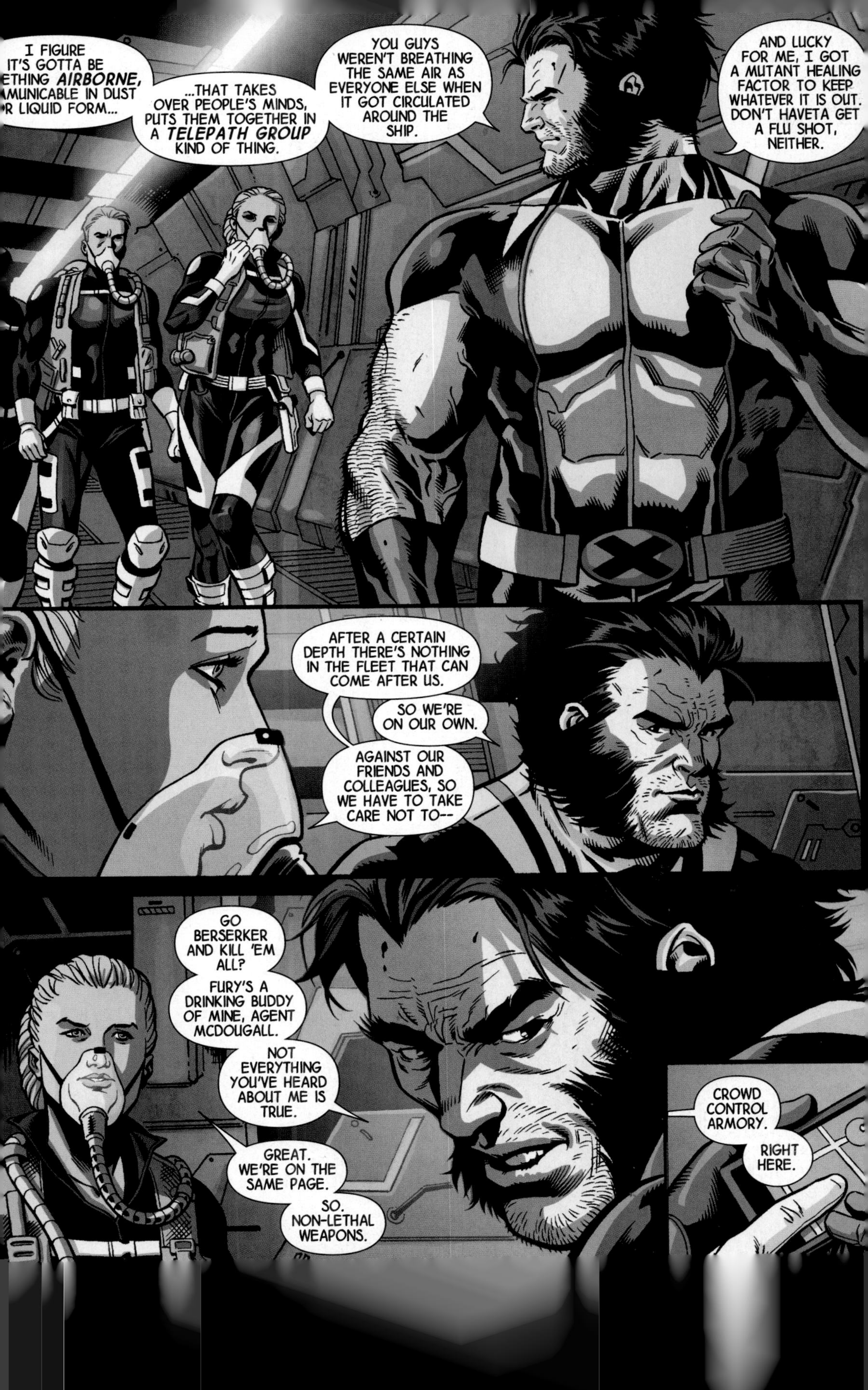
I FIGURE IT'S GOTTA BE ...ETHING AIRBORNE, ...MUNICABLE IN DUST ...R LIQUID FORM...
...THAT TAKES OVER PEOPLE'S MINDS, PUTS THEM TOGETHER IN A TELEPATH GROUP KIND OF THING.
YOU GUYS WEREN'T BREATHING THE SAME AIR AS EVERYONE ELSE WHEN IT GOT CIRCULATED AROUND THE SHIP.
AND LUCKY FOR ME, I GOT A MUTANT HEALING FACTOR TO KEEP WHATEVER IT IS OUT. DON'T HAVETA GET A FLU SHOT, NEITHER.
AFTER A CERTAIN DEPTH THERE'S NOTHING IN THE FLEET THAT CAN COME AFTER US.
SO WE'RE ON OUR OWN.
AGAINST OUR FRIENDS AND COLLEAGUES, SO WE HAVE TO TAKE CARE NOT TO--
GO BERSERKER AND KILL 'EM ALL?
FURY'S A DRINKING BUDDY OF MINE, AGENT MCDOUGALL.
NOT EVERYTHING YOU'VE HEARD ABOUT ME IS TRUE.
GREAT. WE'RE ON THE SAME PAGE.
SO. NON-LETHAL WEAPONS.
CROWD CONTROL ARMORY.
RIGHT HERE.

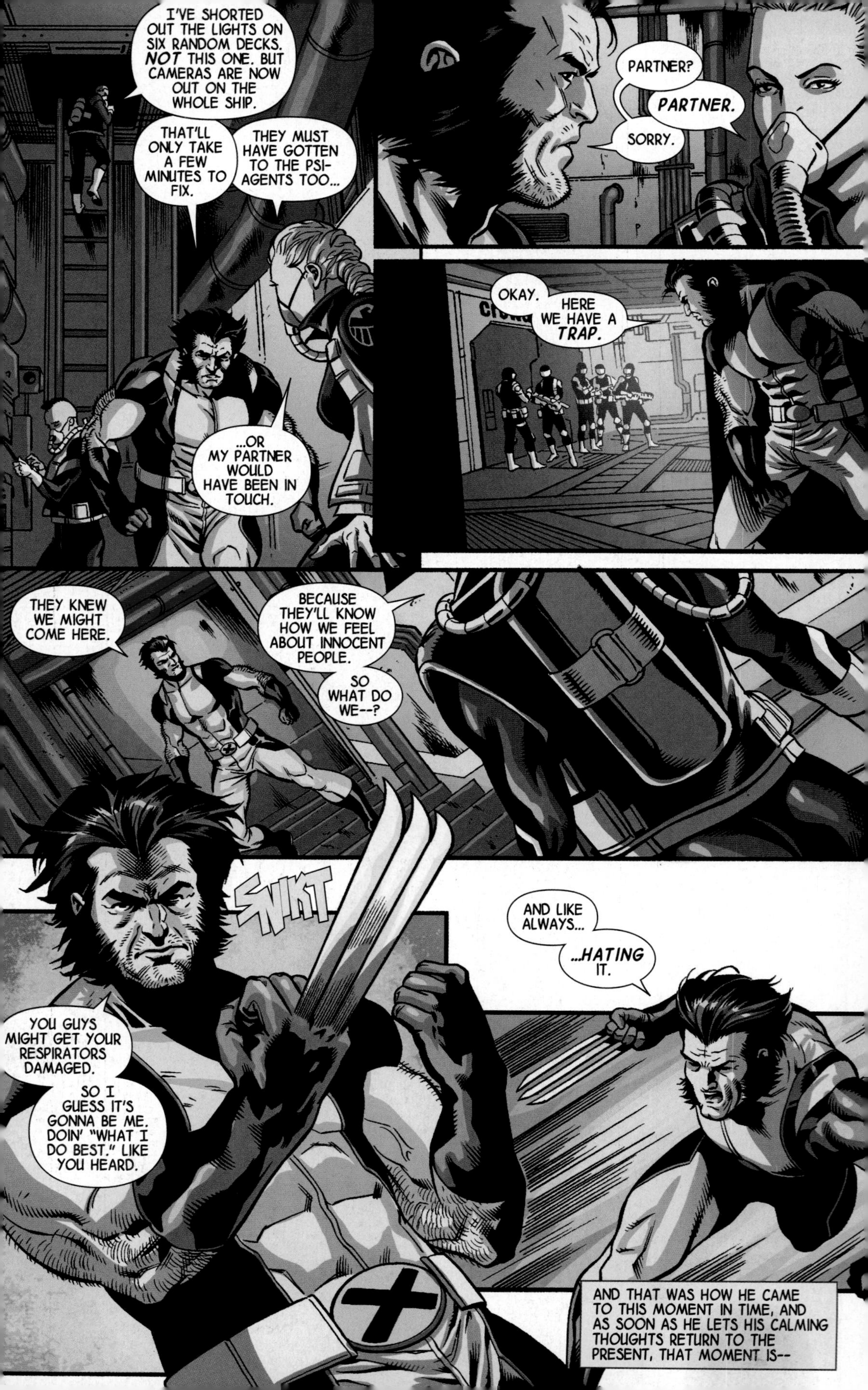
I'VE SHORTED OUT THE LIGHTS ON SIX RANDOM DECKS. NOT THIS ONE. BUT CAMERAS ARE NOW OUT ON THE WHOLE SHIP.
THAT'LL ONLY TAKE A FEW MINUTES TO FIX.
THEY MUST HAVE GOTTEN TO THE PSI-AGENTS TOO...
...OR MY PARTNER WOULD HAVE BEEN IN TOUCH.
PARTNER?
PARTNER.
SORRY.
OKAY.
HERE WE HAVE A TRAP.
THEY KNEW WE MIGHT COME HERE.
BECAUSE THEY'LL KNOW HOW WE FEEL ABOUT INNOCENT PEOPLE.
SO WHAT DO WE--?
SNIKT
YOU GUYS MIGHT GET YOUR RESPIRATORS DAMAGED.
SO I GUESS IT'S GONNA BE ME. DOIN' "WHAT I DO BEST." LIKE YOU HEARD.
AND LIKE ALWAYS...
...HATING IT.
AND THAT WAS HOW HE CAME TO THIS MOMENT IN TIME, AND AS SOON AS HE LETS HIS CALMING THOUGHTS RETURN TO THE PRESENT, THAT MOMENT IS--

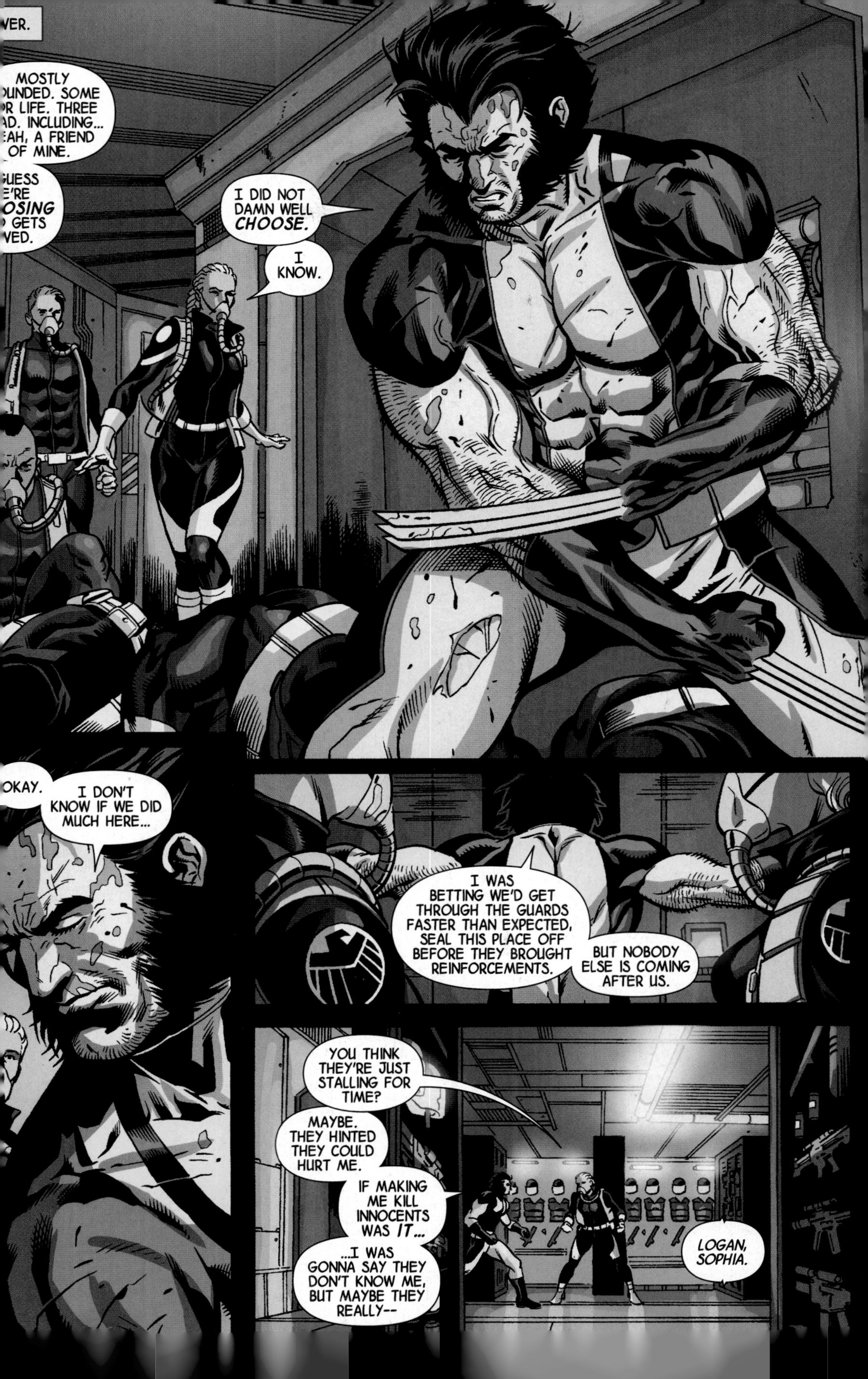

VER.
MOSTLY
UNDED. SOME
R LIFE. THREE
AD. INCLUDING...
EAH, A FRIEND
OF MINE.
UESS
E'RE
OSING
GETS
VED.
I DID NOT
DAMN WELL
CHOOSE.
I
KNOW.
OKAY.
I DON'T
KNOW IF WE DID
MUCH HERE...
I WAS
BETTING WE'D GET
THROUGH THE GUARDS
FASTER THAN EXPECTED,
SEAL THIS PLACE OFF
BEFORE THEY BROUGHT
REINFORCEMENTS.
BUT NOBODY
ELSE IS COMING
AFTER US.
YOU THINK
THEY'RE JUST
STALLING FOR
TIME?
MAYBE.
THEY HINTED
THEY COULD
HURT ME.
IF MAKING
ME KILL
INNOCENTS
WAS IT...
...I WAS
GONNA SAY THEY
DON'T KNOW ME,
BUT MAYBE THEY
REALLY--
LOGAN,
SOPHIA.

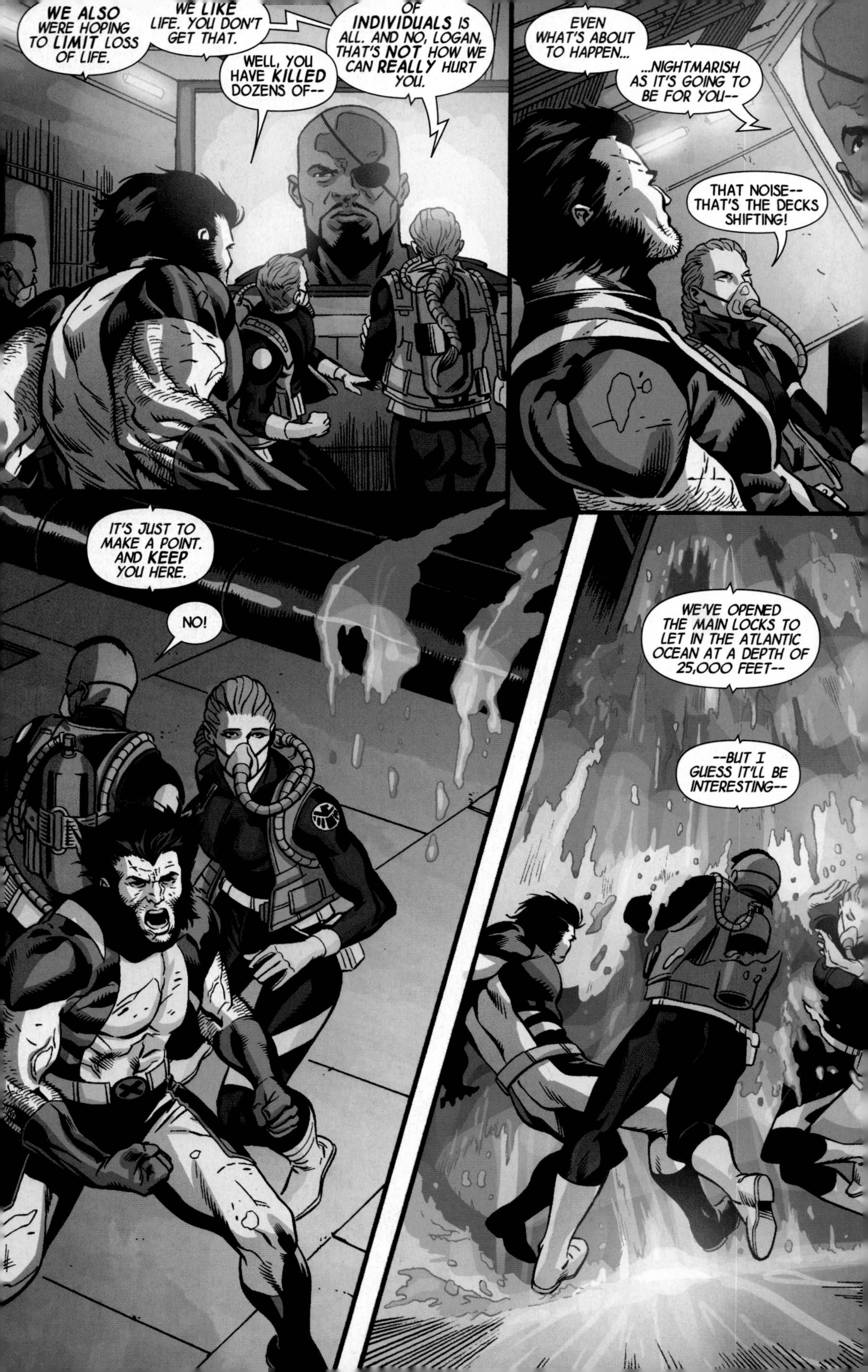
WE ALSO WERE HOPING TO LIMIT LOSS OF LIFE.
WE LIKE LIFE. YOU DON'T GET THAT.
WELL, YOU HAVE KILLED DOZENS OF--
OF INDIVIDUALS IS ALL. AND NO, LOGAN, THAT'S NOT HOW WE CAN REALLY HURT YOU.
EVEN WHAT'S ABOUT TO HAPPEN...
...NIGHTMARISH AS IT'S GOING TO BE FOR YOU--
THAT NOISE-- THAT'S THE DECKS SHIFTING!
IT'S JUST TO MAKE A POINT. AND KEEP YOU HERE.
NO!
WE'VE OPENED THE MAIN LOCKS TO LET IN THE ATLANTIC OCEAN AT A DEPTH OF 25,000 FEET--
--BUT I GUESS IT'LL BE INTERESTING--

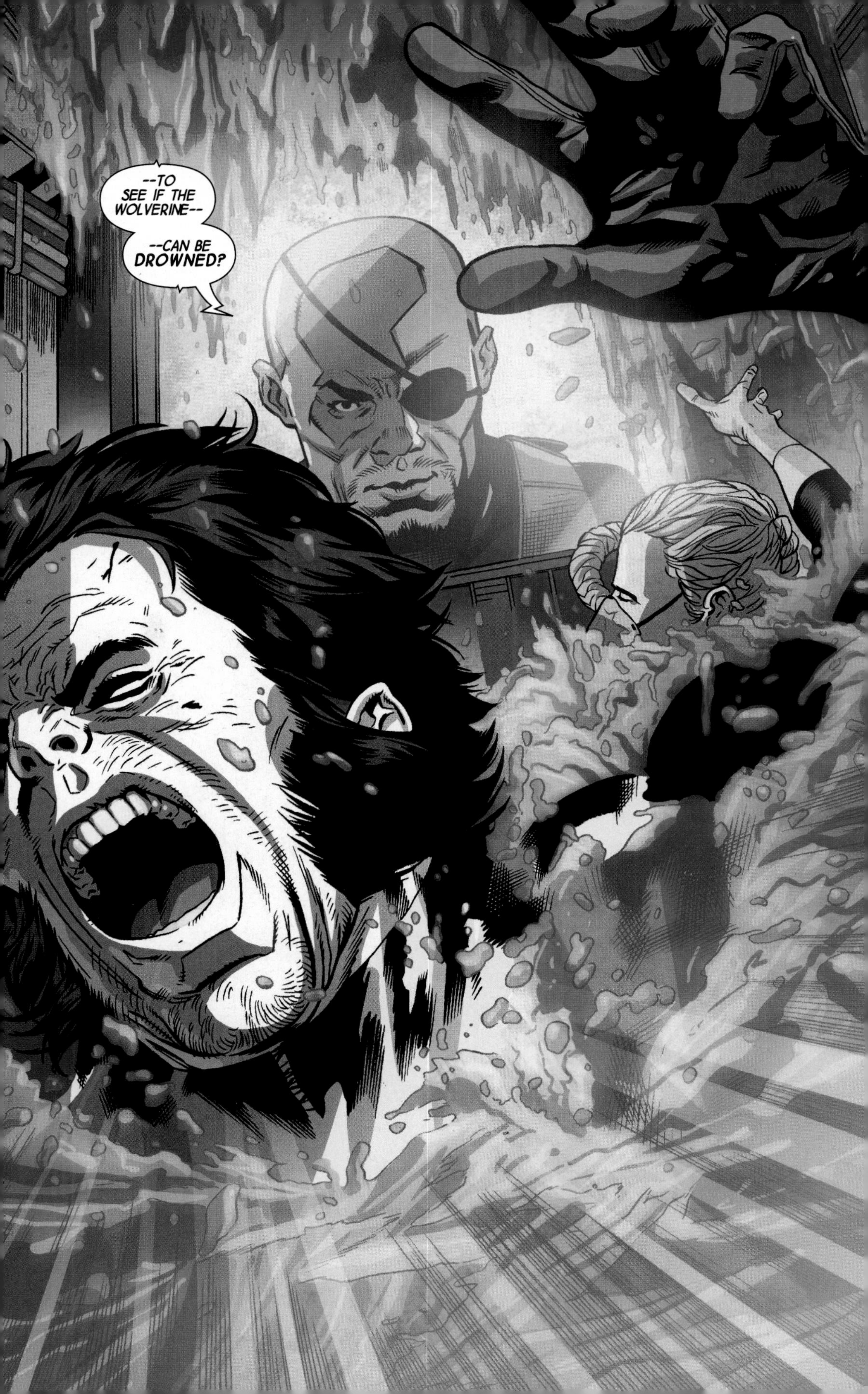
--TO SEE IF THE WOLVERINE--
--CAN BE DROWNED?

SIX

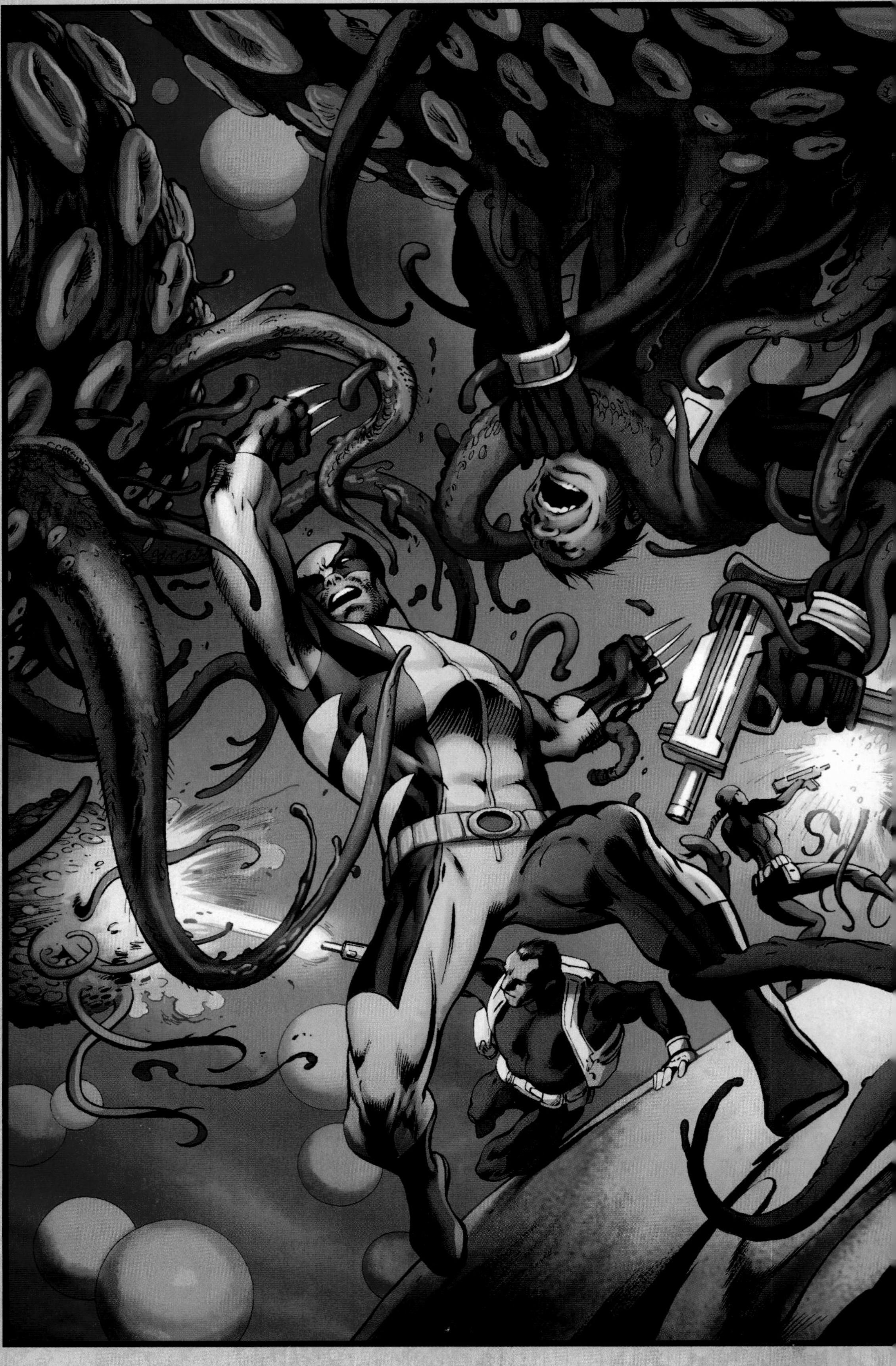

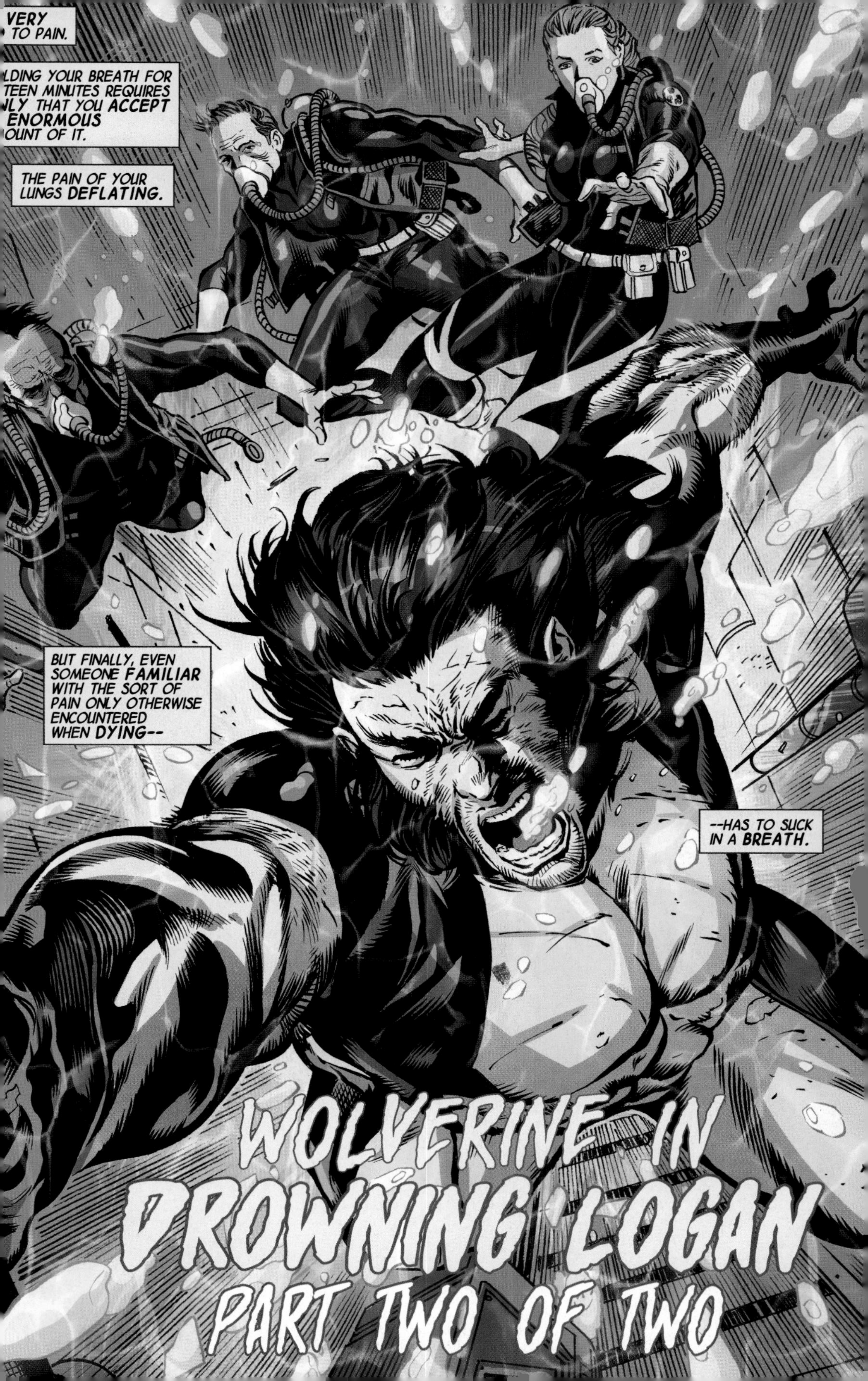
VERY
TO PAIN.
LDING YOUR BREATH FOR TEEN MINUTES REQUIRES NLY THAT YOU ACCEPT ENORMOUS OUNT OF IT.
THE PAIN OF YOUR LUNGS DEFLATING.
BUT FINALLY, EVEN SOMEONE FAMILIAR WITH THE SORT OF PAIN ONLY OTHERWISE ENCOUNTERED WHEN DYING--
--HAS TO SUCK IN A BREATH.
WOLVERINE IN
DROWNING LOGAN
PART TWO OF TWO

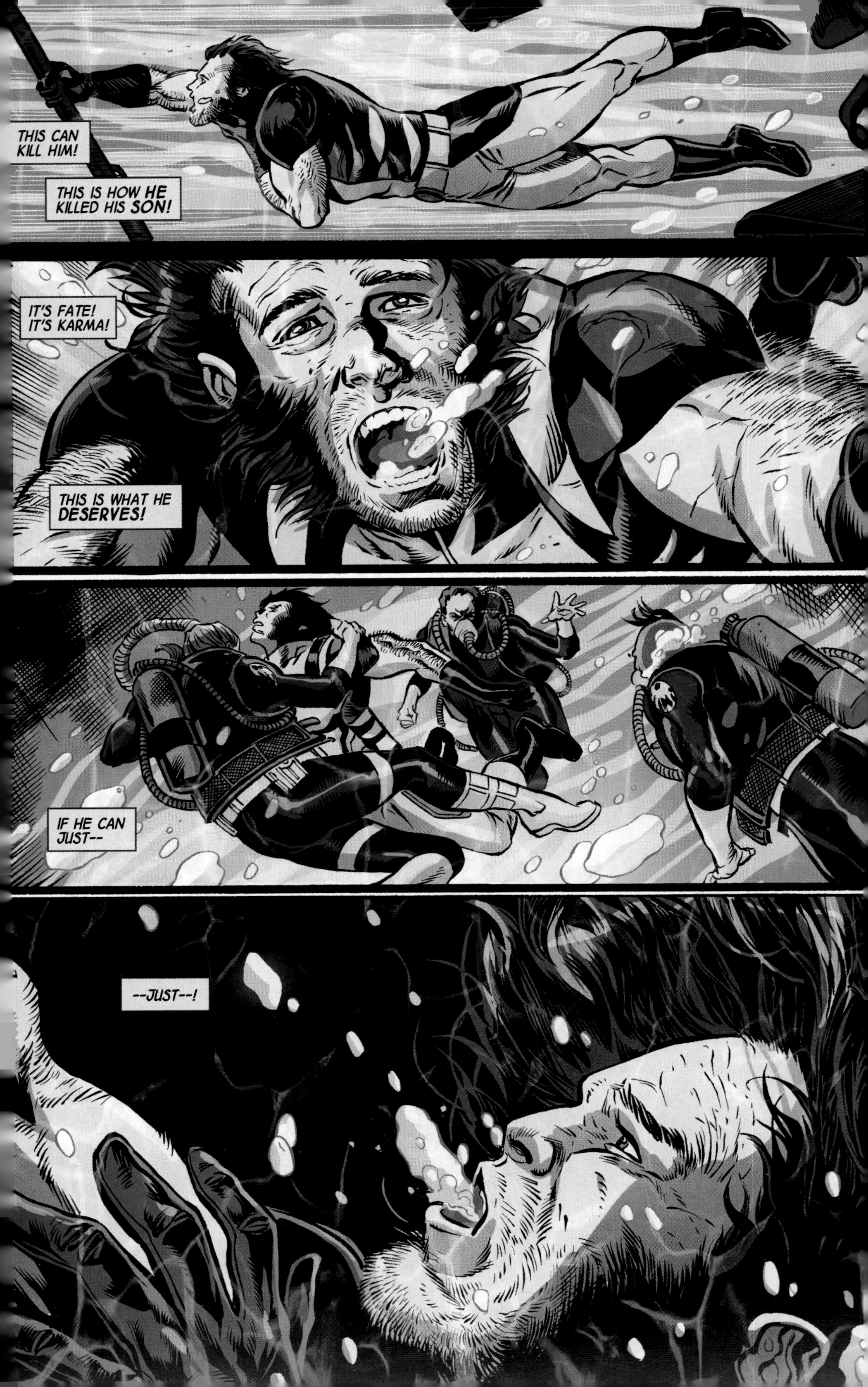

THIS CAN KILL HIM!
THIS IS HOW HE KILLED HIS SON!
IT'S FATE! IT'S KARMA!
THIS IS WHAT HE DESERVES!
IF HE CAN JUST--
--JUST--!

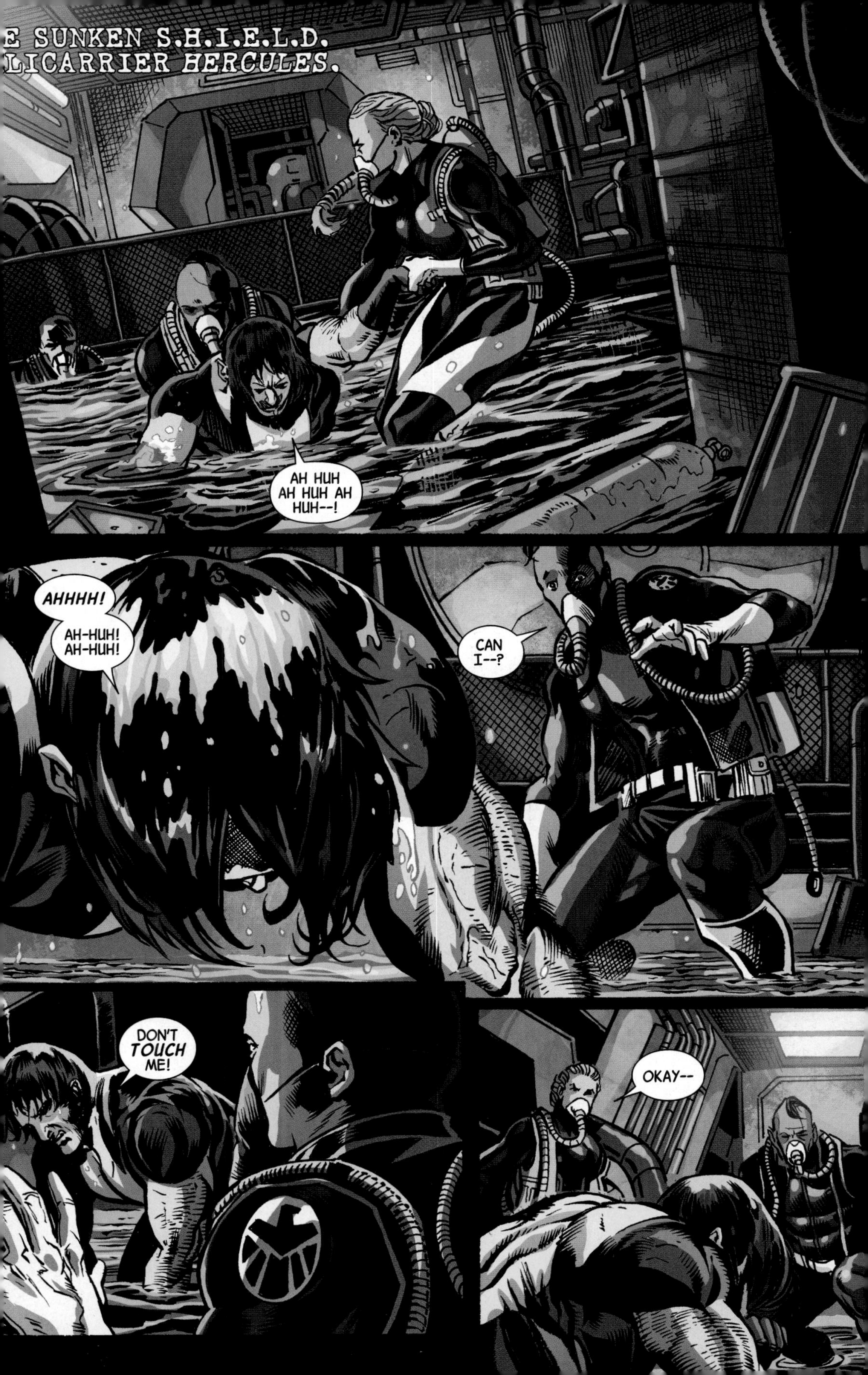

E SUNKEN S.H.I.E.L.D.
LICARRIER HERCULES.
AH HUH AH HUH AH HUH--!
AHHHH!
AH-HUH! AH-HUH!
CAN I--?
DON'T TOUCH ME!
OKAY--

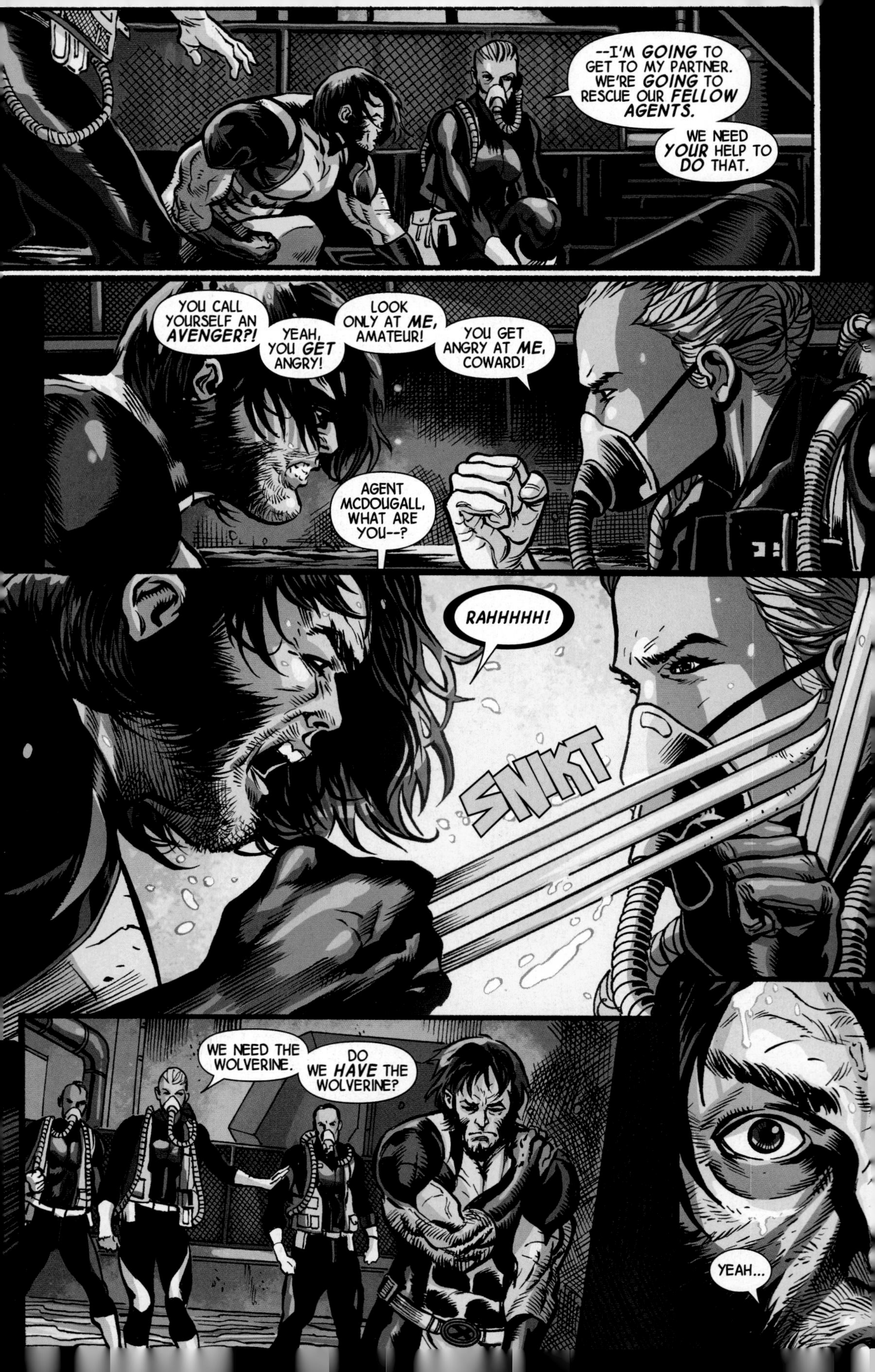
--I'M GOING TO GET TO MY PARTNER. WE'RE GOING TO RESCUE OUR FELLOW AGENTS.
WE NEED YOUR HELP TO DO THAT.
YOU CALL YOURSELF AN AVENGER?!
YEAH, YOU GET ANGRY!
LOOK ONLY AT ME, AMATEUR!
YOU GET ANGRY AT ME, COWARD!
AGENT MCDOUGALL, WHAT ARE YOU--?
RAHHHHH!
SNIKT
WE NEED THE WOLVERINE.
DO WE HAVE THE WOLVERINE?
YEAH...

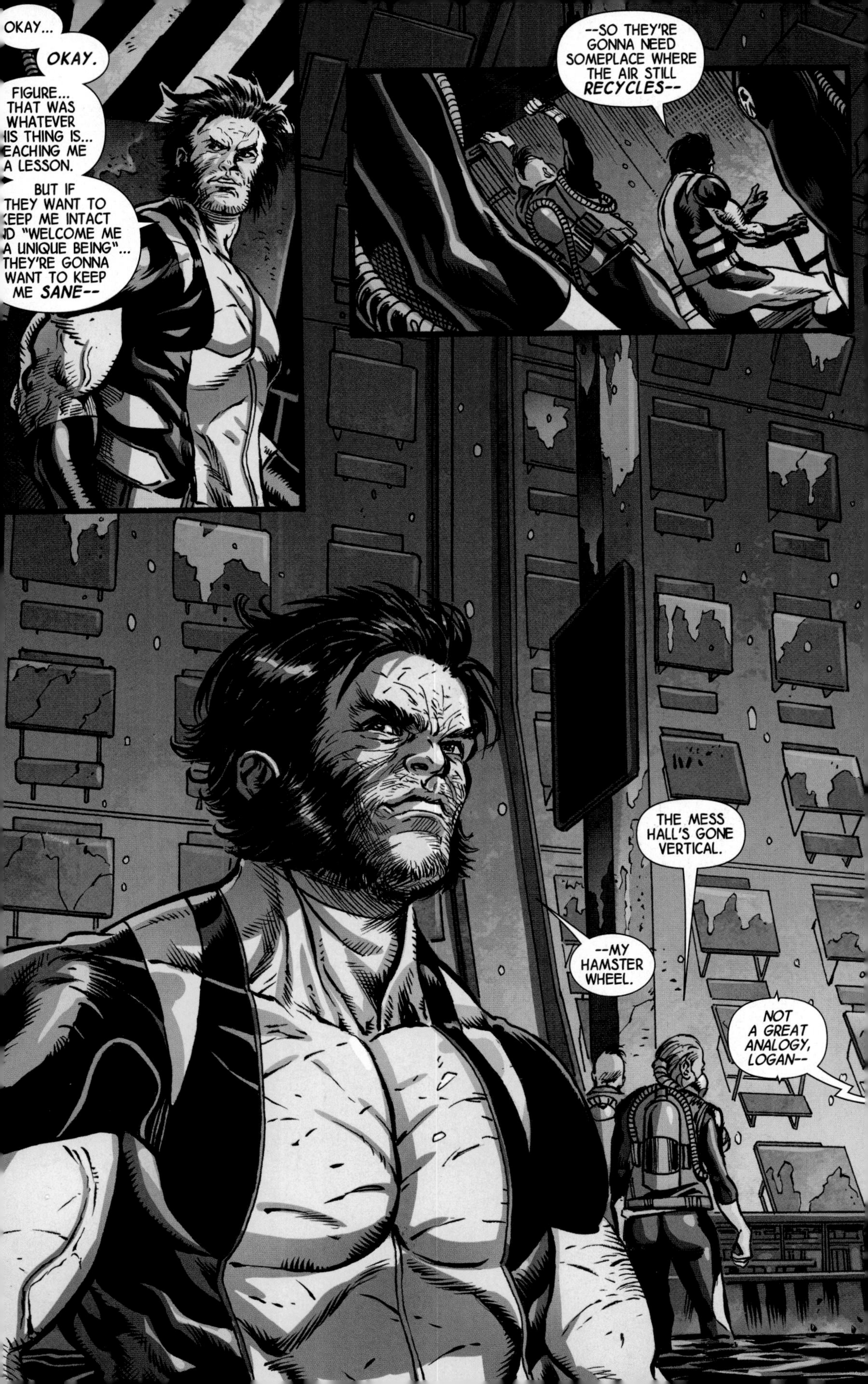
OKAY...
OKAY.
FIGURE... THAT WAS WHATEVER
BUT IF THEY WANT TO
THEY'RE GONNA WANT TO KEEP ME SANE--
--SO THEY'RE GONNA NEED SOMEPLACE WHERE THE AIR STILL RECYCLES--
THE MESS HALL'S GONE VERTICAL.
--MY HAMSTER WHEEL.
NOT A GREAT ANALOGY, LOGAN--

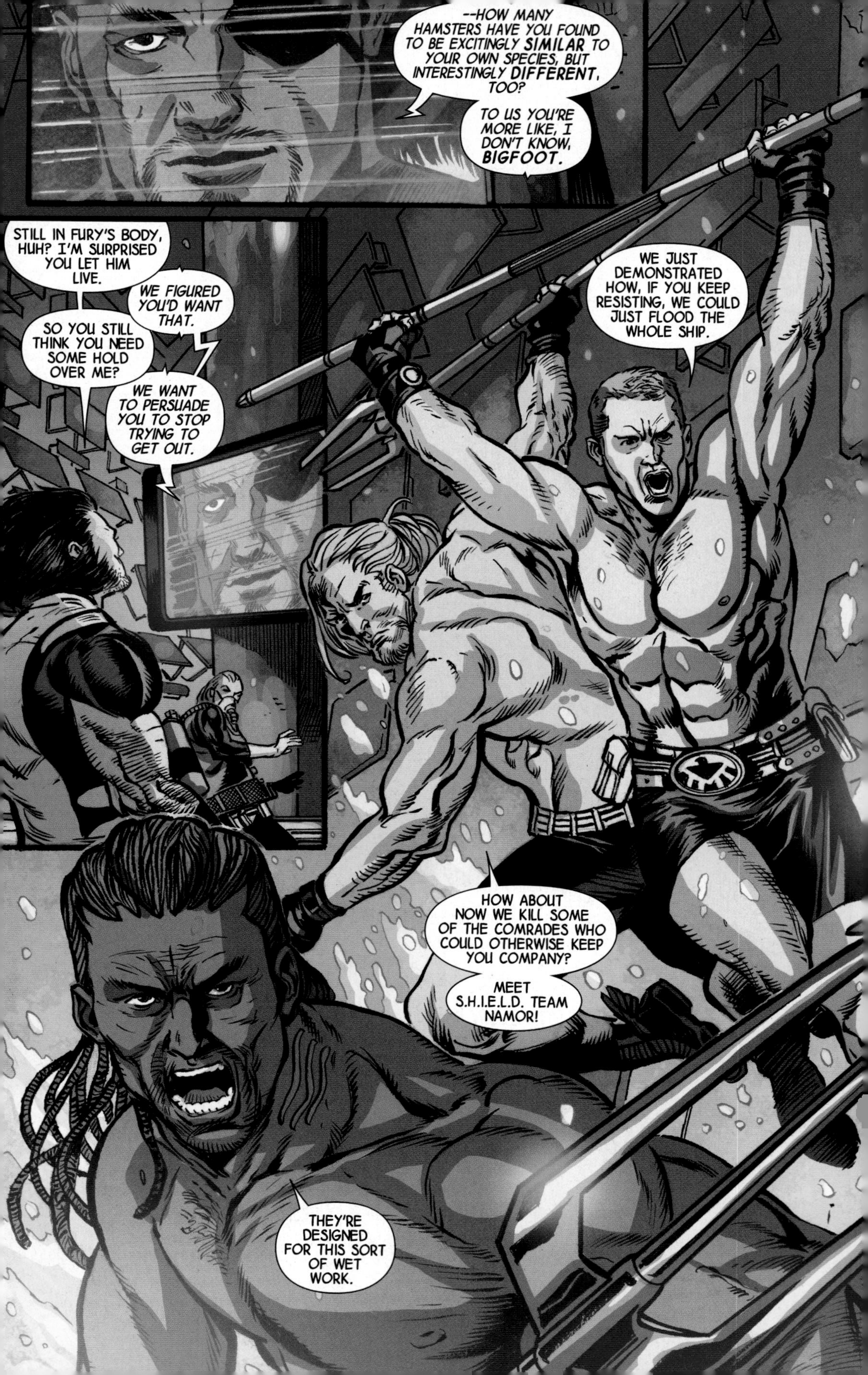
--HOW MANY HAMSTERS HAVE YOU FOUND TO BE EXCITINGLY SIMILAR TO YOUR OWN SPECIES, BUT INTERESTINGLY DIFFERENT, TOO?
TO US YOU'RE MORE LIKE, I DON'T KNOW, BIGFOOT.
STILL IN FURY'S BODY, HUH? I'M SURPRISED YOU LET HIM LIVE.
WE FIGURED YOU'D WANT THAT.
SO YOU STILL THINK YOU NEED SOME HOLD OVER ME?
WE WANT TO PERSUADE YOU TO STOP TRYING TO GET OUT.
WE JUST DEMONSTRATED HOW, IF YOU KEEP RESISTING, WE COULD JUST FLOOD THE WHOLE SHIP.
HOW ABOUT NOW WE KILL SOME OF THE COMRADES WHO COULD OTHERWISE KEEP YOU COMPANY?
MEET S.H.I.E.L.D. TEAM NAMOR!
THEY'RE DESIGNED FOR THIS SORT OF WET WORK.

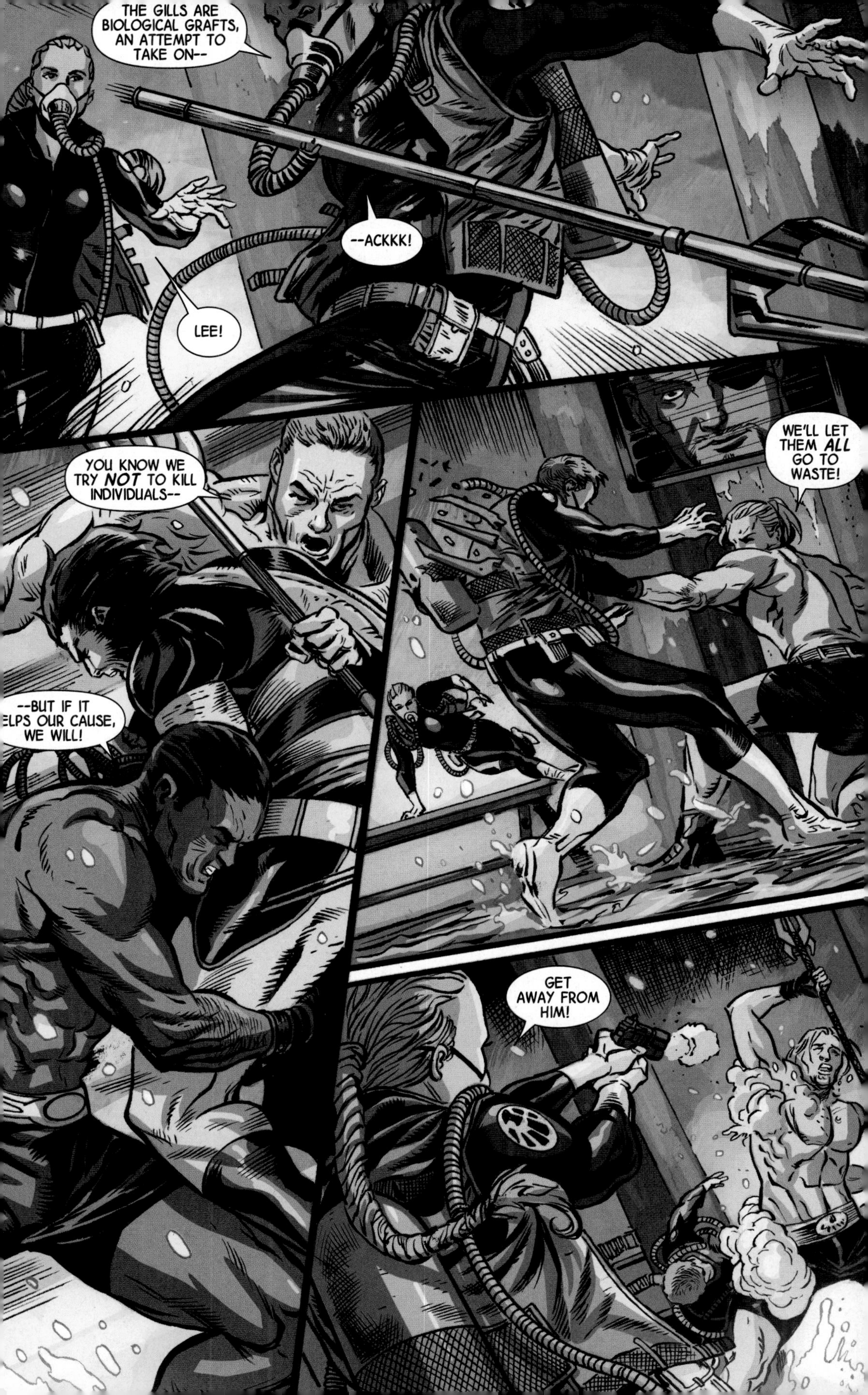
THE GILLS ARE BIOLOGICAL GRAFTS, AN ATTEMPT TO TAKE ON--
--ACKKK!
LEE!
YOU KNOW WE TRY NOT TO KILL INDIVIDUALS--
--BUT IF IT ELPS OUR CAUSE, WE WILL!
WE'LL LET THEM ALL GO TO WASTE!
GET AWAY FROM HIM!

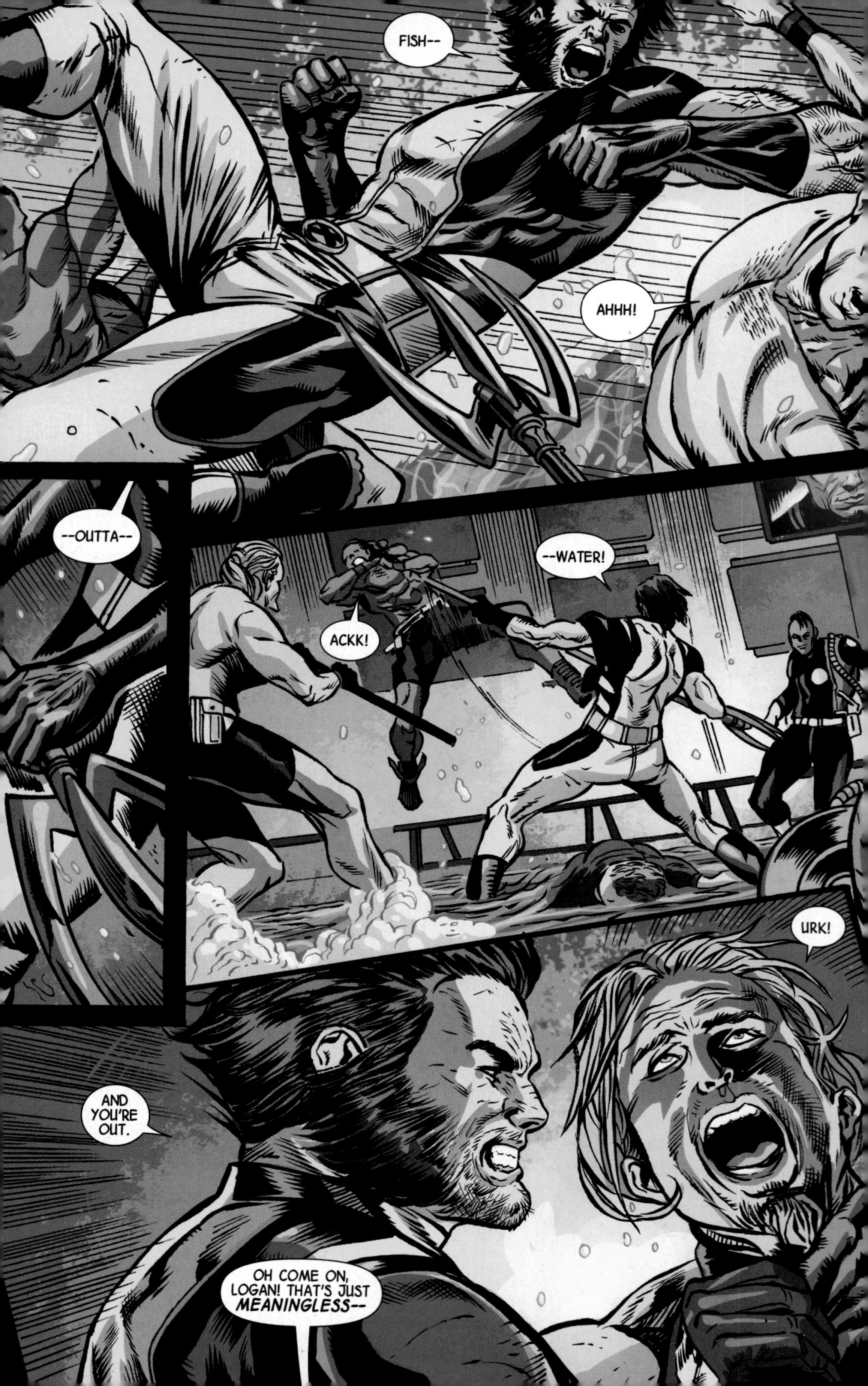
FISH--
AHHH!
--OUTTA--
ACKK!
--WATER!
URK!
AND YOU'RE OUT.
OH COME ON, LOGAN! THAT'S JUST *MEANINGLESS*--

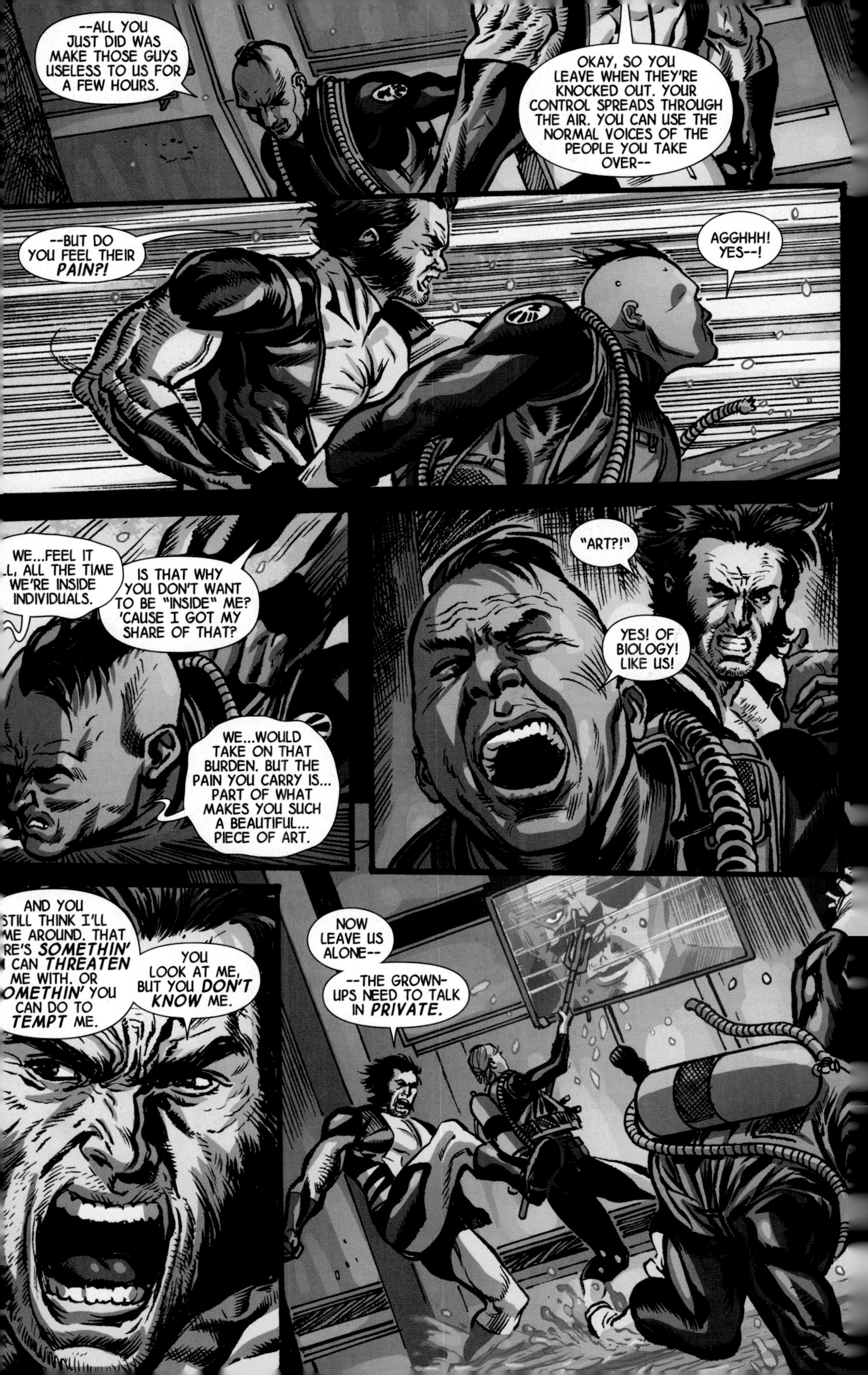
--ALL YOU JUST DID WAS MAKE THOSE GUYS USELESS TO US FOR A FEW HOURS.
OKAY, SO YOU LEAVE WHEN THEY'RE KNOCKED OUT. YOUR CONTROL SPREADS THROUGH THE AIR. YOU CAN USE THE NORMAL VOICES OF THE PEOPLE YOU TAKE OVER--
--BUT DO YOU FEEL THEIR *PAIN?!*
AGGHHH! YES--!
WE...FEEL IT ...L, ALL THE TIME WE'RE INSIDE INDIVIDUALS.
IS THAT WHY YOU DON'T WANT TO BE "INSIDE" ME? 'CAUSE I GOT MY SHARE OF THAT?
WE...WOULD TAKE ON THAT BURDEN. BUT THE PAIN YOU CARRY IS... PART OF WHAT MAKES YOU SUCH A BEAUTIFUL... PIECE OF ART.
"ART?!"
YES! OF BIOLOGY! LIKE US!
AND YOU STILL THINK I'LL ...ME AROUND. THAT ...RE'S *SOMETHIN'* ... CAN *THREATEN* ME WITH. OR ...*OMETHIN'* YOU CAN DO TO *TEMPT* ME.
YOU LOOK AT ME, BUT YOU *DON'T KNOW* ME.
NOW LEAVE US ALONE--
--THE GROWN-UPS NEED TO TALK IN *PRIVATE.*

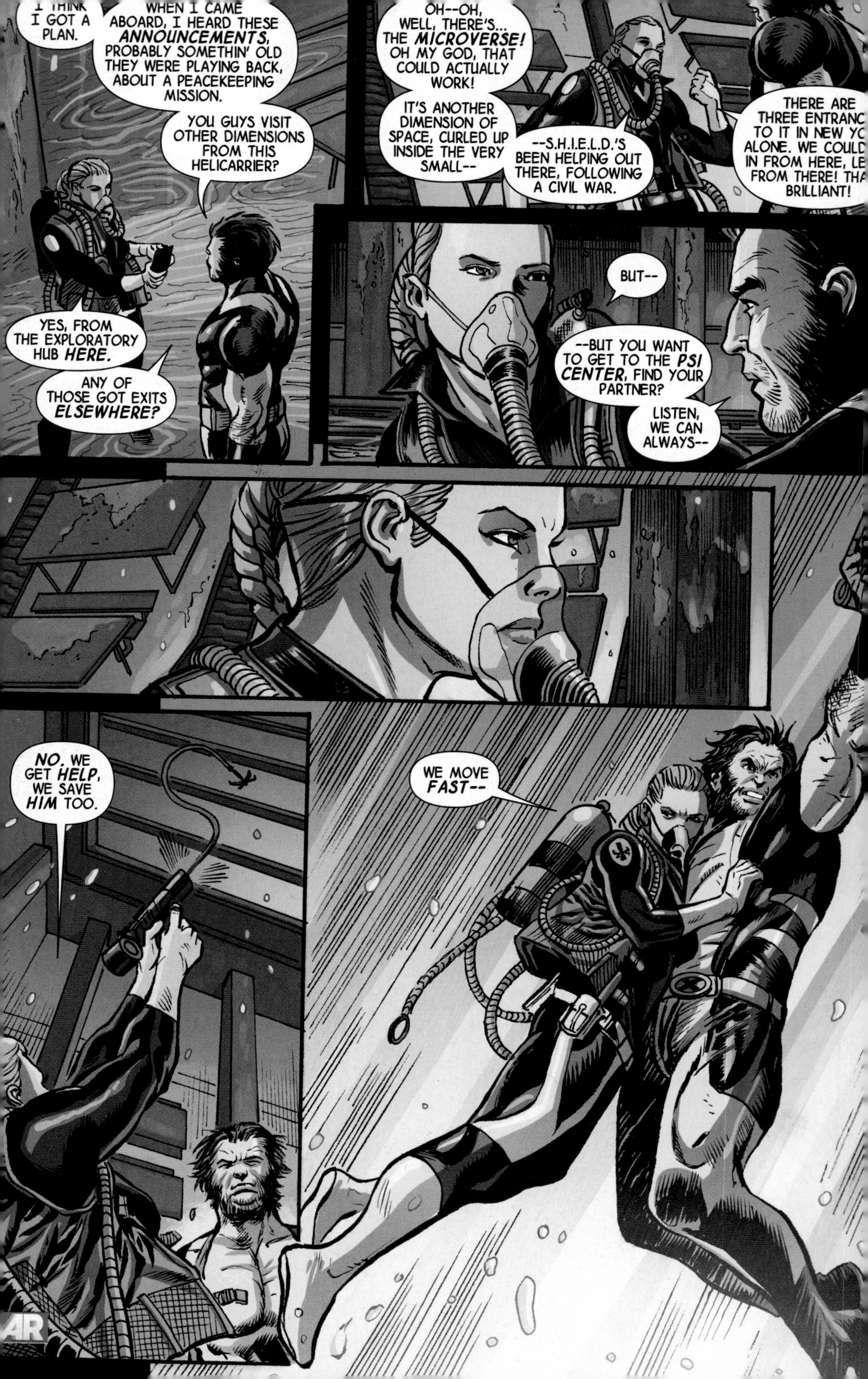
I THINK I GOT A PLAN.
WHEN I CAME ABOARD, I HEARD THESE ANNOUNCEMENTS, PROBABLY SOMETHIN' OLD THEY WERE PLAYING BACK, ABOUT A PEACEKEEPING MISSION.
YOU GUYS VISIT OTHER DIMENSIONS FROM THIS HELICARRIER?
YES, FROM THE EXPLORATORY HUB HERE.
ANY OF THOSE GOT EXITS ELSEWHERE?
OH--OH, WELL, THERE'S... THE MICROVERSE! OH MY GOD, THAT COULD ACTUALLY WORK!
IT'S ANOTHER DIMENSION OF SPACE, CURLED UP INSIDE THE VERY SMALL--
--S.H.I.E.L.D.'S BEEN HELPING OUT THERE, FOLLOWING A CIVIL WAR.
THERE ARE THREE ENTRANC TO IT IN NEW YO ALONE. WE COULD IN FROM HERE, LE FROM THERE! THA BRILLIANT!
BUT--
--BUT YOU WANT TO GET TO THE PSI CENTER, FIND YOUR PARTNER?
LISTEN, WE CAN ALWAYS--
NO. WE GET HELP, WE SAVE HIM TOO.
WE MOVE FAST--

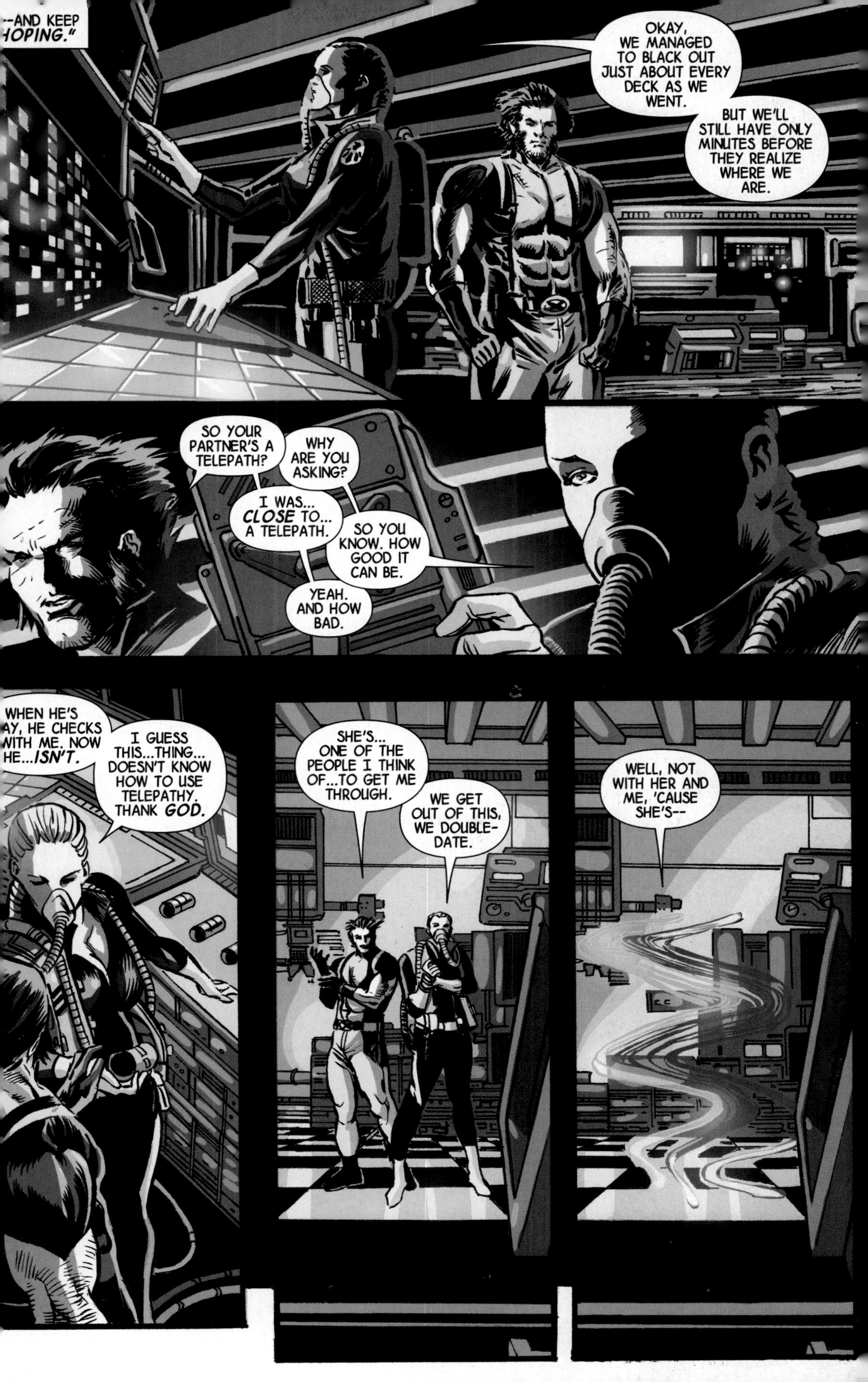
--AND KEEP HOPING."
OKAY, WE MANAGED TO BLACK OUT JUST ABOUT EVERY DECK AS WE WENT.
BUT WE'LL STILL HAVE ONLY MINUTES BEFORE THEY REALIZE WHERE WE ARE.
SO YOUR PARTNER'S A TELEPATH?
WHY ARE YOU ASKING?
I WAS... CLOSE TO... A TELEPATH.
SO YOU KNOW. HOW GOOD IT CAN BE.
YEAH. AND HOW BAD.
WHEN HE'S AY, HE CHECKS WITH ME. NOW HE...ISN'T.
I GUESS THIS...THING... DOESN'T KNOW HOW TO USE TELEPATHY. THANK GOD.
SHE'S... ONE OF THE PEOPLE I THINK OF...TO GET ME THROUGH.
WE GET OUT OF THIS, WE DOUBLE-DATE.
WELL, NOT WITH HER AND ME, 'CAUSE SHE'S--

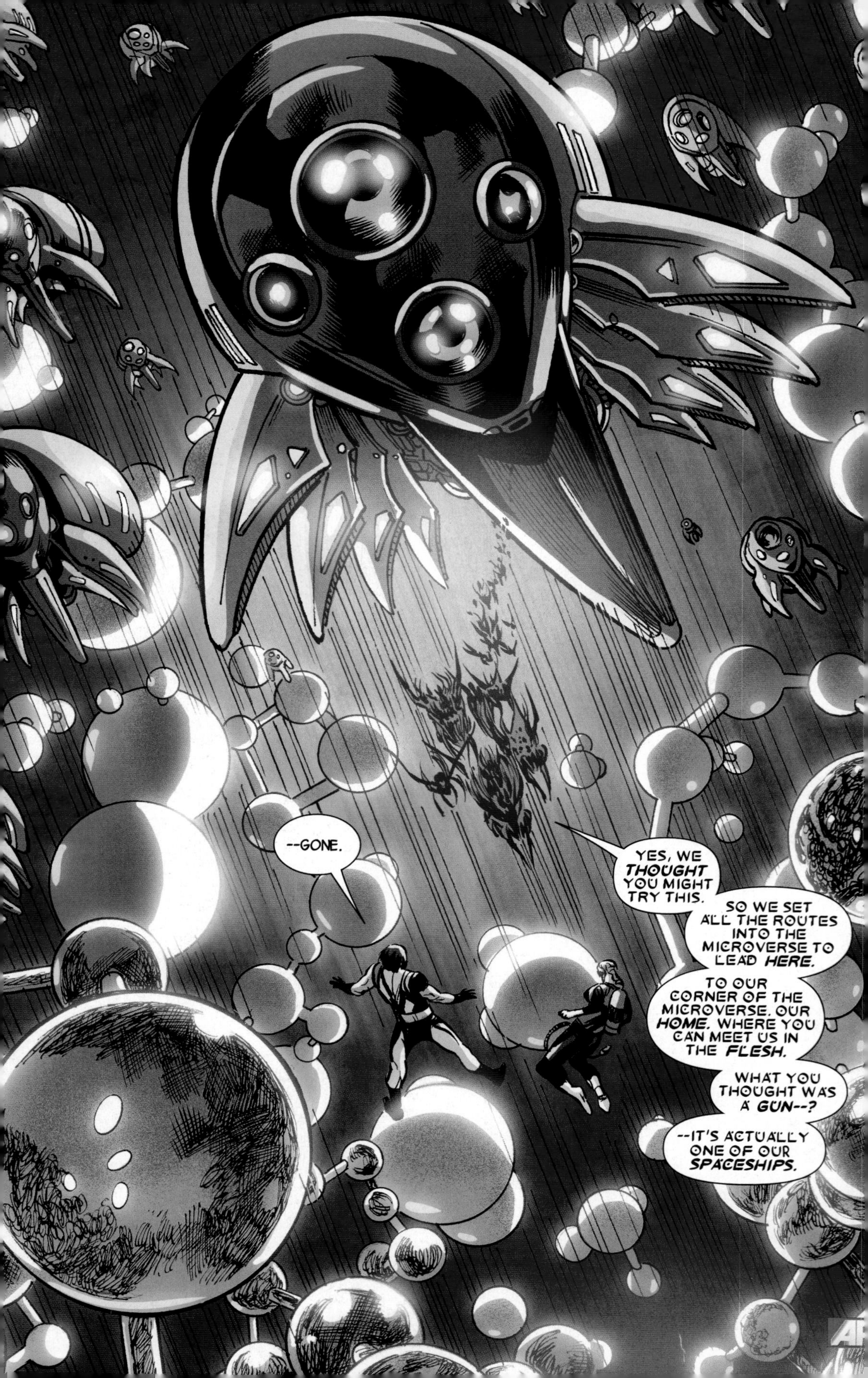
--GONE.
YES, WE THOUGHT YOU MIGHT TRY THIS.
SO WE SET ALL THE ROUTES INTO THE MICROVERSE TO LEAD HERE.
TO OUR CORNER OF THE MICROVERSE. OUR HOME. WHERE YOU CAN MEET US IN THE FLESH.
WHAT YOU THOUGHT WAS A GUN--?
--IT'S ACTUALLY ONE OF OUR SPACESHIPS.

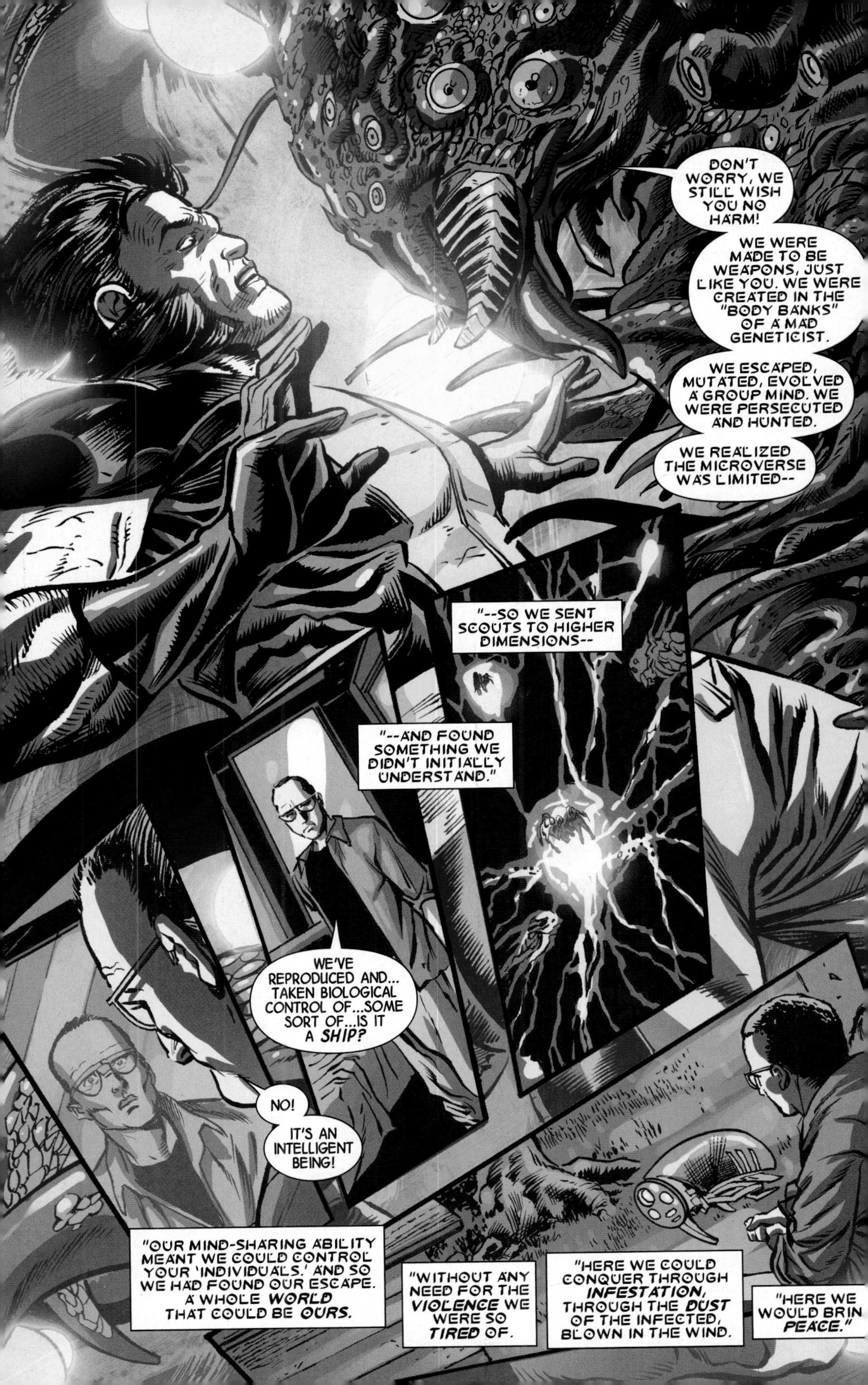
DON'T WORRY, WE STILL WISH YOU NO HARM!
WE WERE MADE TO BE WEAPONS, JUST LIKE YOU. WE WERE CREATED IN THE "BODY BANKS" OF A MAD GENETICIST.
WE ESCAPED, MUTATED, EVOLVED A GROUP MIND. WE WERE PERSECUTED AND HUNTED.
WE REALIZED THE MICROVERSE WAS LIMITED--
"--SO WE SENT SCOUTS TO HIGHER DIMENSIONS--
"--AND FOUND SOMETHING WE DIDN'T INITIALLY UNDERSTAND."
WE'VE REPRODUCED AND... TAKEN BIOLOGICAL CONTROL OF...SOME SORT OF...IS IT A *SHIP?*
NO!
IT'S AN INTELLIGENT BEING!
"OUR MIND-SHARING ABILITY MEANT WE COULD CONTROL YOUR 'INDIVIDUALS.' AND SO WE HAD FOUND OUR ESCAPE. A WHOLE *WORLD* THAT COULD BE *OURS.*
"WITHOUT ANY NEED FOR THE *VIOLENCE* WE WERE SO *TIRED* OF.
"HERE WE COULD CONQUER THROUGH *INFESTATION,* THROUGH THE *DUST* OF THE INFECTED, BLOWN IN THE WIND.
"HERE WE WOULD BRIN *PEACE."*

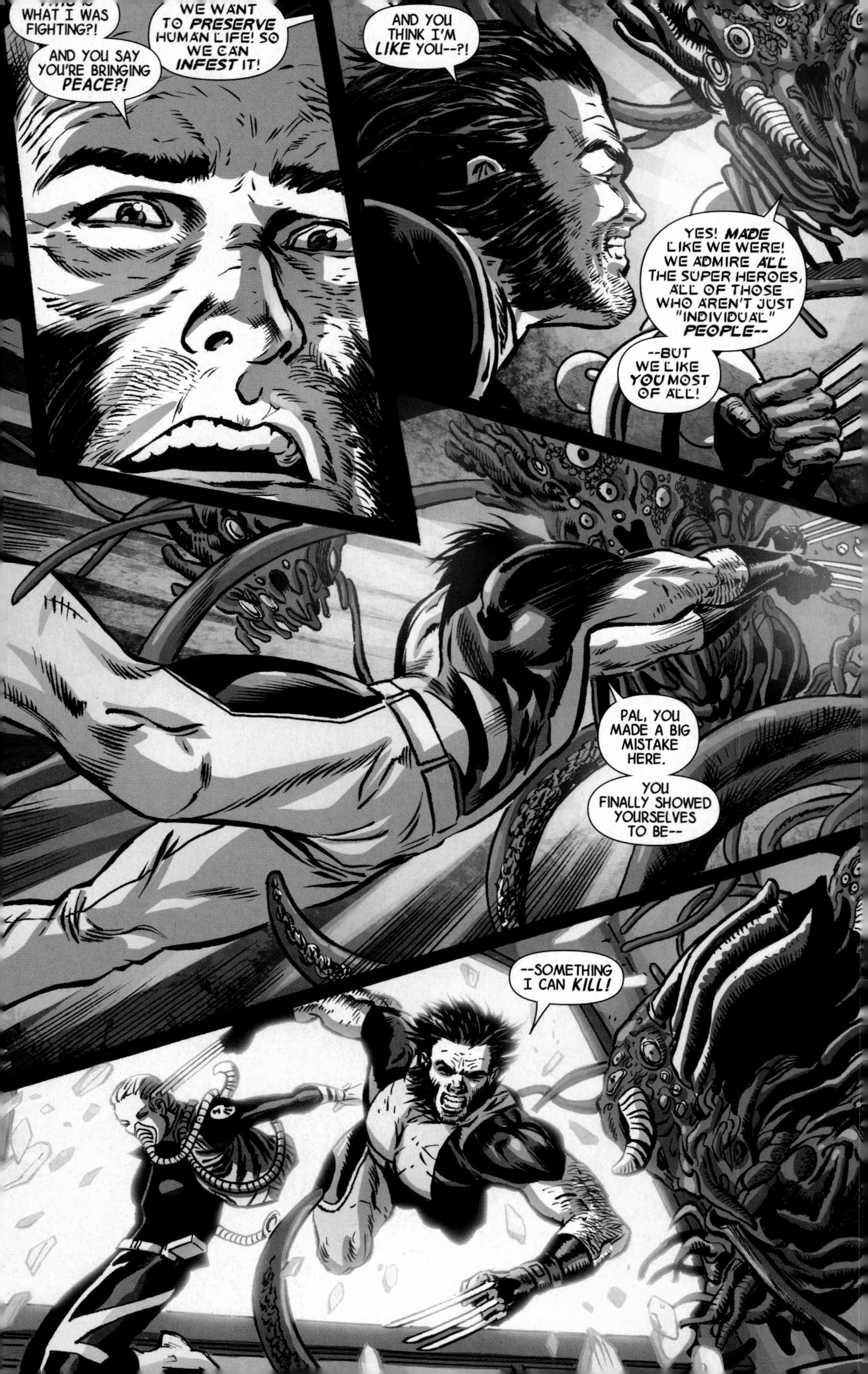
WHAT I WAS FIGHTING?!
AND YOU SAY YOU'RE BRINGING PEACE?!
WE WANT TO PRESERVE HUMAN LIFE! SO WE CAN INFEST IT!
AND YOU THINK I'M LIKE YOU--?!
YES! MADE LIKE WE WERE! WE ADMIRE ALL THE SUPER HEROES, ALL OF THOSE WHO AREN'T JUST "INDIVIDUAL" PEOPLE--
--BUT WE LIKE YOU MOST OF ALL!
PAL, YOU MADE A BIG MISTAKE HERE.
YOU FINALLY SHOWED YOURSELVES TO BE--
--SOMETHING I CAN KILL!

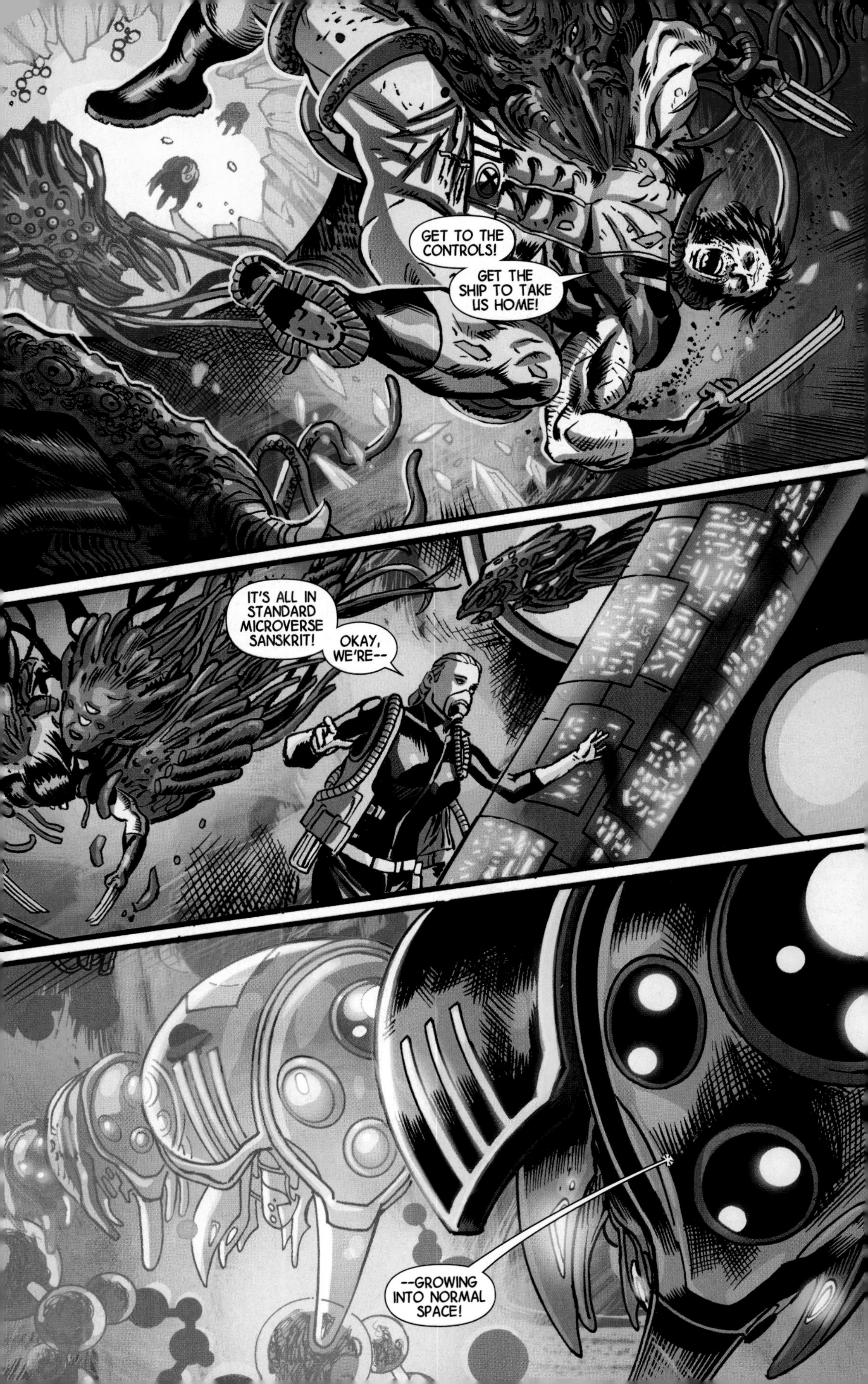
GET TO THE CONTROLS!
GET THE SHIP TO TAKE US HOME!
IT'S ALL IN STANDARD MICROVERSE SANSKRIT!
OKAY, WE'RE--
--GROWING INTO NORMAL SPACE!

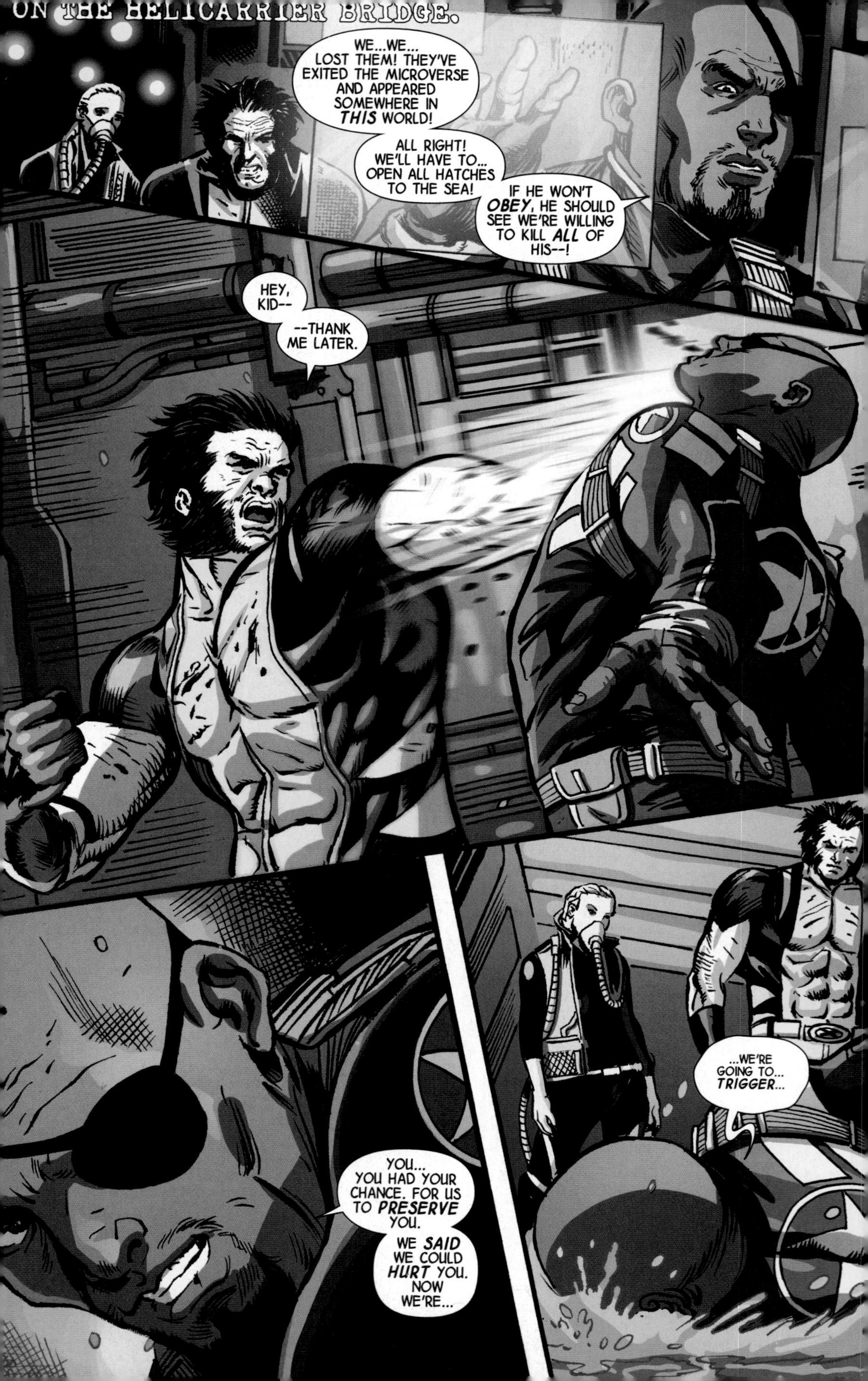
ON THE HELICARRIER BRIDGE.
WE...WE... LOST THEM! THEY'VE EXITED THE MICROVERSE AND APPEARED SOMEWHERE IN THIS WORLD!
ALL RIGHT! WE'LL HAVE TO... OPEN ALL HATCHES TO THE SEA!
IF HE WON'T OBEY, HE SHOULD SEE WE'RE WILLING TO KILL ALL OF HIS--!
HEY, KID--
--THANK ME LATER.
YOU... YOU HAD YOUR CHANCE. FOR US TO PRESERVE YOU.
WE SAID WE COULD HURT YOU. NOW WE'RE...
...WE'RE GOING TO... TRIGGER...

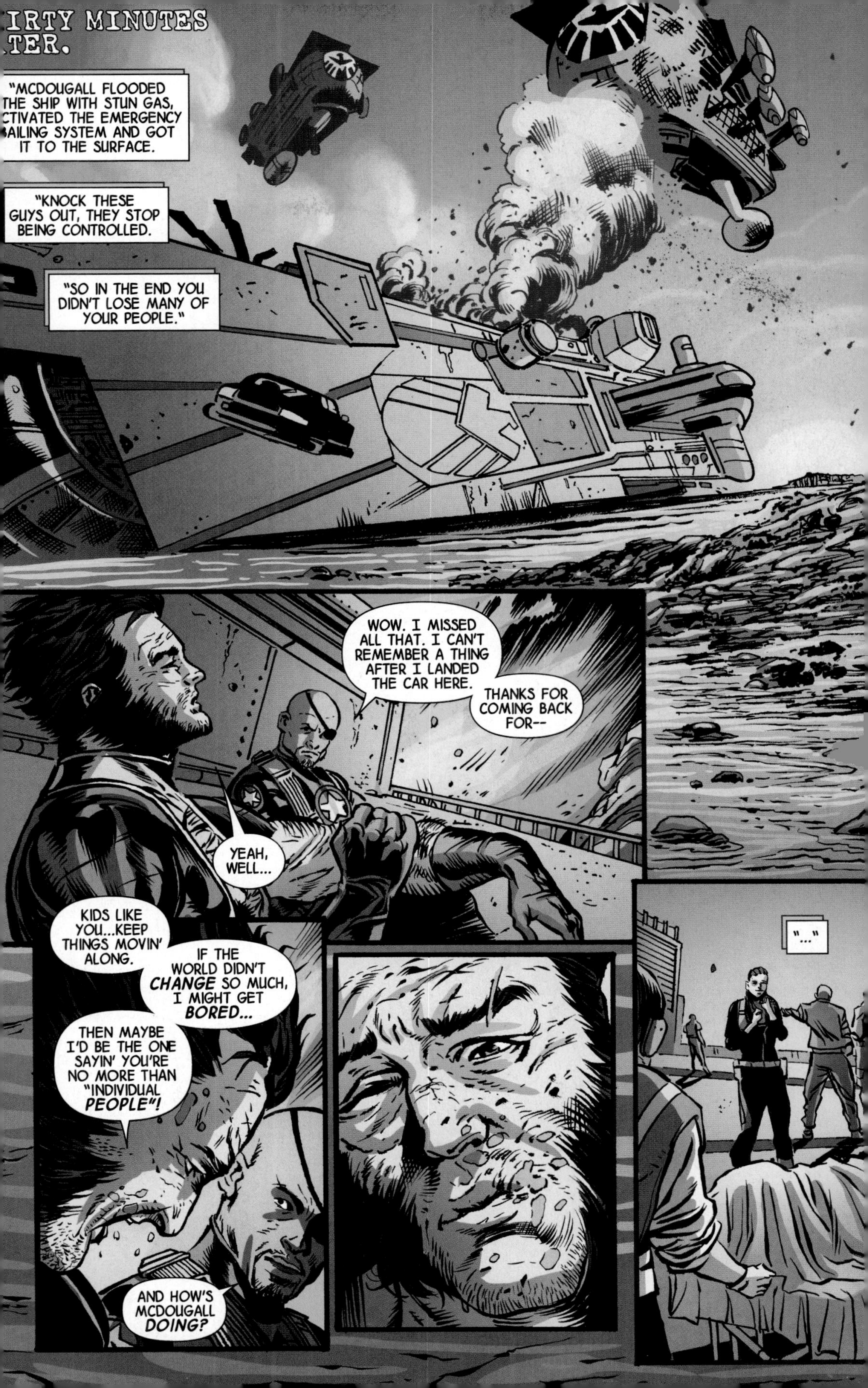

IRTY MINUTES
TER.
"MCDOUGALL FLOODED THE SHIP WITH STUN GAS, CTIVATED THE EMERGENCY AILING SYSTEM AND GOT IT TO THE SURFACE.
"KNOCK THESE GUYS OUT, THEY STOP BEING CONTROLLED.
"SO IN THE END YOU DIDN'T LOSE MANY OF YOUR PEOPLE."
WOW. I MISSED ALL THAT. I CAN'T REMEMBER A THING AFTER I LANDED THE CAR HERE.
THANKS FOR COMING BACK FOR--
YEAH, WELL...
KIDS LIKE YOU...KEEP THINGS MOVIN' ALONG.
IF THE WORLD DIDN'T CHANGE SO MUCH, I MIGHT GET BORED...
THEN MAYBE I'D BE THE ONE SAYIN' YOU'RE NO MORE THAN "INDIVIDUAL PEOPLE"!
AND HOW'S MCDOUGALL DOING?
"..."

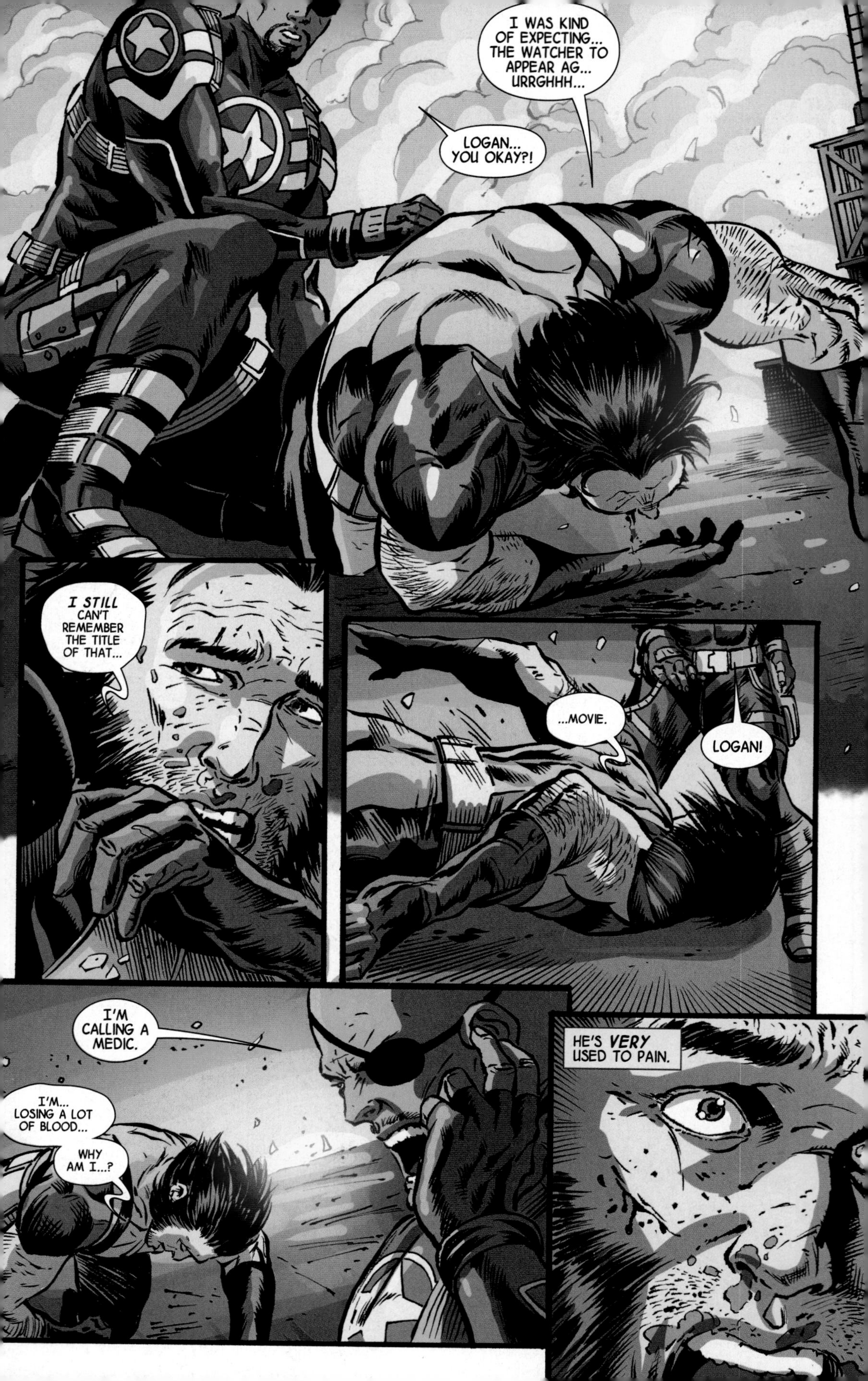
LOGAN... YOU OKAY?!
I WAS KIND OF EXPECTING... THE WATCHER TO APPEAR AG... URRGHHH...
I STILL CAN'T REMEMBER THE TITLE OF THAT...
...MOVIE.
LOGAN!
I'M CALLING A MEDIC.
I'M... LOSING A LOT OF BLOOD...
WHY AM I...?
HE'S VERY USED TO PAIN.

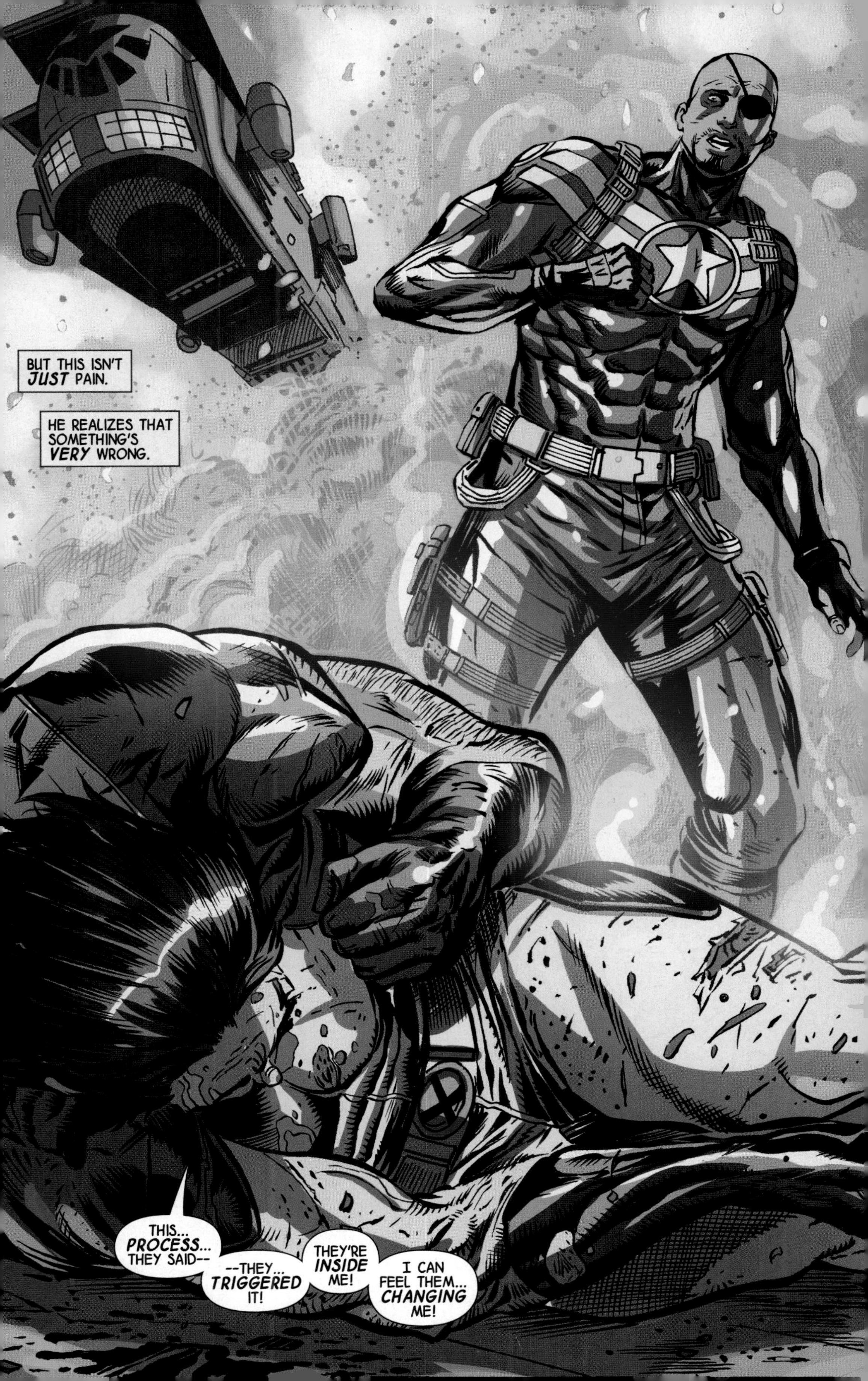
BUT THIS ISN'T JUST PAIN.
HE REALIZES THAT SOMETHING'S VERY WRONG.
THIS... PROCESS... THEY SAID--
--THEY... TRIGGERED IT!
THEY'RE INSIDE ME!
I CAN FEEL THEM... CHANGING ME!

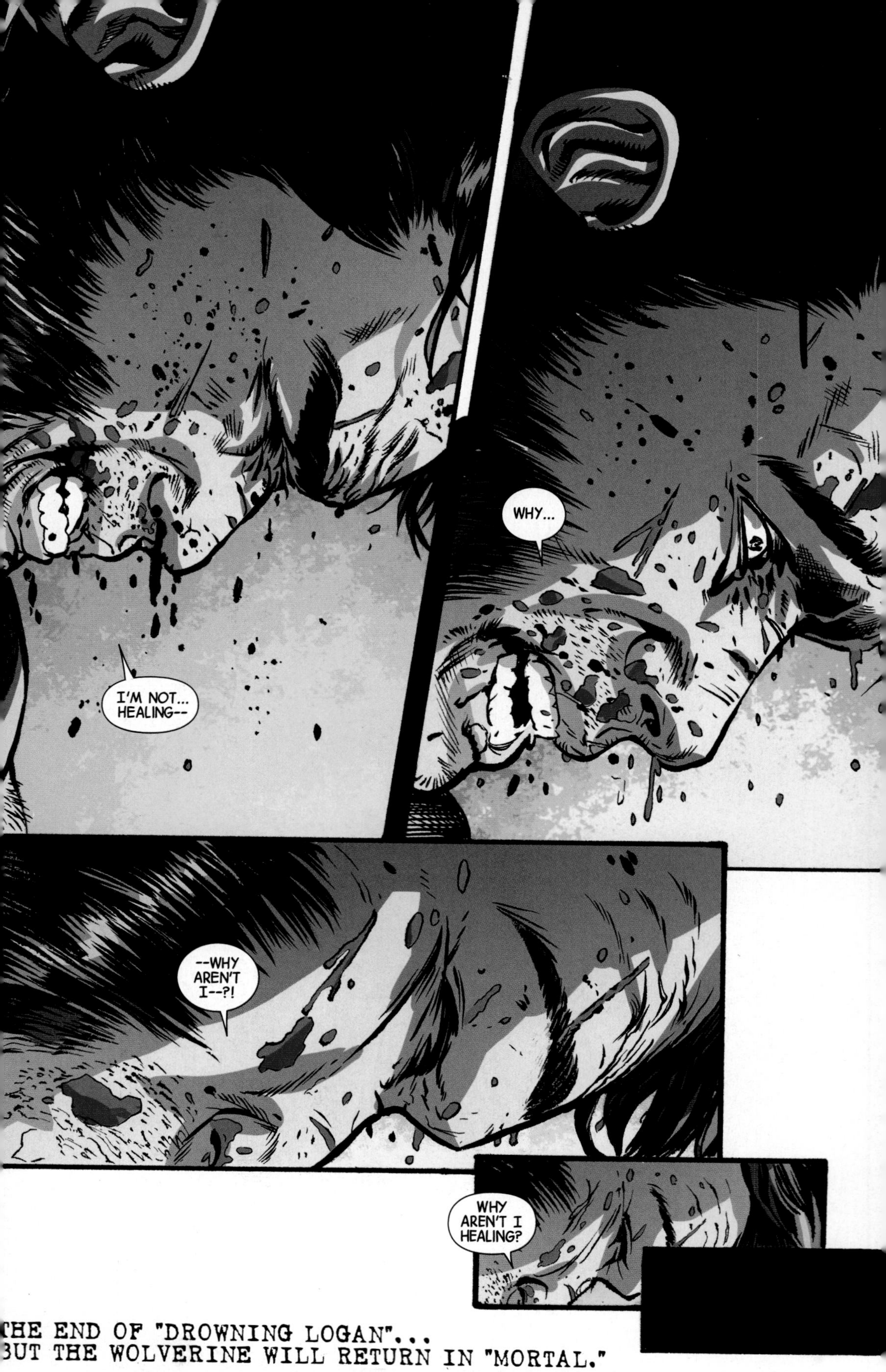
I'M NOT... HEALING--
WHY...
--WHY AREN'T I--?!
WHY AREN'T I HEALING?

THE END OF "DROWNING LOGAN"...
BUT THE WOLVERINE WILL RETURN IN "MORTAL."

#1 VARIANT BY OLIVIER COIPEL

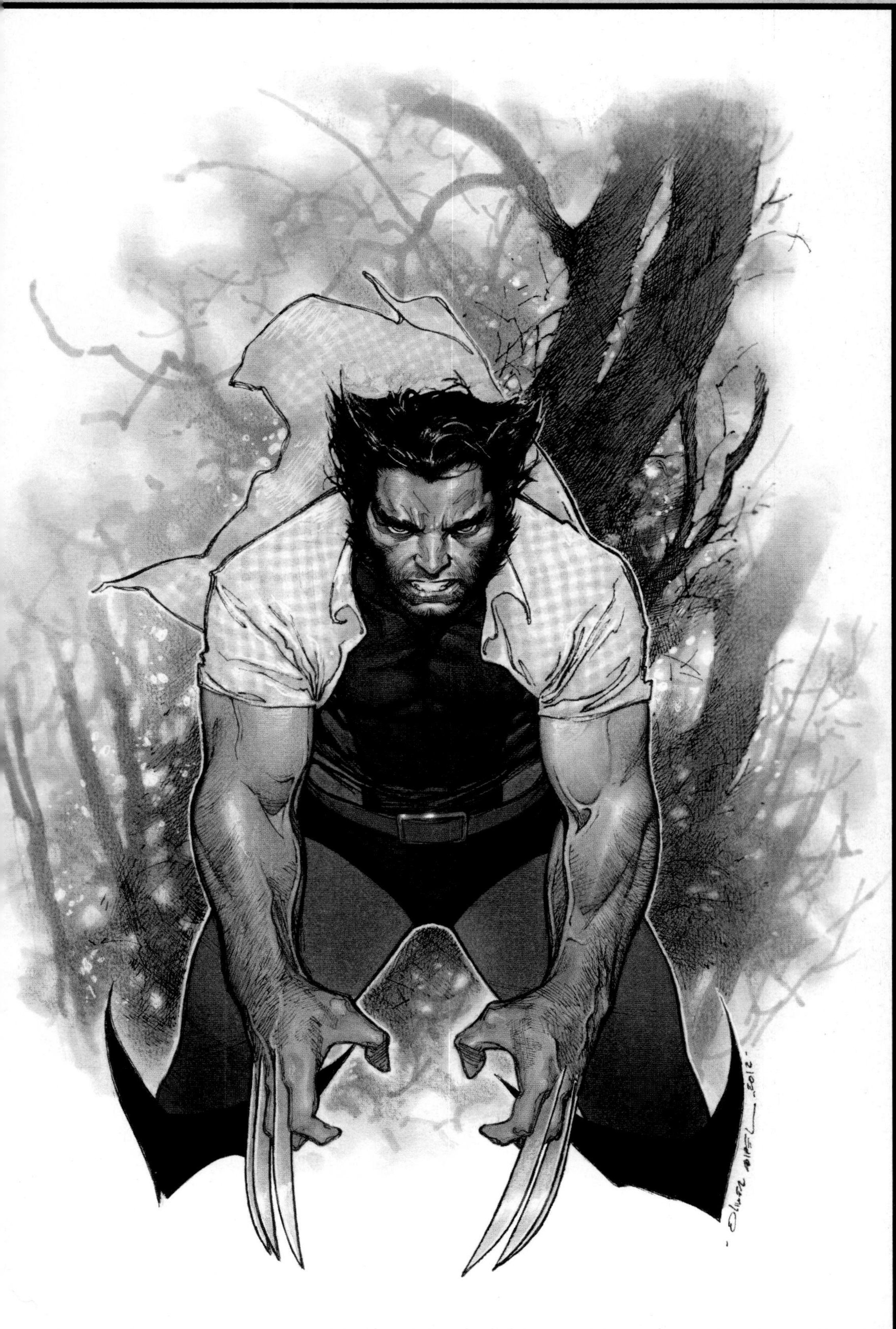

#1 VARIANT BY SKOTTIE YOUNG

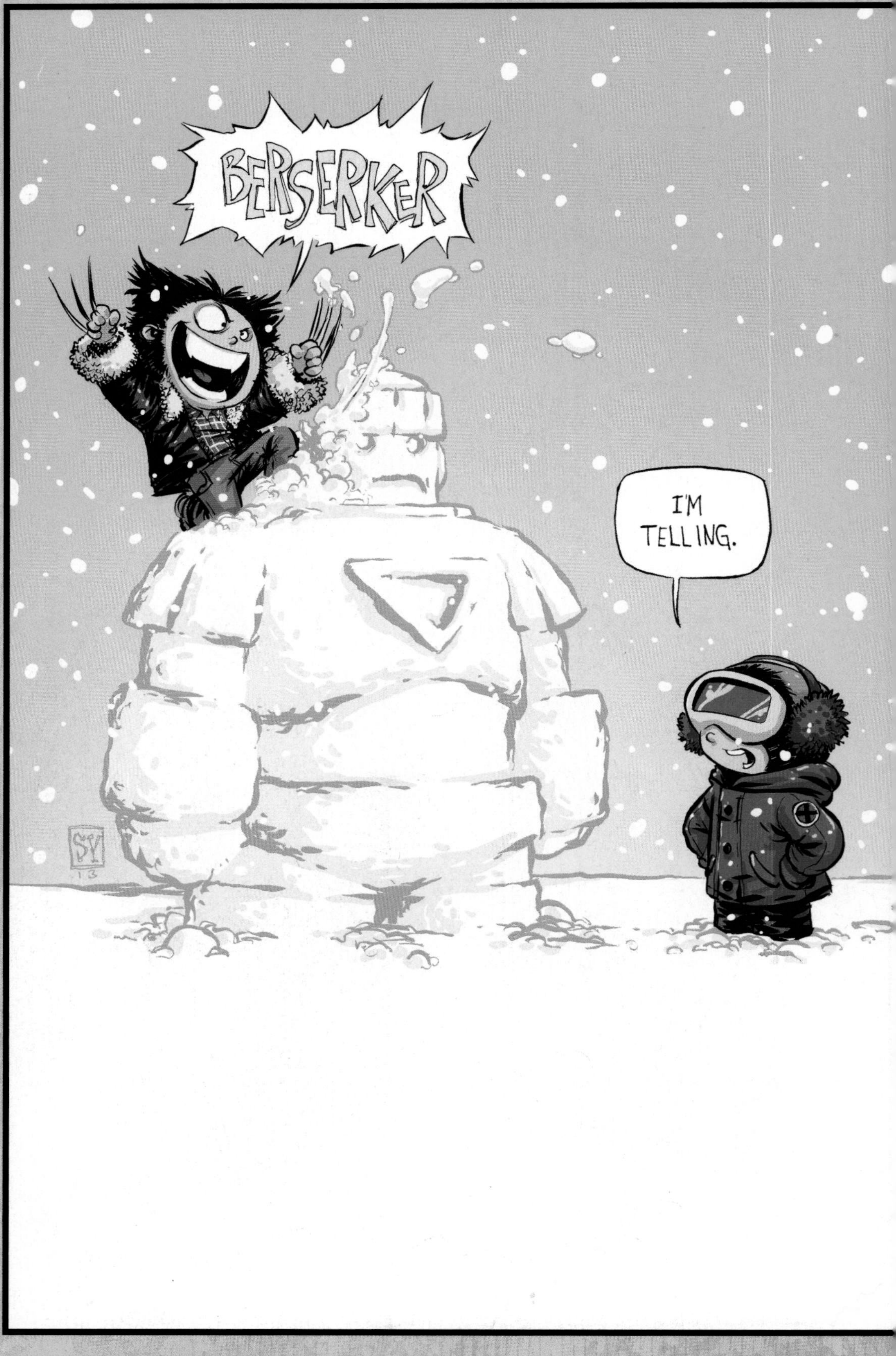
BERSERKER
I'M TELLING.
SY 1.13

#1 MILE HIGH VARIANT BY HUMBERTO RAMOS & EDGAR DELGADO

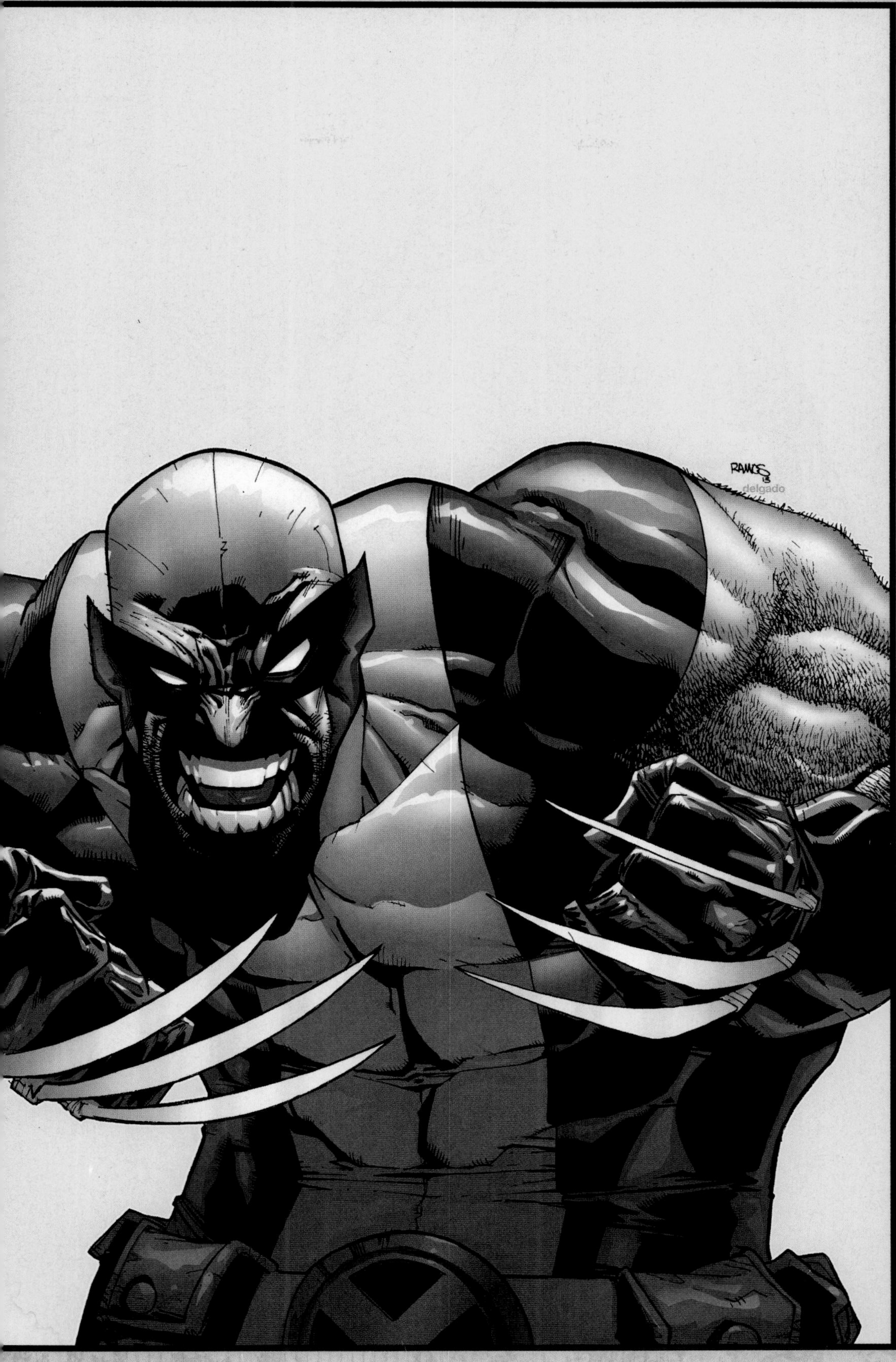

RAMOS 13
delgado

#1 FORBIDDEN PLANET VARIANT BY SALVADOR LARROCA & FRANK D'ARMATA

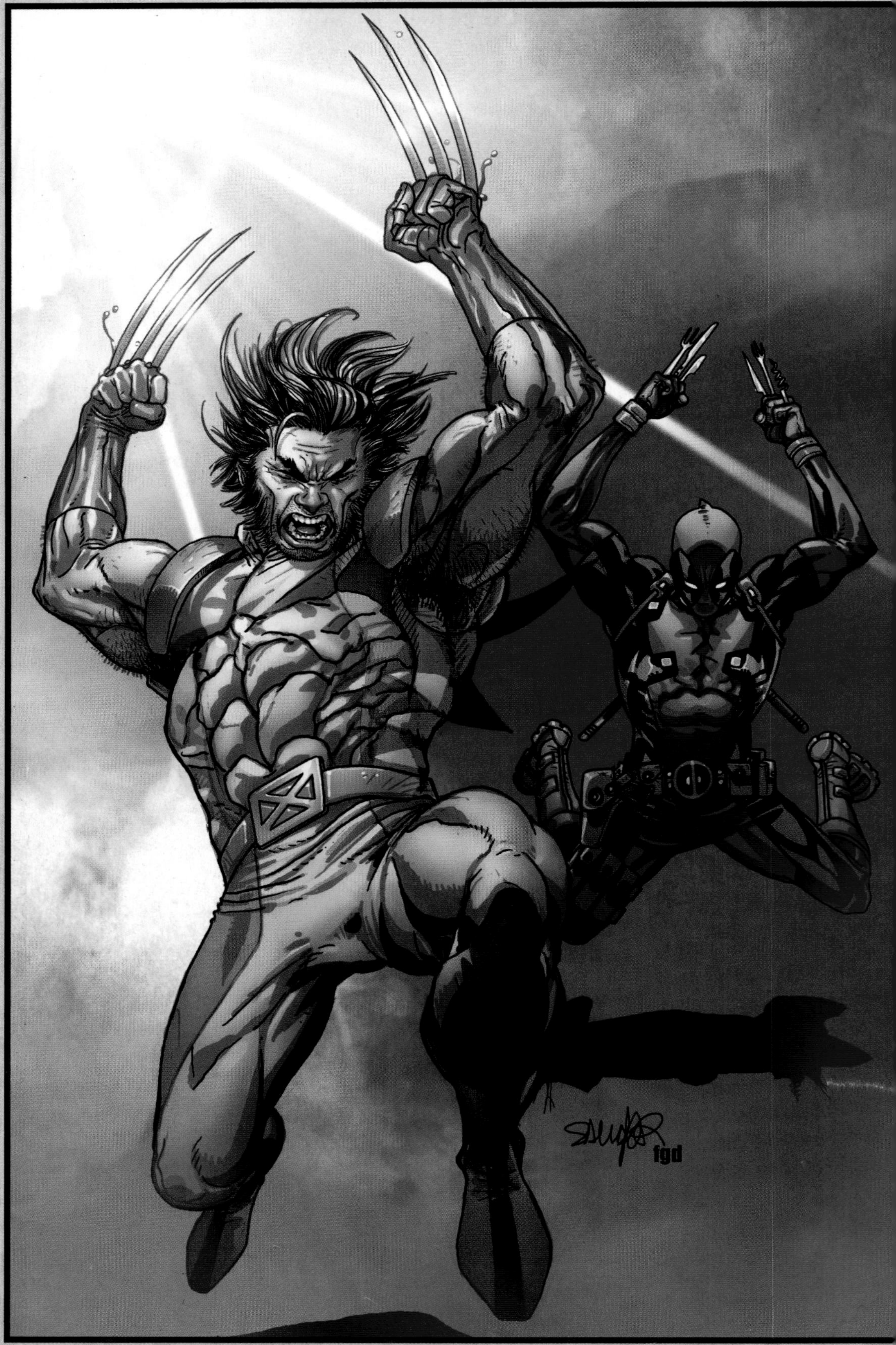

1 SKETCH VARIANT
BY ALAN DAVIS & MARK FARMER

2 VARIANT BY
MIKE DEODATO & RAIN BEREDO

#3 VARIANT BY ED McGUINNESS

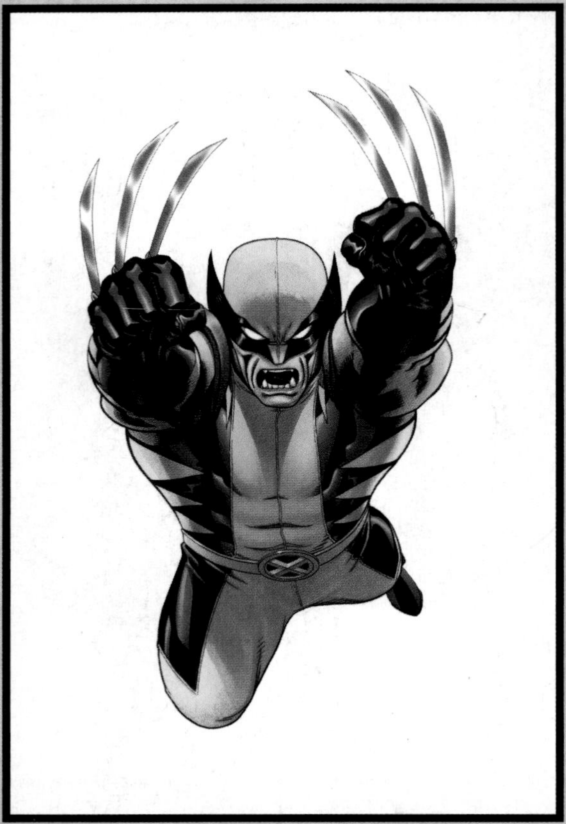

#4 VARIANT BY SALVADOR LARROCA & DAVID OCAMPO

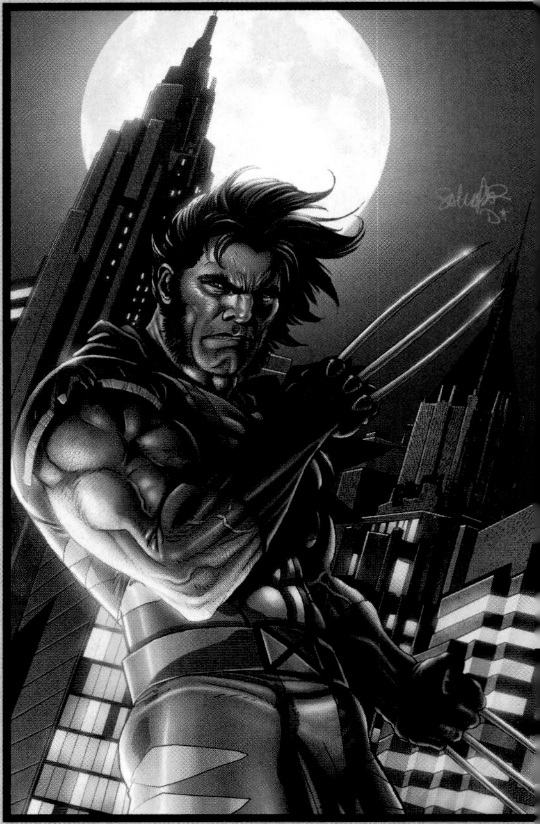

#4 WOLVERINE THROUGH THE AGES VARIANT BY PASCAL CAMPION

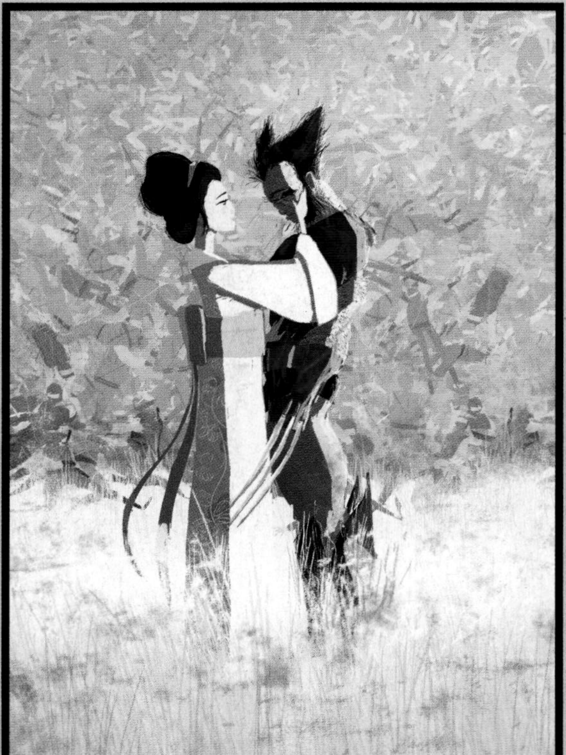

#5 VARIANT BY OLIVIER COIPEL

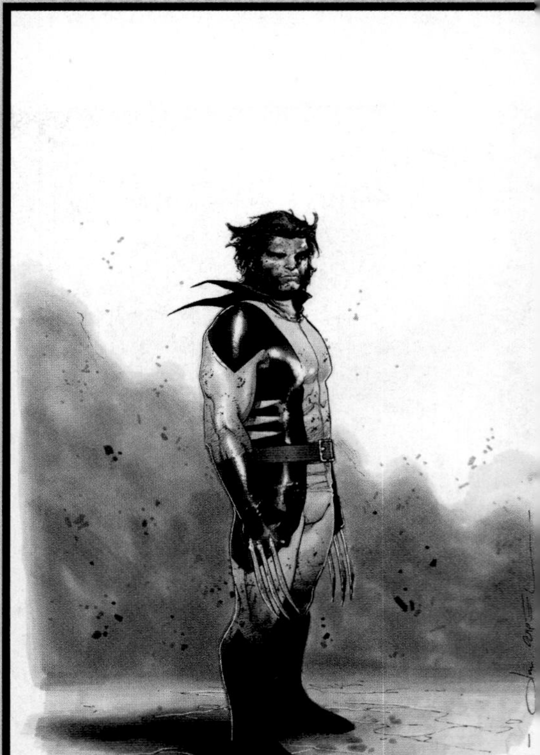

TO ACCESS THE FREE *MARVEL AUGMENTED REALITY APP* THAT ENHANCES AND CHANGES THE WAY YOU EXPERIENCE COMIC

1. Download the app for free via marvel.com/ARapp
2. Launch the app on your camera-enabled Apple iOS® or Android™ device*
3. Hold your mobile device's camera ov any cover or panel with the AR grap
4. Sit back and see the future of comics in action!

*Available on most camera-enabled Apple iOS® and Android™ devices. Content subject to change and availability.

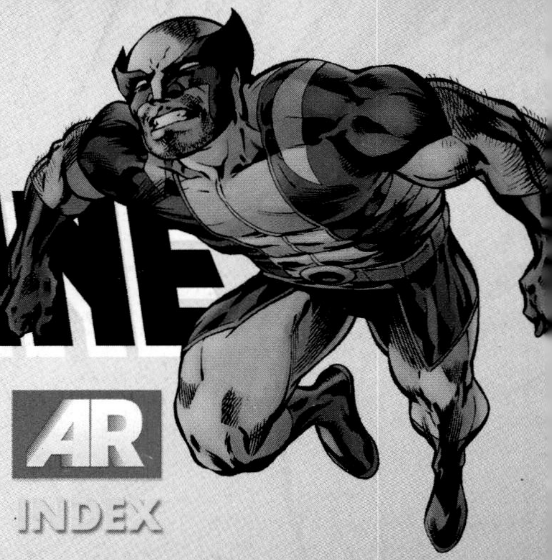

AR INDEX